CONSIDER NO EVIL

Consider No Evil

Two Faith Traditions and the Problem of Academic Freedom in Religious Higher Education

BRANDON G. WITHROW
and MENACHEM WECKER

CASCADE *Books* · Eugene, Oregon

CONSIDER NO EVIL
Two Faith Traditions and the Problem of Academic Freedom
in Religious Higher Education

Cascade Books
An Imprint of Wipf and Stock Publishers
199 W. 8th Ave., Suite 3
Eugene, OR 97401

www.wipfandstock.com

ISBN 13: 978-1-62032-489-9

Cataloguing-in-Publication data:

Withrow, Brandon.

Consider no evil : two faith traditions and the problem of academic freedom in
religious higher education / Brandon G. Withrow and Menachem Wecker.

xviii + 198 pp. ; 23 cm. Includes bibliographical references and index.

ISBN 13: 978-1-62032-489-9

1. Academic freedom. 2. Scholars—Religious life. 3. Universities and colleges—
United States—Religion. I. Wecker, Menachem. II. Title.

LB2324 .W58 2014

Manufactured in the U.S.A.

To my father, Greg:

You taught me to think for myself,
but I've never felt that meant to think alone.
Thanks for the spirited discussions over breakfast at "the cafe."

—BGW

To my grandfather:

Although we didn't always agree on every religious topic,
you were an inspiration to me always.
I miss you every day.

—MW

Contents

Acknowledgments

From both authors:

We are deeply appreciative of the magic that Mindy Rice Withrow introduced to our chapters. She truly has all of the gifts of the Greek Muses, and it seems criminal for her name not to appear on the cover as well.

From Brandon:

Sitting across from my bookshelves, I imagine the horde of names that fill those acknowledgments—hundreds of people without whom my shelf would be bare. The same could be said for this book, which would not be possible without those whose personal stories gave me cause to write it (Peter Enns, Sam Logan, Steve Taylor, and Doug Green).

I'm grateful to my coauthor, Menachem, whose friendship was unexpected but now prized. We discuss religion 140 characters at a time; it may not be efficient, but it is always illuminating.

My thoughts have repeatedly turned to my fellow students and administrators, especially those who uniquely understand this book because of our shared grief, particularly Mark and Karyn Traphagen, whose abilities to chart new paths are inspiring, and Art Boulet, whose snark will always get a like on Facebook. I'm similarly grateful to Diana and Jeff Frazier for the many Friday nights talking near the pool. Nothing makes a controversy go down better than a finger of scotch.

To my family, who make an appearance in the first chapter: I love you dearly and wouldn't change a thing (well, maybe just one or two).

Thanks to my newest community of friends, who have nothing to do with these controversies; you're a breath of fresh air. To my research assistant, Brandon Goodling: thank you for your careful sleuthing; you're a fantastic scholar. MaryAnn Mead, you'll find what you are looking for in chapter 3.

Finally, I'm grateful to Paul Raushenbush, my editor at *The Huffington Post*; to Jahnabi Barooah, former assistant editor at *HuffPost*, whose work has modeled for me how modern religious thinkers can contribute to the betterment of society; and to the editors at Cascade, Charlie Collier and Christian Amondson, for having faith in another volume.

From Menachem:

I am very thankful to my many friends, relatives, and teachers who have allowed me to speak freely and endured my often misguided notions and theories, and—perhaps most importantly—to all the rabbis, teachers, administrators, and others who have, inadvertently, showed me the value of academic freedom by so skillfully exhibiting the inverse. I would also like to acknowledge the input of the many people I interviewed for this book, many of whom asked not to be named.

Above all, I am extremely grateful to Brandon for his careful readings of my chapters and for holding my hand (so to speak) as I waded through the scary waters of academic citations and footnotes.

Introduction

Brandon G. Withrow

Buridan's ass is a classic tale—a dilemma—of a donkey that is equally hungry and equally thirsty. Walking along the center of a path, he discovers an alluring pail of water on one side and a hearty bucket of hay on the other, but each was equally distant from where he stood. What does he do?

"Water is the logical priority, I assume," one student says as I present this tale in a philosophy class. Students automatically think of the donkey as a person, as if it has a rational mind.

"Remember what happens when we assume," I remind the students. They chuckle. The point of the story is that a donkey is not rational, and without an overwhelming desire for either water or food, or a rational mind to push it one way or another, it will die in the path.

Human beings, so goes the point, are not like donkeys. None of us can have a Buridan's ass moment. We have motivations for what we do, and there is no truly libertarian free will. Decision-making motivators may be encoded in our genes or introduced by outside forces, but at some point we are pushed one way or the other off the path and toward the logical destination.

Likewise, academic freedom can never be absolutely free. Many of us in academia might imagine a moment when we could say and do whatever we think best without overt influence by others. But the reality is that we are limited—limited by the vision of a school's administration, by the professional standards of our specific specializations, or, if in a religious institution, by the boundaries of the faith statement of our tradition.

In this book, Menachem and I set out to look at the restrictions placed on the academic freedom of students and professors by the traditions of their communities. We each look at stories of those within our respective traditions who have come under suspicion, been disciplined or fired for their challenges to the status quo of their universities, colleges, and seminaries. These are tragic stories—real conflicts within communities, affecting the everyday lives of real people—set in both Christian and Jewish worlds; they demonstrate that despite the differences between these religions, there are shared themes and concerns when it comes to religious education today.

An outsider's view on these situations may give the impression that these are simple cases of semantics, or good guys defending a tradition from cultural takeover, or entitled faculty members complaining about a loss of privilege. But an insider's view reveals the historical nuances, the unique considerations of academia, the damage caused by strong-willed leaders making unilateral decisions, the malignancy of a community turned upon itself, and the complexities of the human element present in every situation.

The Human Dilemma of Today's Academy

It's the human side of these stories that so many overlook. Why, someone once asked me, would anyone stay at a seminary when they question its confession of faith? Why don't they just leave? Where is that person's integrity? The answer is complex. So from the start of this discussion, it is important to understand why the loss of a faculty position may be devastating, and why the chance to avoid such a situation might compel someone to remain silent about her sexual orientation or his changing beliefs. Students may see faculty as intellectuals with significant power on the world stage, but the reality is that our worlds are very fragile, and that fragility is increasing every year. In fact, that is why a book like this is necessary.

There is no job hunt like the hunt for a faculty position. If you've had this experience, then you understand why I bring it up as an example of the tenuousness of academic life; and if you haven't had this experience, putting yourself in the shoes of the faculty position seeker will go a long way in helping you understand the concerns of this book.

Institutions generally begin their searches at least a year or more from their hire date, which means unemployed faculty applying for these positions have a long wait. For employed faculty whose conflicts involve theological disagreement with their institutions, the length alone of this process makes the prospect of finding a new position daunting and encourages silence. (That silence may be a possible solution in some instances, as not all mountains are worth dying on—and I'll address this more in chapter 7—though it rarely ends well.)

Unlike many jobs familiar to the public, most academic positions require a significant application process that goes well beyond a *curriculum vitae* (an academic resume) and application letter. A bundled faculty application may include significant statements on teaching philosophy, research plans, and multiple recommendation letters from colleagues (which can be complicated to obtain for those who don't want to draw attention to their impending exits). They may also include writing samples, demonstrations of teaching competency, sample syllabi, and sample student evaluations. Most require transcripts from all higher educational institutions attended, and if copies do not suffice, applicants likely must pay for official copies.[1]

After the extended preparation of this overstuffed manila envelope, the hopeful candidate is greeted by deafening silence. Depending on how the search committee is managed, that silence may continue for months, resolved only by the dreaded form letter or email. That pain is only increased if the candidate has already invested in the hope of interviewing for the position at his or her annual professional association meeting—a common interview location for many hiring schools—and unemployed academics often drop $1,500 to $2,500 on a credit card to cover hotel, flight, and meeting registration, only to discover that they won't be invited to interview there after all.

What do you do then? Apply for another position. Weep. Repeat.

I'm not trying to overdramatize this common experience but to point out how it contributes to the situations described in this book. Part of the problem in the academic job market today is one of production. The number of new PhDs continues to outpace the number of available academic posts each year. Like scavenger birds fighting over a fresh corpse along the interstate, academics eagerly push their way in, hoping to peck away at a small piece of the carcass. But the numbers are against them.

Consider a PhD in history, for example. According to the American Historical Association (the primary professional society for many historians), the number of advertised positions during the 2011–12 academic year was 740 (627 jobs were posted in the previous year). The number of new PhDs granted in the same academic year was approximately 1,100 (a year

---

1. Transcripts at some institutions are free for the first few requests; at others they cost anywhere from two to ten dollars each. Multiplied by thirty or fifty or a hundred applications, this can become a financial burden for the unemployed academic.

earlier that figure was 1,066).[2] Now figure in that new PhDs are competing with existing and still unemployed PhDs who lost their positions during the economic downturn. If you're not yet sufficiently depressed by the numbers, consider that more and more colleges and universities are hiring contingent faculty (adjuncts and shorter-term, contract-based employment), rather than traditional full-time, tenure-track professors. Adjunct faculty are now a collective of PhDs in poverty, cobbling together part-time teaching posts without benefits and hoping to make their rent. The abundance of production and the decreased demand for full-time faculty has turned academia into an intellectual version of the dollar store.

At Kalamazoo Valley Community College, for example, which hires more than 300 part-time faculty members who earn approximately $2,400 per course (for 15 weeks of work), adjunct work is nothing more than a poorly paid internship. Full-time faculty at Kalamazoo, recognizing that their contingent colleagues would not receive their first paychecks until a full month after the start of class, pooled together a pantry of food items, gift cards, and cash to help them get through the dry weeks of work without pay.[3]

Aside from the dreaded job market, there also may be conflicting considerations of integrity that can impact one's decision to leave. To those well suited to their school's faith statements, it may look like a lack of integrity if a faculty member remains in a position even when his or her changing beliefs conflict with those espoused by the school. But it is a problem of cognitive dissonance, that is, two points of concern that appear at odds and make a clear decision feel impossible. Is it more important to resign over some degree of doctrinal disagreement or to feed, clothe, and shelter your family? What if you have a sick spouse or child and you need to keep your health insurance? What responsibility do professors have to the students who traveled across the country to study with them specifically, or to those whose dissertations or theses they are chairing? Is it worth it to uproot children, pulling them from their grandparents or schools, and incur significant expenses in order to move across the country for a temporary or adjunct position?

There are no simple solutions for faculty who must leave their teaching posts, and that anxiety can be increased significantly when the leaving is involuntary. For those who work in schools where new leadership or

2. June, "Jobs for Historians," para. 3.
3. Dunn, "Part-Time Faculty Wait for Payday," para. 11.

growing donor influence are driving changes in what faculty suddenly must now affirm in their beliefs, lifestyle, or sexual orientation, there may be little time on the clock to find an amicable solution. Even worse, since many religious institutions are exempt, they do not contribute to unemployment, meaning that when a professor is let go for ideological reasons there is no public help to offset the attending financial difficulty.

And a faculty member who feels he or she was unjustly fired, based on beliefs, gender, or race, cannot necessarily sue for damages. In 2009, two tenured professors, Laurence H. Kant and Jimmy Kirby, were let go from Lexington Theological Seminary for reasons of financial exigency, according to the seminary. Both faculty members sued, asserting that they believed race played a role (Kant is Jewish and Kirby is black). But the courts refused to hear their cases even upon appeal. In order to uphold the Establishment Clause, U.S. courts treat religious faculty as ministers, even though no denomination assumes official ordained roles of professors just because they are faculty at their schools. (Being Jewish, as Kant noted, meant he would not have been considered a minister in any Christian church.) But the courts interpreted the case as a religious matter in which they could not get involved. So proving discrimination or enforcing tenure contracts may be impossible if, as in this case, an institution can convince a court that it is a religious matter.[4]

Leaving an academic position—voluntarily or involuntarily—is therefore neither easy nor simple. The examples in this book of faculty (and students) who have run afoul of the religious limitations of their institutions are intended to demonstrate the real problem of academic freedom in a religious context. We put these situations into a historical framework and attempt to offer some potential solutions to help individuals and institutions avoid such situations in the future.

The Story of This Book

Menachem and I met in 2008. After I had written a piece for *The Chronicle of Higher Education* on being a PhD in a world of social media, blogging, and online education,[5] he contacted me to do an interview, first for his blog and then for the *Houston Chronicle*. We've been friends ever since, chatting weekly through Twitter and Facebook. I went on to become an assistant

4. Basu, "Tenure at Risk," paras. 3–4, 10, 15.
5. See Withrow, "Not Your Father's PhD."

professor of the history of Christianity and religious studies, teaching at a seminary and a university; he became an education reporter for *U.S. News & World Report* and freelanced as an arts and religion reporter. We finally met in person late in the summer of 2012 over dinner at the National Press Club in Washington, DC, where we signed the contract for this book.

The idea for the book came from a piece I wrote, in 2011, for *The Chronicle of Higher Education* titled "Finding Empathy in Religious Studies." Menachem and I had a long conversation about the article and how it related to experiences we had had within our own faith traditions. When he suggested that the themes of the article deserved a book-length exploration, I agreed to pursue it if he would join me as the coauthor. Thus *Consider No Evil: Two Faith Traditions and the Problem of Academic Freedom in Religious Higher Education* was born.

How to Read This Book

This volume is a personal, analytical look at higher education. Menachem and I were raised in very conservative households and attended conservative educational institutions. Our two personal stories make up Part One of this book. While we were raised according to different religious traditions—his Orthodox Jewish, mine conservative Evangelical Christian—we discovered many similarities in what we experienced with our families, in our educational endeavors, and in our current trajectories. So the two chapters in Part One may be read as our memoirs, offering some insight into the worlds in which we were raised and the presuppositions that guided our educational pursuits. They also connect our stories to controversies at the educational institutions we attended, laying the foundation for analysis in subsequent chapters.

In Part Two, we turn to the history of education in each of our traditions. My chapter explores the world of Western education and its entanglement in Christian theology. Menachem's chapter focuses on the Jewish story of education in exile, where scholars learned in community, without the brick and mortar that laid the foundation for the established schools of Western Christianity.

Part Three jumps ahead to more recent history, where we examine controversies at universities, colleges, and seminaries since the turn of the millennium. These stories return to schools we know well, looking at controversial professors and institutional revolutions that turned life upside down for faculty and students. Here we attempt to diagnose some of the problems that lead to faculty terminations and student confrontations.

And finally, Part Four ventures into the world of potential solutions. While not at all exhaustive, our comments call for a reexamination by religious institutions of their priorities, and encourage faculty and students to take stock of the reality they embody.

This book is not designed to be comprehensive. Menachem and I intentionally set out to stick closely to the traditions we know best. We discovered that across our religious traditions we had common experiences and concerns about religion and higher education. We believe that even though we ride close within our narrower traditions, others will—like us—recognize these common threads in their own traditions, and perhaps benefit from our proposals.

So while I discuss the history of Christian education and broad concerns of theology or higher education, I am ultimately tying this to the conservative educational world I know best; and as a professor, my chapters are primarily centered on issues surrounding faculty. But Menachem's chapters closely follow happenings at Yeshiva University, his alma mater, and students and the student experience will feature more prominently in his case studies.

Lastly, there are two ways to read this book, and unlike the example of Buridan's ass, one may be more appealing than the other. The first is to read it from beginning to end, as you read any other book. The second way is to read by author. In the first approach, our topics will be consistent but our distinct voices will be heard from one chapter to the next; in the second approach, our stories will flow more independently and provide a more consistent experience.

However you read, it's our belief that what follows will resonate with many. And it's our hope that it will help prevent more stories like those examined here.

PART ONE

Our Stories

1

No Good Education Goes Unpunished

Brandon G. Withrow

The boy tosses in his bed and calls out to his father. At nine years old, he knows there are no ghosts. He does not need a glass of water. He's not sick. So what's troubling him?

His mind whirls with what-ifs. What if he's not really a Christian? What if his first, second, and third time of receiving Jesus into his heart weren't real? What if hell has a special place just for unrepentant little boys?

His father, a pastor accustomed to addressing the spiritual doubts of others, walks in and places a soothing hand on his shoulder. "Do you want to pray again?" he asks.

"Yes."

And so they do.

Saying "I'm a pastor's kid" is more than a statement of identity; it's a confession. Being around other pastors' kids (PKs for short) resembles an Alcoholics Anonymous meeting. We confess our unhealthy relationship to the church and the damage it has caused. Unlike AA meetings, however, many of us are still in that unhealthy relationship—though there are plenty of PKs who can tell you the exact date of their last "drink."

This chapter is an admission of perspective. I was raised, educated, and now teach in the evangelical world. These pages reflect my time in three conservative evangelical schools, their controversies as experienced through my student eyes, and how these institutions and their controversies shaped my educational and career direction. It's a story of theologians struggling for control and how theology has served their narratives. My understanding of religious higher education is deeply entwined with these experiences; my conclusions are inseparable from this phenomenology. For that reason, I begin with a short memoir, and a fair warning: it's not always a positive story.

In the Beginning

My father, born William Gregory, is Greg to his friends. Like his father before him, he struggled with alcohol abuse in early adulthood. When I was around three years old, he and my mother were on the verge of separation, thanks in part to his drinking. Unfortunately, there's nothing unusual about that. Countless Sunday morning services since the dawn of "the testimony" genre have started this way.

Faced with the possibility of repeating the mistakes of his alcoholic and drug-addicted father, Dad reached a crisis moment. Late one evening, probably flipping channels on a commercial break during *Barney Miller*, he encountered Billy Graham's sermon on 1 Corinthians 6:10 that "thieves, the greedy, drunkards, revilers, robbers—none of these will inherit the kingdom of God." There was no escaping it; replace "drunkard" with my father's name, and Billy Graham—the evangelical pope with Apostle Paul-like authority—had just condemned him to an eternity in hell. That night, he walked the metaphorical aisle in our living room and fell to his knees before the soft-blue shekinah glory of the television.

This was more than an evening of drunken sadness, phase two of the Sisyphean cycle of drink, repent, repeat. He was determined to find a new path. (Determination is a characteristic of his that I've always tried to emulate.) So shortly after his conversion experience, he found himself active in the Free Methodist Church, a community that became his starting place for exploring his new theological world.

Free Methodists are no strangers to the effectiveness of evangelical guilt. In this circle, Dad faced reminders that his actions could affect his eternal condition. You may be saved today, but grace is only a few sins away from slipping out of one's grasp. While he was concerned about which sins could damn him, he never found an answer that satisfied and he settled firmly on the idea of a grace that never gives up on the sinner. For a recovering alcoholic, this threat of eternal loss is powerful, but for him the security of grace made better sense of Christ's cross. He took cheap beer off his shopping list, threw out his porn and rock music, and made things right with my mother.

Another trait of Methodism is that it doesn't take long before one is pulled into ministry. He began teaching Sunday school classes and soon entertained the idea of a seminary education. One day, after he told my mother he was considering ordination, the denomination's magazine appeared in his mailbox. The words "So you want to be a pastor, but don't know where to begin" ran across the cover, which he took as a possible prompting from God. Within little time, he began working towards ordination, taking a few college classes locally, and making it through the first stages. He didn't have an undergraduate degree, but the Association of Theological Schools allows for a small percentage of students to enter a program based on life experience.

He never finished the process of ordination. Serious theological change sent him down a different path, one that would have a significant effect on me and my educational choices.

The Family Business

My father and several family members who attended the same church eventually left the Free Methodists to form an independent church with congregational governance and a Baptist doctrine of grace. They called it The Assembly of Christians. My father, a mentor of his, and an aunt and uncle were involved in leadership. Dad received his first license to marry at the age of twenty-six, and the first wedding he officiated was his sister's.

My life as a pastor's kid was set in stone.

The family church was conservative, dualistic, and often contradictory, with one foot in mainstream evangelicalism's pop culture and the other firmly planted in stricter fundamentalist doctrine. Alcohol and secular music were taboo, but the church loved its Christian hippie music. (The 1970s birthed an industry of Christian alternatives to mainstream music, complete with Christian versions of popular songs, the advent of praise music, and Christian superstars—big fish in a relatively small pond.) Compared to many fundamentalist Baptist preachers, my father's long Sonny Bono hair and wash-worn blue jeans made him stand out in the pulpit. But as progressive as the church's look may have been, its theology was generally conservative.

I've never been able to paint my father and "The Assembly," as they still call themselves, with a broad brush. There were moments when their independent mindset and their disconnect from the historical tradition defied strict categories. "One man's conservative is another man's liberal" is an aphorism of my father's that continues to prove itself.

In those early years, to those outside of our conservative world, he was no doubt a fundamentalist preacher, but for those on the inside, he was far from being a real conservative. In fact, among the parents at my Baptist grade school, Dad was considered a liberal. Who but a liberal would have "long" hair (reaching the collar of his shirt)? Who but a liberal would prefer contemporary Christian music to the hymns of the faith? Who but a liberal would take his kids to see *Indiana Jones* in the theater? (Many of our Baptist friends refused to buy the local newspaper because it advertised movies.) Being a "liberal," my father was rarely welcome at PTA meetings.

But there were areas of life and belief where we were clearly closer to fundamentalism. We were young-earth creationists, rejecting evolution as "only a theory," which we defined as "a guess." The Assembly, then and now, maintained the view that it is not biblical for women to be in pastoral ministry, hold the office of deacon, or serve as ushers. In the early years, our apocalyptic imagination was held captive by the dispensational view of the end of the world, most familiar today as the theology of the *Left Behind* novels. It was common for me to join the adults in regular weekly Bible studies, during which we scanned the newspaper for signs of the coming antichrist and compared what we found with the predictions of book of Revelation.

In addition to this progressive-fundamentalist duality, our lonely congregation had times of stability and times of great tumult. In the earliest years, The Assembly met in several odd locations, including the office of a chiropractic center, the basement of our house, the back room of a laundromat, an old school, and then above a Tupperware office. We eventually made it to our own building, where the congregation grew to around 150 members.

And it was a family church, by which I mean it was eventually filled with and run by my father's sisters, their husbands, and friends. Church equaled family, and vice versa. This was often beneficial for my brother and me, since both The Assembly and our immediate family moved around the Toledo area with some regularity. At the time, Toledo was not small enough to be quaint, but not large enough to have much beyond movie theaters and bowling. The church and its connection to my extended family offered stability.

It also baptized me into the gladiatorial world of Christians eating Christians. We attracted families that were looking for a place to worship and find community, but we also had a knack for collecting those who'd left a wake of trouble at previous churches. Plenty of self-proclaimed prophets showed up at our doors peddling their apocalyptic schisms. There were groups who thought Christ would return in 1988 and 1994 and every year between and after. They brought with them a persecution complex that was generally self-fulfilling. And in each case, the church leaders felt the need to protect the congregation, while the prophets felt their authoritative messages from God were being ignored.

But the two largest catastrophes came not from outsiders but from within—disputes over authority that involved members of my extended family. The first occurred when I was a child, in 1982. My most vivid memory was sitting in the family van while my parents and my father's siblings argued loudly in the front yard of the building the church rented. I remember a close friend of my father's jumping into the van to distract my brother and me and keep us from getting upset. The dispute lasted for a while, leading to my father seeking advice from a seasoned minister and the congregation voting to install more of my uncles as leaders, with one as the music minister. When the dust settled, my father's mentor and an aunt and uncle were gone. It would be years before that first rift healed.

Then when I was fifteen, a second debate over doctrine and church authority embroiled the remaining family members. It began with a cousin who ran into trouble with the law, leaving the leadership of an uncle (who was also a minister in our church) in question. This time my paternal grandmother left with the rest of my aunts and uncles. It was a devastating moment in the history of The Assembly, and I watched my father break down in tears. He tendered his resignation, only to have it refused by the remaining (non-family) leadership. The last of the family disappeared out the doors, never to return. There were no awkward Thanksgivings or Christmases after that, because the connection was severed completely.

It might seem unbelievable that a grandmother would cut off her grandsons because of a disagreement, but at the time my grandmother felt her bread and butter were with the departing family members, and so went her allegiance. She also really knew how to hold a grudge. This was a woman who'd once had a bad experience at a shoe store, and after it went out of business and was replaced by a series of other businesses, she refused to buy anything from any store that occupied the same building.

The summer after she left the church, I frequently rode my bike to her place, hoping to keep that relationship fresh, but I was always greeted at her door by "the grudge." Years passed without birthday cards, Christmas cards, or even an acknowledgment of my existence if we happened to run into her somewhere. Even on her deathbed, as my father sat next to her in quiet conversation, she refused to make her peace with him.

Countless family dinners were disrupted by congregants calling for my father. He gave hours of counsel to people with troubled relationships, spent long days in the hospital with the sick and grieving, shared financial resources with others in need even though we didn't have much—only to discover that one day they, too, would leave the church over a theological disagreement. Whenever I hear the advice not to go into business with family, I immediately think of those early years in my father's church. Twenty-five years later, no divisions of this magnitude have occurred again in his congregation, though plenty of friends have come and gone, and there are still moments when a member of the congregation is formally disciplined for adultery or causing division. Nevertheless, my first impressions of Christianity were formed in these rough, early years.

Yes, I have great memories too—regular church picnics, friendly pranks, talent shows that showcased the bizarre humor of our congregation, close friends who graciously put up with my overly pious teenage opinions, food and comfort regularly offered by good people.

But looking back over my experiences in theological higher education, and all the disputes over church authority and theology, it's not surprising that those experiences resemble the most formative ones of my upbringing.

A New Identity

The biggest theological change for The Assembly came shortly after the second family split. Our Baptist roots had been firmly planted in a tradition that emphasized free will, an unchallenged remnant of the Free Methodist tradition. But in the years following the second split, that ideology was displaced by a Calvinist perspective, nudging us into more of a Reformed Baptist tradition.

There were many reasons for this transition, one of which might have been a desire to understand how God could allow—or was it ordain?—such painful interpersonal conflicts, and I welcomed this perspective with all the fervor of a young man searching for answers to life's hardest questions. Looking back, I realize that, to me, one of the most significant outcomes of this theological shift was the people it brought into our circle.

I'm no longer a Calvinist but I'm happy that I inhabit the place in the multiverse where this change occurred. Because at nearly the same time that The Assembly embraced Reformed doctrines, a new family arrived looking for a church that shared their Calvinist convictions. The oldest daughter was sixteen, homeschooled with her four siblings, and raised on an apple orchard where her father had painted "Jesus Saves" in giant letters across the roof of his barn. I was nineteen, schooled by the state, and had never had more than an eighth of an acre for a backyard. When we met, I was dating the music minister's daughter, but apparently it had been predetermined that I'd break up with her and fall in love with Mindy, the orchard girl, because within a few years we were married and enrolled at Moody Bible Institute in Chicago.

You'd think that as a pastor's kid—after a childhood of rising early for Sunday services and filling the rest of every week with Wednesday night services, Bible studies, youth group meetings, potlucks, and service projects—an early retirement from the church experience would be a reasonable desire. Many children of ministers want nothing to do with the church community or theology by the time they reach college.

But not me. I went on to earn a bachelor of arts in theology. And the theological disputes of my early years would prove to be like high school preparatory programs for my higher educational experiences.

Schooled in Chicago

Mindy and I, both theology majors at Moody, were deeply apprehensive about our new world. Higher education was not a family tradition. Neither my family nor Mindy's had set aside funds for it. In fact, my grandparents on both sides of the family had fourth-grade educations at best, and my dad worked as a precision grinder while pastoring before becoming a full-time minister later in life.

Chicago was (at first) a large cement monster. We spent four years downtown, and then another two a little further north. Exposed to a new abundance of other cultures and church traditions, we began to read and think more broadly and eventually to establish theological perspectives distinct from our communities of origin.

In what was a radical shift for us then (though looking back it was probably imperceptible to outsiders), we moved from being Reformed Baptist Calvinists to Presbyterian Calvinists. Among other things, this meant that to our Baptist parents, who looked forward to grandchildren, we would be committing the sin of baptizing infants. We now followed the Westminster Confession of Faith—a second Bible for Presbyterians—and no longer embraced what we felt was the science fiction of dispensationalism.

We also underwent a significant change of view on the role of women within the church. Despite the fact that Moody was a mostly patriarchal institution (Exhibit A: as a male theology major, I took a preaching class called "Homilectics" while Mindy, as a female theology major, took a preaching class called "Sermon Preparation for Women"), Mindy found professors there who helped her rethink her place in the world. She joined a literary discussion group led by a feminist English professor who mentored her honors students. The group was entirely female; some male students, undoubtedly echoing the sentiments of their professorial mentors, spread the rumor that the group's members were lesbians. (Apparently, in a conservative Christian school only lesbians are smart.)

This situation was followed by a walkout protest sparked by an invitation to Anne Graham Lotz to speak at Moody's yearly student conference. Several male students were appalled that a woman would be allowed to speak publicly. Though required to attend, they sat in the front row of the auditorium and made a show of marching out when she stepped into the pulpit. The following year, the school's leadership invited only men to speak. In protest over the administration's tacit support of misogyny, Mindy and I wrote a letter to the school's president. When he did not reply, we published it as an open letter in the campus newspaper—and only then received a personal reply. We became known as activists for gender equality.

During our time at Moody, feminism was not the only divisive force among faculty and students. The real controversy was about which type of dispensationalist you were. Half of the faculty members were Classic Dispensationalists, while the others were Progressive Dispensationalists. Classics understood the promises of the Old Testament to be offered to Israel alone and the fulfillment of the Davidic throne in the Messiah to be realized only in the future millennial reign of Christ after the second coming. The Christian church is a gap in the plan of God, they argue, a parenthetical moment between the promises to Israel and their ultimate fulfillment. Classic Dispensationalism was deeply ingrained in Moody's history.

But in the early 1990s, Progressive Dispensationalists were looking to reimagine dispensationalism by emphasizing the progressive nature of the promises of God. Rather than postpone the fulfillment of the Old Testament promises of a Davidic reign to the millennial kingdom, they concluded that the promises of God were fulfilled progressively, meaning partially now (already) and partially in the future (not yet). They wanted to transform Moody's tradition to welcome the progressives.

Obviously, all hell broke loose.

Faculty began fretting over this new travesty of theology, secretly posting negative comments and articles to their colleague's corkboards outside of their offices, trash-talking each others' books in classes, and decrying what they believed was a horrendous theological lie. The devil was in the details of Progressive Dispensationalism. (Both sides believed in a literal devil.)

As students always do, they began taking sides. Some went as far as posting protest signs in the windows of their dorms and writing op-ed pieces in the student paper. "Why have us read the books of other views if you don't want us to ever consider those views?" asked one student. Another student lampooned the divided professors in his student paper cartoon "Calvin and Hodge"—i.e., John Calvin and Charles Hodge—an obvious parody of *Calvin and Hobbes.*

The feverish dispute wasn't just an argument between faculty colleagues; it had serious ramifications for students. Every student had to sign a doctrinal statement demonstrating his or her "orthodoxy" in order to graduate. My final semester, as I walked through the halls of the Sweeting Center reading the statement that fit easily on a three-by-five card, I was intercepted by the professor who was leading the charge to require a more thorough statement in order to limit the graduation of progressives.

"You know what that means," he told me, pounding his fingers into the statement hard enough to leave indentations. His eyes never blinked. "You know what that means and if you can't sign it, you can't graduate."

But I walked away, sure of one thing. If I had failed to learn and change from my time in this institution, I thought, then what was the purpose of being here? Being able to sign the statement in the way that I understood it would mean that my education enabled me to be my own person, not a carbon copy of one man. So I signed it and graduated.

As deeply provincial as that debate was, it was merely a reminder of what I was already well versed in from my time as a pastor's kid: many Christians are adept at eating each other alive. The real crime there was the failure of some professors to be educators instead of theological hall monitors.

Watching the dispute among faculty and experiencing the pressure over perceived orthodoxy led me to a new appreciation for theological diversity. This is not to say that I became a freethinker, in the traditional sense, but I discovered a desire to be among those who were less afraid of other opinions.

And as ironic as it may sound, that conclusion meant I'd be taking up with evangelicals for my next degree.

The Evangelicals

A Moody professor introduced me to the broader evangelical world and suggested I consider Trinity Evangelical Divinity School at Trinity International University (Deerfield, Illinois), where I earned a master of arts in the history of Christian thought. Compared to Moody, Trinity had plenty of diversity within its faculty and was therefore a breath of fresh air. While the divinity school's tradition was the Evangelical Free Church, many traditions are represented. Faculty do have to sign a doctrinal statement, but not students.

My first experience with theological controversy at Trinity was the result of a movement known as Evangelicals and Catholics Together (ECT). Unlike the conflict at Moody, however, the fighting was not between "colleagues" of the same department; this fight covered a swath of the larger evangelical world.

ECT was an attempt between ecumenically minded evangelical leaders like my advisor in the church history department, Dr. John Woodbridge, to open up discussions between evangelicals and Catholics on the idea of Christian unity. For nearly two years, during my weekly advisee meetings with Woodbridge, we were immersed in discussion about whether Catholics and evangelicals could and should find a place for peaceful conversation to resolve their differences for the sake of joint missions and in opposition to secularism.

Unlike Catholic Christians, evangelicals have no hierarchal authority to help moderate and support these types of discussions. When evangelical leaders attempt to engage in a dialogue of this magnitude, they often find themselves embroiled in debates with each other. Those evangelicals who opposed the conversation appeared to see themselves as defending the

Protestant Reformation and therefore the gospel. Any attempt for evangelicals to work with Catholics, as they saw it, compromised doctrines of grace and justification by faith.

This very public controversy led to a number of reactionary books and articles splashed across the pages of *Christianity Today*. Those promoting evangelical and Catholic dialogue included leading Catholic thinkers like Jesuit priest and later cardinal Avery Dulles, and former Lutheran-turned-Catholic priest and founding editor of the journal *First Things*, Richard John Neuhaus. Well-known evangelical cosigners and contributors to the movement were former Special Counsel to President Nixon, Chuck Colson; Campus Crusade's Bill Bright; Christian Broadcasting Network's Pat Robertson; historian and then Wheaton College professor Mark Noll; Calvinist icon and professor J. I. Packer; the executive editor of *Christianity Today* and academic dean of Beeson Divinity School, Timothy George; and my professor at Trinity, John Woodbridge. Those evangelicals opposed to the effort were best known in Reformed evangelical circles, and included Ligonier Ministries' R. C. Sproul; Grace Community Church pastor, John F. MacArthur; televangelist John Ankerburg; professor Michael Horton; and the now deceased D. James Kennedy and John H. Gerstner.[1]

The controversy over ECT officially and publicly began in March 1994 with the joint statement of purpose "Evangelicals and Catholics Together: The Christian Mission in the Third Millennium." Initially, this was an affirmation of a common faith for the sake of proclaiming "the good news" and contending "for the truth that politics, law, and culture must be secured by moral truth." Signers wanted to reverse the advancement of secularism, outlaw abortion, and promote religious freedom. They ran into difficulty with other evangelicals when they also affirmed together that "we are justified by grace through faith because of Christ."[2]

Opposition evangelicals, many of whom were members of Christians United for Reformation (CURE), believed this statement ignored real differences between the Protestant and Catholic doctrines of justification. Protestant emphasis on imputed and alien righteousness was essential to counter a Catholic view of infused righteousness, which they believed was contrary to the Pauline doctrine of grace. In an attempt to maintain evangelical unity, both sides of the dispute drafted a joint document called

---

1. This is a partial list. Gerstner passed away in the early stages of this discussion.

2. Colson and Neuhaus, *Evangelicals and Catholics Together*, ix, xxii–xxvi. A copy of the statement may be found online: http://www.firstthings.com/article/2007/01/evangelicals--catholics-together-the-christian-mission-in-the-third-millennium-2.

"Resolutions for Roman Catholic and Evangelical Dialogue," which affirmed that "while both Evangelicals and Roman Catholics affirm the ecumenical Creeds, we do not see this catholic consensus as a sufficient basis for declaring that agreement exists on all the essential elements of the Gospel."[3] This attempt to reaffirm evangelical unity on the doctrine of justification was only a temporary truce.

Over the next three years, the evangelical and Catholic dialogue continued, and concerned opponents were now under the banner of The Alliance of Confessing Evangelicals. They drafted "The Cambridge Declaration" (1996), which sounded an alarm that evangelicals were abandoning the doctrines of grace found in the Protestant Reformation.[4]

By December 1997, evangelicals and Catholics signed a new ecumenical statement known as "The Gift of Salvation," making it clear that they were "speaking not for, but from and to" their "several communities."[5] The Alliance once again countered with "An Appeal to Fellow Evangelicals" (1998), which indicated that they were "profoundly distressed" by "The Gift of Salvation," as it was "seriously flawed" on the Protestant teaching of the gospel.[6] The debate went on for a few years, resulting in several books and articles and eventual splits between former allies on the issue.[7]

While some students experienced the debate as a novelty, my connection went beyond being an advisee of ECT proponent John Woodbridge. Before arriving at Trinity, my new Reformed Presbyterian affiliation put me on the side of the opposition; but via my studies at Trinity, Woodbridge introduced me to an entirely new world of thinking. Christians did not have to agree on the fine details of how justification worked (infused or imputed), so as long as they agreed on the source of salvation (Jesus' death on the cross). While five hundred years of Reformation division between Catholics and Protestants was not meaningless, as he explained it to me, it

3. A copy of the statement may be found online: http://www.modernreformation.org/default.php?page=printfriendly&var2=876.

4. Alliance, "Cambridge Declaration," 14.

5. Evangelicals and Catholics Together, "Gift of Salvation," 35.

6. Alliance, "Appeal to Fellow Evangelicals," 29.

7. For a partial history of ECT, see my MA thesis, "Jonathan Edwards as a Resource for Current Evangelical Discussion over the Language of Justification" (1999). One Alliance member did change sides in this discussion. John H. Armstrong of *Reformation and Revival Journal* (who also gave me one of my first publishing opportunities) took a more ecumenical position, eventually forming an organization for ecumenical work and writing his book *Your Church Is Too Small: Why Unity in Christ's Mission Is Vital to the Future of the Church* (2010).

was also not an excuse to avoid Christ's ultimate desire expressed in John 17:21 that Christians be "one."

Even in agreeing with this new perspective, I remained strongly connected to the Reformed world that opposed ECT. A few members of the local Orthodox Presbyterian church I attended wondered how I could keep studying with Woodbridge given his obvious heresy. I received emails from Reformed friends—and from people I didn't really know, but who found my personal website where I wrote about theology—asking me to step away from the theological ledge of ecumenism.

Back home, The Assembly held yearly conferences called Toledo Reformed Theological Conferences (TRTC). The 1990s saw a revival of the conference movement among Reformed Christians. Among those invited to speak at TRTC were those named above who stood in opposition to ECT, though they were invited to speak on other theological issues. When I attended, I was often invited by my dad to join him and the speakers for lunch; and these occasions provided windows into how they understood ECT supporters. In short, the way they understood ECT was not my experience with it.

I became passionate about the subject, actively keeping documents and links to articles on my website, with the hope of combating misinformation. (It would not be the last time I did this for a cause.) As I worked in Trinity's alumni department, I helped organize a public lecture for Woodbridge to clarify the work of ECT. I wrote my MA thesis on the subject, published two related journal articles, and carefully worked the discussion into my introduction to a new edition of van Mastrich's *Treatise on Regeneration*.[8]

My childhood church introduced me to controversy on the congregational level, and Moody showed me how to apply it to a theology department. Trinity was my first real exposure to broad theological dispute across campuses, publishing houses, and theological traditions. But the real blood-thirsty division occurred at the last of my theological schools, Westminster Theological Seminary.

---

8. I wrote the introduction to and edited an edition of Dutch theologian Peter van Mastricht's *Treatise on Regeneration* (2002).

The Truly Reformed

Despite the ECT debate, I remained interested in the Presbyterian tradition. I arrived in Philadelphia shortly before September 11, 2001, to start a PhD in the history of Christianity. The program was historical and theological, and I hoped it would help resolve whether I was really Presbyterian. As it turned out, I was not.

Westminster was founded as the result of a dispute at Princeton Seminary in the early days of the fundamentalist-modernist controversy. The first few decades of the twentieth century left evangelicals with a fear that liberalism was taking over the educational world. Between 1910 and 1915, former president of Moody Bible Institute, R. A. Torrey, and the Baptist minister and evangelist A. C. Dixon put their opposition to liberalism in print by editing several volumes of *The Fundamentals: A Testimony to the Truth*. Each chapter defended their definition of Christian orthodoxy against their liberal enemies and included affirmations of the inerrancy of the Bible, the historicity of the miracles of the Bible, and the resurrection of Jesus from the dead. A symbol of the era was the media circus known as the Scopes Monkey Trial (1925), popularized by the movie *Inherit the Wind* (1960), in which John Scopes was accused of violating the law by teaching evolution in the public schools. The fundamentalist saw evolution as a liberal rejection of the inerrant authority of the Bible.

In New Jersey, Princeton Seminary was experiencing its own fears of encroaching liberalism. As conservative professors saw it, liberals were replacing the "Old Princeton" of Charles Hodge and Benjamin Warfield. Professor and Presbyterian minister J. Gresham Machen (1881–1937) wanted to return Princeton to its conservative roots, and his famous book *Christianity and Liberalism* (1923) was his call to rally. In the 1920s, Machen became a major evangelical leader. Moody Bible Institute invited Machen to speak at conferences and James M. Gray (academic dean at Moody) had suggested that Machen might replace him.[9] Machen's effort to keep Princeton Seminary conservative failed when the school reorganized in 1929, officially creating more room for his feared liberal opponents.

At this defeat, Machen and three other Princeton faculty members (Robert Dick Wilson, Oswald T. Allis, and Cornelius Van Til) decided to form Westminster Theological Seminary in Philadelphia (1929). Machen was also concerned that his denomination, The Presbyterian Church

---

9. Harris, *Fundamentalism*, 20; Carpenter, *Revive Us Again*, 41.

(USA), had given way to the liberal Social Gospel of Baptists like Walter Rauschenbusch and Harry Emerson Fosdick, and so he, along with others, founded the Independent Board for Presbyterian Foreign Missions (1933), an act that brought him up for disciplinary charges by his denomination.[10] Charles Woodbridge (father of John Woodbridge) represented him before the denomination, but they both found themselves disciplined and stripped of ordination. This led Machen to push for the formation of The Presbyterian Church in America, which eventually became the Orthodox Presbyterian Church.

For decades, Westminster had a reputation for controversy. When I graduated from Trinity and hoped to learn more about Presbyterianism, Westminster was one of the names I had heard, though I did not fully understand its culture. I was also under the impression that it had been slowly becoming more open to the broader evangelical world. In a private letter, conservative Presbyterian theologian John Gerstner warned me against attending Westminster since they had recently invited ECT signer Chuck Colson to speak in chapel. Given my new perspective on this subject, however, I did not see this as a bad thing. And as it happened, Westminster would soon turn back to its conservative roots.

By 2005 a full-blown controversy had broken out over a book by Peter Enns, a tenured faculty member in biblical studies, resulting in a major rift in the faculty and a dispute that spilled over into the broader evangelical and Presbyterian world. It was a dispute that clearly struck at the history of Westminster and pushed almost every creative theologian out, setting the school back on a path toward fundamentalism.

Enns's notorious book, *Inspiration and Incarnation: Evangelicals and the Problem of the Old Testament* (2005), addresses the concerns evangelicals often have on issues of higher criticism. When the Bible is subjected to the same scrutiny that is given to any ancient text, it is evident that its stories and texts reflect and borrow from the cultures of the day. The Mosaic law code, for example, is clearly connected to, or at least shares a very close historical trajectory with, the centuries-older Code of Hammurabi (eighteenth century BCE), a Babylonian legal code. The wording of the two law codes is very close. One might imagine the problem this poses for evangelicals, who stress the unique, inerrant, and divine origin of the Bible. If the Mosaic law is said to be by divine inspiration, yet it clearly borrows from a pre-existing legal culture, then one might argue that Scripture is not

10. Sweeney, *American Evangelical Story,* 101.

truly God's words. These conclusions had been central to the concerns of the fundamentalist-modernist controversy earlier in the century, leading to the formation of Westminster.

Enns recognized that evangelicals could not continue to ignore these points of higher criticism and remain academically relevant. So he proposed a better way to look at the issue, a way he dubbed the incarnational analogy. According to this thinking, as Christ is said to be fully divine and fully human but one person, so too one could see the Bible as (by way of analogy) divinely inspired while not disconnected from its human context. "To work within an incarnational paradigm means that our expectations of the Bible must be in conversation with the data," writes Enns, "otherwise we run the very real risk of trying to understand the Bible in fundamental isolation from the cultures in which it was written—which is to say, we would be working with a nonincarnate understanding of Scripture."[11]

This was only intended to be an analogy and never a precise, one-to-one comparison. Enns hoped to show a side of the Bible that would allow for critical analysis of its sources, while remaining respectful of its authority and place in theology. This includes recognizing that myth plays a role in the Bible, especially in Genesis. For evangelicals, the idea of myth carries with it the connotation of a "lie" or "deceptive story," but from an incarnational perspective, myths are designed to speak about a greater reality from within a prescientific community. God sees no need to correct these myths, as it is more important that his ideas communicate in a language understood by his people. "This is what it means for God to speak at a certain time and place—he enters *their* world," Enns writes. "He speaks and acts in ways that make sense to *them* . . . he accommodates, condescends, meets them where they are."[12]

The theologians exploded in response. Attacks on Enns's book ran the gamut from challenging the incarnational analogy by questioning its orthodoxy on christological discussions to arguing over doctrines of inerrancy. But *Inspiration and Incarnation* was clearly an attempt by Enns to develop ideas already present in the "theological tradition, represented by . . . [his] colleagues at Westminster Theological Seminary, past and present."[13] John Calvin's doctrine of divine accommodation, which is a strong part of that tradition, used very similar language to that of Enns.

11. Enns, *Inspiration and Incarnation*, 168.

12. Ibid., 56.

13. Ibid., 9.

In a later chapter, I will go into further detail about this dispute, but for now it is sufficient to say that part of the controversy centered on who properly represented the theological standards of the seminary, that is, the Westminster Confession of Faith. Many on faculty supported Enns, but others saw themselves as being the "truly Reformed," defenders of Westminster in the tradition of Machen. They were fighting the new liberalism.

The entire campus was caught up in the controversy. It drove conversations at the café, in the bookstore, during long conversations over scotch, and on the Internet. The same faculty that took aim at Enns also pushed out the president. It was clear that the plan was not only to address the theological position of *Inspiration and Incarnation* but also to restructure and reorganize the seminary with a fundamentalist agenda—the inverse of what had happened at Princeton Seminary earlier in the century.

A change in faculty and administration became the full agenda. Samuel T. Logan, who was also the chair of my dissertation committee, was removed from the presidency. In his place was installed Peter A. Lillback, whose presidential agenda included returning the school to a strong inerrancy, promoting his Reclaim America message (based on his Providence Forum ministry), and fighting the dangerous message of Dan Brown's *Da Vinci Code*.

Rather than Westminster's traditional mission of training ministers, the focus fell on Lillback's obsession with proving that George Washington was an orthodox Christian, eventually landing him the role of guest on then Fox News host Glenn Beck's show. Westminster became a platform for his self-published book, *George Washington's Sacred Fire* (2006). When students and employees expressed to the board their concerns about the direction of the school, they felt their degrees or jobs were on the line. Students published an online "Save Our Seminary" petition and took to their blogs to vocalize their fear over Westminster's new fundamentalist direction.

As a student, I did what I knew best (and what my embedded justice meter called for): I documented on my blog the events as they occurred.[14] I kept records and copies of every article published in journals, official and unofficial school records and statements on the situation, and even streamed secretly recorded audio of a meeting between the faculty and students. To their credit, the seminary never asked me to shut down my activity, though some faculty made it clear they were keeping tabs on my activities.

---

14. "Justice meter": the name Mindy and I have given to the unstoppable feeling that "somebody has to do something about this!"

As these events unfolded, I realized that I was making another intellectual and theological transition. Every day on campus presented new grist for the rumor mill. Between my connections as a student and Mindy's position directing the seminary's marketing communications office, it was impossible to avoid encountering more horror stories. The atmosphere was becoming intolerable. Then her boss was terminated unjustly and suddenly, with the swiftness of an amputation. Mindy felt she could no longer do her job promoting and speaking on behalf of the school.

By the end of 2006, my dissertation was complete; I'd be graduating in a few months and no longer needed to remain in residence. So the timing was perfect when I received an offer to be a visiting instructor at Samford University's Beeson Divinity School in Birmingham, Alabama. It provided a chance to work with Timothy George, and while we knew it would provide only a semester's worth of employment, we decided it was time to reinvent our daily life and find some peace of mind.

As with any controversy, it can be hard to hear about the problems of an institution day in and day out, especially when it involves people you love and respect. Our move to Birmingham gave us a chance to refocus our priorities, and it gave us both time to write. We were in the middle of writing (together) a five-volume history of Christianity, and I was publishing a book on Katherine Parr, the last wife of Henry VIII. We needed to be away from Philadelphia and the Westminster decline to make that happen. And we needed the geographical space to rethink our theological affiliations and reconsider why we consistently found ourselves in dog-eat-dog communities.

When I first arrived at Westminster, I thought I was finally evading the trappings of the fundamentalism that had marked my early years. I didn't understand then that my shift to Presbyterianism was, in part, a confusing of fundamentalism with specifics of theology rather than a way of seeing the world. I had simply swapped one fundamentalism for another.

But that time was over. We devoted our season in Birmingham to exploring other traditions. Our exposure to Cathedral Church of the Advent, Birmingham's Episcopal center, eventually led us to affiliate with the Episcopal Church, leaving the Reformed world behind.

Lessons Learned

At the end of my visiting post at Beeson, we returned to Ohio while I applied for permanent positions. The U.S. economy was tanking, and openings in my field rapidly dried up. I became active in the American Academy of Religion, applying my background in religious history to developing a career in religious studies. My goal was no longer theology but the academic study of religion.

I secured a position at Winebrenner Theological Seminary (Findlay, Ohio) as assistant professor of the history of Christianity and religious studies. Compared to Westminster, Winebrenner is theologically diverse. And the position provided the opportunity to teach at the University of Findlay as an adjunct in the religious studies program.[15] I headed up the online education committee at Winebrenner, took part in the hiring of the new university librarian, and became director of a master of arts program. These were opportunities to start developing a professional life away from the theological world I knew and no longer respected.

The full story of my intellectual journey is beyond the scope of this chapter, but my time teaching religious studies, contributing to the religion section of *The Huffington Post*, the local hub of the Religion News Service, and *The Chronicle of Higher Education* has provided a new academic perspective and a broader appreciation of interreligious dialogue.

In reflecting on these past controversies, as well as current situations experienced by colleagues in other institutions, I've discovered a number of takeaways. I'll explore these in greater detail in a later chapter of this book, but three are worth noting here.

Disputes Are Foremost about Control

Whether you're a child in a church or a student in higher education, never underestimate the need for others to have control. At Moody, Classic Dispensationalists demanded control over the theology department, while progressives sought to maintain control over their academic freedom. Evangelicals and Catholics Together opened a feud over who truly represented evangelicalism and was authorized to speak for the Protestant Reformation. Westminster had a heritage of creativity and scholarship to

---

15. Winebrenner is associated with the University of Findlay, sharing a campus and an ecclesiastical history.

which Peter Enns believed he was contributing, much to the chagrin of those who wanted to control the seminary's story and keep it firmly within its fundamentalist origins.[16]

Divisions like these are fueled primarily by the desire to control a community or movement or to maintain control over one's rights and freedoms within a community. Whether or not the cause is just, power grabs always hurt people and wither communities.

Theology Is the Justifying Narrative for Maintaining Control

Before it was called "An Appeal to Fellow Evangelicals," The Alliance of Confessing Evangelicals called their document "The Battle for the Gospel."[17] The title was changed after the initial publication when ECT members took offense to the idea that they were somehow against the gospel of Jesus in wanting to work with other self-proclaimed Christians. But that original title is telling: the theological narrative was that of a battle, and in that battle one was either for or against the gospel. If there is anything evangelicals cannot abide, it's the idea of a false gospel. Theology became the justifying narrative for control of evangelicalism.

Similarly, Westminster's story was about far more than doctrine. Doctrinal differences alone would not have left employees feeling targeted or moved the board of trustees to bring in a ministry called Peacemakers to heal community rifts. The public face of the story was theological, as seminary representatives portrayed themselves as defenders of the trustworthiness and divine inspiration of the Bible. But Enns had never rejected these doctrines. Why then, after he left, did Westminster start its "Full Confidence Tour" to defend the Bible against criticism?[18] It became the theological narrative for the controversy.

In all of the situations I've recounted, a theological narrative aided power and control. One side was orthodox and the other was near heresy;

16. See Peter Enns's inauguration address as Professor of Old Testament and Biblical Hermeneutics from March 2006, published as Enns, "Bible in Context." See chapter 3 for an analysis on the rhetoric of the Westminster story.

17. While a student of Woodbridge, I alerted him to my discovery that The Alliance document, "Battle for the Gospel," had gone online under that title, even though ECT members had previously requested that the title be changed, given its inflammatory nature. The title was quickly altered, but it gave away their true perspective.

18. For information about Westminster Theological Seminary's "Full Confidence Tour," see http://www.wts.edu/alumni/events/fullconfidencetour1.html.

one was either on the side of God or on the side of the devil. Which side you were on depended solely on who was in control.

All Controversies Are More Complicated than We Realize

Recounting these controversies with a black-and-white simplicity would be a disservice. These stories are always far more complicated than they seem to be. While control plays a significant role in these divisions, there is no doubt in my mind that many of the individuals involved believed they were working for the greater good. After all, who wants the devil in control of a theological institution? And while theology serves the purpose of control, it would be grievous to leave the impression that all theologians in these disputes were simply, and consciously, making things up for the sake of a power grab. Most theologians would not frankly admit to using theology to manipulate others, because most of them likely believe that the theology they espouse is truly worthy of a cause such as the inerrancy of the Bible. But this is also not to say that everyone was above board; there are always the manipulators, the abusers, and the self-servers.

And looking back at my experiences growing up in the church and taking three degrees in theological higher education, I'm aware that my sympathies went to those with whom I felt the most theological kinship and who appeared to me to get the raw end of the deal. I've always rooted for the underdog. My experience may justify that position, but it cannot be said to be neutral in relationship to it.

So it is wise to acknowledge that in every situation, whether it is true injustice, cognitive dissonance, confirmation bias, or a host of other factors, the waters of truth are muddy. But if we are to continue to carry out religious education, we must understand what is driving these disputes and identify principles around which academic freedom, or whatever version of it is possible in the religious academy, may flourish.

That is the purpose of this book.

2

The Paradox of Modern and Orthodox

Menachem Wecker

I can still remember my 2001 conversation about art and the second commandment with a prominent rabbi almost like it was yesterday. I was spending my freshman year as an undergraduate at Yeshiva University—an Orthodox Jewish institution in Manhattan that regularly scores in the top fifty in the *U.S. News & World Report* Best Colleges rankings—studying abroad at a Jewish theological seminary, or *yeshiva*, called *Sha'alvim*. If you asked me at the time, I would have said I planned to major in psychology and art, naïvely thinking that I could spend my career looking at Rorschach tests and Kinetic House-Tree-Person drawings; when I later learned there was a good deal of hard science I would have to memorize, my major would change to classical languages (Greek and Latin) and then philosophy, finally settling on English literature. But none of those things were on the curriculum at Sha'alvim, where students' days are packed with intensive private and group study of ancient Hebrew and Aramaic texts—breaking only for prayer, meals, and sleep.

The Israeli school's claim to fame, of which its faculty and administration are very proud, is its identification in Joshua 19:42.[1] The nearby valley *Ayalon*, which readers of the King James Bible may recognize as Ajalon, will remind astute Old Testament students of the story of the fall of the

---

1. All quotations of Hebrew Scriptures that appear in my chapters are my own translation.

five Amorite kings—of Jerusalem, Hebron, Jarmuth, Lachish, and Eglon—
wherein Joshua commanded the sun to stand still in Gibeon (*Givon*, in
Hebrew) and the moon to halt in the valley of Ajalon (Josh 10:12). This
unlikely and miraculous celestial arrangement, or perpetual suspension,
allowed the Jewish armies to prolong their bombardment of the multi-
army coalition that had assembled against the Jewish ally, Gibeon. Without
night-vision goggles and drones, ancient warfare had to abide, evidently, by
the natural ebb and flow of daylight.

The Joshua war reference is particularly appropriate for Sha'alvim,
which was the setting of the so-called tractor battle two years before the
Six-Day War. As the *New York Times* reported on November 1, 1965,[2] Jordanians and Israelis were engaged in a "plowing contest which turned into
a fierce gun battle" in the Ayalon (the *Times* referred to it as "Aiyalon")
Valley, midway between Jerusalem and Tel Aviv. Concerned that the Jordanians were strategically planning a land grab scheduled around Jewish holy
days, the Israelis were even willing to violate the sacred Sabbath. "Among
the Israeli tractor drivers were bearded men from the Kibbutz Shalabin
[Sha'alvim], an Orthodox community where respect for the Sabbath forbids
Saturday work," according to the *Times* article. "On this Sabbath, however,
a rabbi, Meir Schlesinger, told the farmers that he had obtained a special
dispensation based on a long session with Talmudic scholars."

The scene, the *Times* continued, recalled "the blood feud of the Hat-
fields and the McCoys, the 60 tractors began plowing amid a rain of rifle
fire. The Israelis say the Jordanians opened up on Israeli positions; the
Jordanians make the opposite claim. Soon the bark of automatic-weapon
fire filled the valley." Forty years later, Sha'alvim the rabbinical school, the
kibbutz, and the nearby village of *Nof Ayalon* (Hebrew for "Ayalon view")
remain fervently nationalistic, and that came through in the coursework in
the classes I occasionally attended.

According to the school's website,[3] the "high-level *hesder* yeshiva," or
religious school that marries Jewish studies and military service, "is known
for its dynamic and high-level learning program, unique educational philosophy, and accomplished graduates," if it does say so itself. The school,
according to its site, prepares students for their commitments to the Jewish
people and the Torah. The description then introduces the school's location
and history, particularly:

2. See *New York Times*, "U.N. Plea," 14; also referenced in Gross, "Bittersweet," 6.

3. See Yeshivat Sha'alvim, "Overview," para. 1.

> Sha'alvim is nestled in the natural beauty of central Israel, along the fertile fields of the Ayalon Valley, halfway between Jerusalem and Tel Aviv. Surrounded by nature and removed from the distractions of a busy city, the Sha'alvim student can blossom and grow to reach his fullest potential as a ben Torah ["son of the Torah"]. Yeshivat Sha'alvim was established in 1961 as a military outpost yeshiva. With the liberation of Jerusalem, Judea, and Samaria in 1967 Sha'alvim became a hesder yeshiva, where Israeli students combine intensive Torah study with active service in the Israeli Defense Forces.[4]

As a student, first in the American program and then the Israeli program (after I was dismissed from the American program for lack of attendance), I was living outside the United States for the first time. The Zionist slant at Sha'alvim—which was a particularly militarist position—wasn't new to me; I had encountered it early and often in my fourteen years at a Jewish day school in Brookline, Massachusetts. But the scope and passion surrounding that position were far more intense than they had been about fifty-five hundred miles away in Boston. Of course there were other new experiences in Israel, such as palm trees (which, to a Bostonian, looked like strategically placed and colorfully dyed icicles), a radically different cuisine (not a good thing, as the Sha'alvim "cafeteria" was rumored to also supply a local jail), and the experience of walking ancient streets whose stones seemed to hold centuries of fascinating, and troubling, stories.

An amateur (at best) painter, I had packed two duffel bags for the trip; one had clothes, and the other contained a roll of cotton duck canvas, tubes and jars of acrylic paint, brushes, a fold-up easel, and other accessories like stretchers, a staple gun, drawing pads, and bulldog clips. (One of my clashes with the institution would arise from my preference for setting up my paints on Tel Aviv beaches and hitchhiking to art museums in Jerusalem rather than attending the more than a dozen hours a day scheduled for class and independent- and peer-study.) Which brings me back to the memorable 2001 conversation that I began with. A prominent rabbi, one Asher Balanson, whose bio on another rabbinical school's website credits him with the somewhat surprising accomplishment of having "his finger on the pulse of the many crucial areas of life,"[5] delivered a *halakhah* (rabbinic

---

4. Ibid., para. 2.

5. See Yeshiva Ohr Yerushalayim, "Faculty," para. 3. For more on the rabbi, see Goldfish, "YoU Are Sub-Parr II," para. 4 and following, although the story may be best taken with a healthy dose of skepticism.

law) class once a week as a guest lecturer. On this particular day, I had approached him after class with a question.

Balanson would likely strike many readers as a character who had just stepped off the *Fiddler on the Roof* set. Like all of the rabbis at the school, he wore a black hat and a suit, and he also had long *payos* (side curls) and peppered his regular speech with Hebrew and Aramaic words and phrases. Like Tevye, the rabbi was a large man, but he would have never tolerated Tevye's "on the other hand" increasingly liberal stances in the face of the evolving shtetl. Balanson was one of the most right-wing rabbis in the establishment, and his size, coupled with his reputation as a great legal mind and a *possek*—a rabbi whose expertise empowers him to be a religious judge—made him even more intimidating to an eighteen-year-old.

"What does the rav [rabbi] think about the apparent clash between making art and the second commandment," which prohibits making or worshipping idols or images of "anything" in the heavens above or the earth below, I asked. I made sure to refer appropriately and respectfully to him in the third person. "Is it *assur* [forbidden] to paint?"

The interaction, as I remember it, could almost have come out of a Woody Allen film. The rabbi thought for a minute, and there may have been some stroking of his long white beard. Finally, in a soft voice, he said something along the lines of, "It's unclear if it's permissible to paint, but since we are dealing here with an issue like idolatry that has to do with heaven and hell,[6] isn't it better to be safe than sorry?"

For a rabbi who has no inclination for or interest in painting, the better-safe-than-sorry[7] argument surely made perfect sense—a sort of rabbinic adaptation of Pascal's Wager. So what if I didn't try my painting arm at becoming a follower of Rembrandt; the enormity of the punishment that

---

6. It may surprise some readers to hear an Orthodox rabbi refer to hell, but in my experience, many, many rabbis referred to hell as a literal place where evildoers are punished for eternity. There are countless references to a literal hell—which goes by a variety of names, from *She'ol* to *Gehinnom*—in the Talmud and in later rabbinic writings, and as I have noted elsewhere, Jewish art often depicts hell, particularly with reference to the earth swallowing up Korah and his sons (Num 16) and the Egyptians perishing in the Red Sea (Exod 14).

7. This approach is embodied by the charge in *Ethics of Our Fathers*, or *Pirkei Avot* (*m. Avot.* 1:1), where one of the three main teachings of the Men of the Great Assembly is to "make a fence around the Torah." That fence-making has been interpreted as placing barriers, or safety nets, between Jews and potential opportunities for sin, although the rabbis do often reject some actions as being out of hand. One fence is deemed wise and commendable, but a fence around a fence around a sin is viewed as excessive.

would await me when I met Rabbi Peter at the pearly gates, if indeed painting was anathema, would be much worse than the disappointment I would
feel if the celestial Jewish saint told me, after I had lived the artless life of a
Philistine, that I could have picked up a palette knife after all, wouldn't it?
But for an immature young man who felt the urge to paint like a religious
calling, worshipping at the altar of Apollo wasn't an easy habit to break,
and, frankly, it could often feel more fulfilling, creative, and meaningful
than bowing my head in synagogue.

"A Carob Tree Isn't a Valid Testimony"

How did things get to this point? In his excellent book *The Artless Jew:
Medieval and Modern Affirmations and Denials of the Visual*,[8] Kalman P.
Bland, a religion professor emeritus at Duke University, dispels the bizarre
rumors that Judaism is aniconistic, or anti-images, but evidently Bland's
book isn't required reading in Orthodox schools and his view hasn't perme-
ated the walls of Jewish seminaries. And to understand some of the factors
that led up to this broader, conservative, better-safe-than-sorry approach to
Orthodox Jewish life, it's informative to turn to a particular story from the
Talmud that has always made an impression on me.

To imagine the setting of the fierce rabbinic debate between Rabbi
Eliezer and his colleagues, one must forget about iPads and Facebook, cars
and airplanes, and instead consider first-century Jerusalem. The subject
at hand in the academy that day was a particular type of oven, and the
question was whether Jewish law allowed for the contraption in question
to become ritually impure (*tameh*). In what must initially have seemed to
be the ultimate trump card in a public debate, Rabbi Eliezer marshaled a
miraculous sign from heaven to demonstrate that his legal position on the
oven was correct, and that the sages he was refuting were mistaken.

"If I'm correct, let the carob tree be my witness," Eliezer dramati-
cally declared, as the Babylonian Talmud tells it.[9] Sure enough, the tree
was uprooted and relocated one hundred—or, as some rabbis said, four
hundred—cubits away.[10] But the sages were unimpressed. "A carob tree isn't
a valid testimony," they assured Eliezer.

8. Bland, *The Artless Jew*.

9. See *b. B. Metz.* 59b. Online translation: http://www.come-and-hear.com/babam-
ezia/babamezia_59.html.

10. For comparison's sake, Moses, according to rabbinic tradition, was the absurdly
tall height of 10 cubits (or *amot*).

"If my position is right, let the river prove it," the rabbi countered, and the river began to flow backward. But the rabbis wouldn't budge despite the miracle, since, they said, rivers aren't empowered to be judges even if they have a poor sense of direction.

"If my argument is true, let the walls of the academy prove it," Rabbi Eliezer responded, apparently failing to pick up on the already blatant pattern that had emerged. The walls started to incline and threatened to cave in, but Rabbi Joshua, one of the sages, rebuked them. "What business is it of yours when scholars argue?" he demanded of the walls. Not wanting to shame either of the rabbis, the walls remained suspended—neither collapsing altogether nor returning to their full upright position.

Unfazed, Rabbi Eliezer called upon the heavens themselves to bear witness, and a divine voice (literally *bat kol* in Hebrew, or a daughter-voice) testified that Rabbi Eliezer's ruling reflected God's own perspective on the matter. Rabbi Joshua would have none of it, however, and surely with a good deal of *chutzpah*, he cited Deuteronomy 30:12: "It [the Torah] is not in the heavens."

Rabbi Joshua's implication was that the delivery of the Law to the Israelites in the revelation at Mt. Sinai functioned somewhat like the ritual wherein a painter or sculptor serves up her or his artwork to the public and undergoes a symbolic "death of the artist." Perhaps God in heaven held a monopoly on the interpretation of laws, such as those governing the oven in question, before Sinai, but once the Law was revealed, Joshua was suggesting, some kind of biblical version of "no backsies" went into play. Human courts and earthly academies, it would seem, could overrule and reverse celestial judgments, and in fact, as the Talmudic narrative continues, Rabbi Nathan met the Prophet Elijah (Hebrew *Eliyahu*) and asked him what transpired in heaven while the debate was unfolding in the religious academy. "God laughed and said, 'My sons have defeated me. My sons have defeated me,'" the prophet said.

The way my father always explained that divine statement of conquest came from the rabbi who gave him his *smicha*, or rabbinic ordination—Rabbi Moshe Feinstein (1895–1986), widely regarded as a "giant in intellect" and "the leading *halachic* [legal] authority of his generation, and his *p'sakim* (halachic rulings) were accepted worldwide."[11] The way Feinstein explained God's statement that His sons had defeated Him, my father would say, is that God had initially meant the Deuteronomy verse to mean

---

11. See, for example, the bio at Orthodox Union, "Great Leaders," para. 1.

that human courts would define and interpret earthly laws only when they had no alternative, but of course if God interceded and told them what the law was, they should follow that divine directive. God's laughter, according to Feinstein, and his defeat lay in His human children using that verse to essentially cut Him out of the judicial process. Evidently, if Nathan and Elijah can be trusted, that loss of power amused, rather than offended, God.

Jewish schools, like theological seminaries of all faiths, have devoted themselves to intense and passionate study of religious doctrines and theory. But Jewish seminaries, at least according to this story (and quite a few others that I could have cited), also set religious precedents that are not only inspired by heavenly courts, but may also decide cases in a manner that binds celestial inhabitants as well. That's a fine thing for a rabbinical academy to aspire to, but it hasn't always played out that way as the centuries have passed since Talmudic times. And it certainly hasn't always worked out that way for me.

A Strictly Observant Upbringing

I and my six siblings grew up in a community utterly devoted to the 613 biblical commandments and countless rabbinical interpretations thereof. We kept strict kosher, which meant that we literally checked every food item we purchased in the supermarket to make sure it had kosher certification, and we ate only at restaurants that were certified kosher (in the entire city of Boston, there was never more than a handful or two). Those laws were not relaxed on vacations, so traveling was much more complicated than it is for most people.

I grew up praying in synagogue at least three times a day (more on holidays), and many of those services were a good deal longer than church. When I pretended to be asleep some mornings in an effort to evade the early morning ark curtain call, my father would humorlessly pour water on my head to get me out of bed, and even pretending to be sick tended not to work. In addition to the synagogue services, there were prayers to be said before and after each meal, as well as for various other regular events, such as seeing a new moon, traveling of any sort that could be dangerous, and after using the bathroom.

Orthodox Jewish laws (*halachot*) are so technical and so all-encompassing that there are even rules on the books governing which shoe to put on first and which lace to tie before the other. I wore a *yarmulke* (skullcap) all the time except when I swam, showered, or slept, and holidays and Sabbaths (which started around nightfall every Friday and went until Saturday night) meant no "work," which included everything from turning on lights and handling money to traveling in a car or bus and writing.

Although my father self-identified as part of a more right-wing community, he taught (and eventually became principal) at the Modern Orthodox day school that I attended for fourteen years, which meant that I was studying in a coed school but attending prayer services on weekends at synagogues where the communities thought it was immodest and sinful for boys and girls to learn together, or to have much interaction at all before marriage. That cognitive dissonance struck me as particularly bizarre and troubling when I couldn't attend my own birthday party one year because some of my female classmates were planning to go to the restaurant. (If memory serves, they celebrated with me *in absentia*.) I was also allowed to attend my friends' bar mitzvahs, but not the bat mitzvahs of my female classmates (except for one, since the classmate of mine was having a joint bat and bar mitzvah with her brother, who was in my brother's class, and it wouldn't do for my brother to attend and me to stay home).

The notion that Judaism is only about cold laws from which one needs to be set free is not quite the entire story. As a writer on religion, I now listen to quite a few sermon podcasts from priests, pastors, imams, ministers, and rabbis on a weekly basis as part of my research, and I often hear Christian leaders and teachers refer to the "legalism" of the Old Testament. With 613 biblical commandments, the Law can sometimes feel like a straitjacket.

Just as pastors, who publicly state that deeds or "works" are irrelevant when it comes to salvation, nonetheless admit that one who truly believes will choose to act in a good manner, the commandments that Orthodox Jews follow aren't part of a grand neurotic obsession, as some outsiders would suspect, but are designed to also work hand in hand with a set of beliefs. Yes, Orthodox Jews believe they are legally bound to recite a blessing before they eat or drink anything and to say grace after they have eaten, but rather than focusing only on the "legalism" inherent in offering so many blessings—with a goal of one hundred a day, according to some commentators—it is important to look at the content of those blessings. Each one recognizes that the food belongs to God rather than to people, and each acknowledges God as the master of the universe, which is a declaration of belief. Incidentally, it is also a commandment for Jews to believe in God, which might surprise some outsiders.

In my eighteen years in Orthodox Jewish private schools (from pre-kindergarten to my senior year at Yeshiva University), however, I often got the impression that only certain kinds of questions were fair game.

Not Quite Modern, Not Quite Orthodox

I went to a Modern Orthodox day school, which is a very complicated beast to define and characterize. With trepidation, I would loosely describe a fundamental mission of Modern Orthodoxy as inspiring Torah-observant Jews who read both Plato and Maimonides' *Mishneh Torah* (a more accessible legal companion to the Talmud) for fun. The great philosophical and legal mind that inspired the movement, Joseph B. Soloveitchik (1903–1993), often referred in his writing and speeches to dualities and dichotomies inherent in living a modern religious life. The late rabbi and PhD's philosophical treatise, *The Lonely Man of Faith*, can be opaque for those who aren't experts in both Western philosophy and Jewish texts.

"I am lonely," Soloveitchik writes early on in the book. "Let me emphasize, however, that by stating 'I am lonely' I do not intend to convey to you the impression that I am alone. I, thank God, do enjoy the love and friendship of many. I meet people, talk, preach, argue, reason; I am surrounded by comrades and acquaintances. And yet, companionship and friendship do not alleviate the passional experience of loneliness which trails me constantly."[12]

A paragraph later, he writes,

> I must address myself to the obvious question: why am I beset by this feeling of loneliness and being unwanted? Is it the Kierkegaardian anguish—an ontological fear nurtured by the awareness of nonbeing threatening one's existence—that assails me, or is this feeling of loneliness solely due to my own personal stresses, cares, and frustrations? Or is it perhaps the result of the pervasive state of mind of Western man who has become estranged from himself, a state with which all of us as Westerners are acquainted? . . . I am lonely because, in my humble, inadequate way, I am a man of faith for whom to be means to believe, and who substituted "credo" for "cogito" in the time-honored Cartesian maxim. Apparently, in this role, as a man of faith, I must experience a sense of loneliness which is of a compound nature. It is a blend of that which is inseparably interwoven into the very texture of the faith gesture,

12. Soloveitchik, *Lonely Man of Faith*, 3.

characterizing the unfluctuating metaphysical destiny of the man of faith, and of that which is extraneous to the act of believing and stems from the ever-changing human-historical situation with all its whimsicality.[13]

Even as a young teenager, I often wondered how practical was such an eloquent and nuanced view of the world—that there was actually religious value, and even a sacred mandate, to enjoy and to delve deep into the Western philosophical, scientific, and artistic canon—as the basis of a large community and an educational system. (The only people I knew who actually seemed to exhibit a genuine passion for reading both sacred and secular texts for fun were my father, the principal of my day school, and perhaps one or two others at most.)

Many higher education public relations shops would no doubt love for the general population, and prospective students and donors in particular, to imagine that their history of music colloquia and their biochemistry courses are packed with students who are filling seats because they genuinely love the material. But that seems like such an implausible scenario that it would seem to render nearly impossible the likelihood that any school has even a small minority of students whose love for learning is manifest in both secular and religious studies, both art and mathematics, both history and political science, for example.

Yet such was the educational mission of the Modern Orthodox day school that I attended in Boston, and of the college I attended, Yeshiva University in Manhattan, often referred to as the flagship Modern Orthodox institution.

As a student at Yeshiva University, I was convinced that about 1 percent of the student body actually wanted to be on campus. It seemed to me that for about half of the student population, it was the most religious school that students could reasonably expect their parents to foot the bill for, and the other half had decided it was the most secular institution to which their parents would agree to send them. The study halls were packed nights with hundreds of students in the former category, who dressed in dark suits, dress shirts, and ties on a daily basis, while the members of the latter group could often be found nights taking the intercampus shuttle that connected the men's and women's campuses of the university. (Did I mention that the campuses were separate and that the men study in roach- and

13. Ibid., 3–5. The full text is accessible here: http://traditionarchive.org/news/article.cfm?id=105067.

mouse-infested dorms in Washington Heights, while the women's campus was on Lexington and Madison Avenues in Midtown Manhattan?)

To call the experience at Yeshiva University—which I will address more in future chapters—schizophrenic is both an understatement and a bit unfair to the institution. YU is a school with an incredibly ambitious mission: "Since its inception YU has been dedicated to melding the ancient traditions of Jewish law and life with the heritage of Western civilization, and each year we celebrate as future leaders make YU their home."[14]

The school's self-identified mission of *Torah U'madda* (Torah and science), according to the website, plays out as follows: "We bring wisdom to life by combining the finest contemporary academic education with the timeless teachings of Torah. It is Yeshiva's unique dual curriculum that teaches knowledge enlightened by values that helps our students gain the wisdom to make their lives both a secular and spiritual success."[15] But those ethical values haven't always shown through so seamlessly, as when the university hurried to remove from its website references to the chairman of its business school's board of directors and the treasurer of the university's board of trustees, one Bernard Madoff.[16]

Occasional high-profile ethical gaps weren't the only incongruous elements at YU, in my experience. One noteworthy event, which is difficult to imagine occurring at many other accredited higher educational institutions, took place when the university was considering a presidential candidate, now the university president, who didn't hold rabbinical certification. In December 2002, rabbis and students held a rally in one of the study halls—which also doubles as a synagogue during prayer times—in which they recited *Tehillim* (Psalms) in an effort to solicit divine intervention to prevent Richard Joel's appointment. The university's official blog[17] even links to a *New York Jewish Week* article that mentions the event:

> Richard Joel is well aware that on the eve of his being chosen president of Yeshiva University last December, a number of students and rabbis were so opposed to his election that they recited *Tehillim* (Psalms), a prayerful response to times of crisis and danger. For some, the fact that Joel was not a rabbinic scholar and,

14. See Yeshiva University, "About," para.1.

15. Ibid., para. 5.

16. For a close look at the references to Madoff on the Yeshiva University website, see Rosenberg, "YU Sanitizes."

17. See Yeshiva University, "Joel Speaks of Moving Forward."

moreover, had for years headed Hillel, the Jewish campus organization that celebrates pluralism, signaled an impending revolution for Yeshiva, away from its Torah roots.

But they will be proven only half-right. Yeshiva under Joel indeed promises much change—in style, substance and outlook. That change, though, will stem not from the direction of secularism but from Joel's commitment to the Jewish people's historic role as a light unto the nations.[18]

Public readings of Psalms in the Orthodox community, it should be noted, are typically reserved for prayers under drastic circumstances—either a member of the community who is dangerously ill, or in response to terrorist attacks in Israel. That faculty members participated in a religious rally designed to prevent—through prayer—the appointment of an Orthodox Jew (who holds a JD) as president of the institution, because he isn't a rabbi, begins to paint a picture of what academic and social life is like on the university's campus.

Another important aspect of campus culture at YU, as well as a modus operandi in the Orthodox community, is the divinely ordained rabbinic authority. Just as the Great Chain of Being that Shakespeare writes of so often represented a hierarchical system that one shouldn't mess with or else, the rabbis, in a somewhat tautological manner, to say the least, interpret a biblical passage to show that God commanded that their leadership be absolutely recognized. The notion, sometimes referred to as *Daat* (or *Daas*) *Torah*, comes from Deuteronomy 17:11, which commands Jews to blindly (literally) follow the rulings of the priests, the Levites, and the judges: "In accordance with their teachings, and in line with the judgments that they decree that you must follow, don't turn from the thing [or word] that they tell you right or left."

Rabbinic interpretations, particularly those of the medieval French rabbi Shlomo Yitzhaki (better known as Rashi), focus on why the verse repeats itself by saying both that one must follow the commandment and that one must not move to the right or the left.[19]

---

18. See Rosenblatt, "Where Will Joel Take Yeshiva U?" paras. 1–2.

19. Rabbinic interpretation often begins with the premise that the Old Testament is absolutely intentional in each letter, and that anything that seems redundant, rather than being poetic or artistic, is intended to teach something new. A central example of this is the repetition three times of the prohibition against cooking a kid in its mother's milk (see Exod 23:19; 34:26; and Deut 14:21), from which the rabbis infer that one cannot (1) cook, (2) eat, or (3) derive benefit from not only a goat in its mother's milk, but also any

According to Rashi, the redundancy in Deuteronomy 17:11 suggests that "even if he [the judge] says to you that your right hand is your left hand, and that your left hand is your right hand [you must listen], and how much more so if he tells you that your right hand is your right hand, and your left hand is your left hand."[20] When one considers that the rabbis (human beings, after all) have decided that the biblical verse empowers them to speak even in contradiction of blatant logic on behalf of the divine, one may further notice a parallel to Homer calling for the choice cuts of meat to be offered to the blind poets.

At least that kind of hypocrisy was how I interpreted it at times, when I increasingly realized with wonder how many of my peers went to rabbis with a wide array of questions, from whether a particular meat dish was kosher after they accidentally dropped some cheese into the pot to very specific questions about what Jewish law had to say about sexual intimacy.[21]

As a student at Sha'alvim, part of my schedule included a pop psychological session with a younger rabbi (who wasn't clinically trained), in which I was asked to reflect on "what I was struggling with today." My peers, who were probably somewhat uncomfortable with the required therapy as well, often responded with atmospheric truisms, such as "I'm trying to improve my connection to *Hashem* [God; literally "the name"]," or "I am working on being more passionate about my studies." I took a different approach and decided I was having a fine day. What, I wondered, was my inquisitor struggling with that day? Needless to say, I was no longer required to attend future sessions of that sort.

Looking back now on many of these experiences with a bit of distance and wiser eyes, I recognize that most of the rabbis I interacted with were genuinely trying to share religious perspectives that they truly believed and felt would benefit others. They were trying to be a light unto my and my peers' nations, as it were. But despite my hindsight, I'm still troubled by the seemingly incongruous views that on the one hand, the rabbis and teachers felt that the biblical and rabbinic perspectives they were sharing

---

combination (with a few notable exceptions) of milk and meat.

20. See a translation, for example, at Chabad, "Devarim," para. 26.

21. Without going too far afield, Orthodox Jewish law forbids any kind of contact, intimate or otherwise, even between husbands and wives at various points during the menstrual cycle. Rabbis are instrumental parts of the process each month, and often need to inspect underwear to determine if the blood is yet of a permissible tone, after which the woman can submerge herself in a ritual bath (*mikveh*) and then commence intimate contact with her husband, until the cycle repeats.

were literally, unequivocally, and absolutely true in all circumstances and forever. Yet, on the other hand, they felt almost equally sure that allowing students to attempt to genuinely understand alternative perspectives was giving a foothold to Satan.

A Plea for Sunlight

It is very difficult for me to imagine being so confident that I had access to the truth that I would construct bulwark after barricade to fortify its position rather than interrogating it. But I do understand conceptually that many religious scholars and teachers must be convinced that it is a waste of time to entertain lies and fictions when the truth is already revealed. (Sadly, the refusal to recognize the importance of fiction tends to lead to the rejection of art, I have found, and, as Brandon mentions in the previous chapter, it leads some to cancel newspaper subscriptions to avoid ads for movies.)

That being said, if higher educational institutions choose to teach from the perspective of apologetics rather than open inquiry—and academic freedom, for that matter—they ought to come clean and be absolutely transparent about what happens (and doesn't happen) in their classrooms and behind closed doors in faculty meetings (or Inquisition-style inquiries). My main talking point is that if the truth sets religious faculty and students free, they really do need to be free.

PART TWO

Our Traditions

3

The Invention of a Christian Education

Brandon G. Withrow

On more than one occasion during the nineteenth century, researchers in Istanbul meticulously cataloged the musty volumes tucked away in the library at the Greek Convent of the Holy Sepulchre. Cataloging was more than an effort to draft an official record of holdings; it also provided the hope of a chance discovery. But every time, the cataloguers failed to recognize the bound treasure right under their noses.

Happenstance has a way of illuminating missed opportunities. And so it was that in 1873, as Bishop Philotheos Bryennios was casually examining the collection, he took up a bound copy of ancient Christian writings and stumbled upon a document, long thought lost, tucked away inside. It was the much-overlooked *Didache,* a church training manual for new converts.[1]

The *Didache* represents one of the earliest recorded attempts outside of the New Testament to instruct Christians in their faith. The first part of the book likely was written in the first century—the section known as the "Two Ways" may have originated with the Essenes, an apocalyptic Jewish sect—and was finished in the second century by Christian authors.[2] It includes instructions for baptism and the Eucharist, a description of the end of time, and the "Two Ways" guide, which proffers the way of life and warns against the way of death.

1. Milavec, *Didache,* xi–xii.
2. Del Verme, *Didache and Judaism,* 140.

That an instruction manual exists at this period in the history of Christianity is far less surprising than the discovery of the manuscript itself. The New Testament is replete with direction for right living and right belief. There's plenty of encouragement to guard the teachings entrusted to these early Christians (e.g., 1 Tim 4:7; 6:20) and warnings about avoiding false knowledge and myths.

From its earliest days, as the New Testament and extrabiblical documents such as the *Didache* confirm, Christianity has been oriented around what the life and mind of the redeemed individual looks like. So it's not surprising, given this history, that such concerns are central to Christian higher education.

And as the rest of this chapter will show, the history of the Western university is inseparable from Christianity and its theological concerns. The fact is that Western higher education is deeply entangled in the theological; and for seminaries, theology is the *raison d'etre*.

Plenty of books have tackled the historical development of a religious, and particularly Christian, education; the rise of the university; and the founding of the seminary. My purpose in this chapter is not to re-examine that history or to immerse the reader in the minutiae of that story, interesting as it is. Neither is my purpose to try to establish the ultimate definition of a university or seminary. Instead, I want to get at a narrower discussion: the relationship between the idea that there is a way of truth and life and the role that idea plays in the history of Christian higher education.

In other words, any conversation on controversies that have occurred within Christian colleges, universities, or seminaries must start by understanding this relationship; and the more we understand it, the more we may find that these controversies—while arguably undesirable, for a host of reasons—perhaps should be expected.

The Catechetical Schools

To understand why Western higher education is so entangled with theology, we have to go back to the beginning of Christianity. In the first and second centuries—the period in which the *Didache* was being written—Christian education came in the form of mentorships. If you wanted to hold a position in the early church, you studied with older church leaders. Similar systems had long existed in Greece and Rome, where students sat at the feet of philosophers, known for "schools" that were less formal institutions than they were mentorships. Zeno, for example, taught students from The Porch (*stoa*), leading to the development of the philosophy of Stoicism.

Similarly, in the early second-century church, those who wanted to become leaders sat under presbyters for theological training, likely modeling the mentoring found within the New Testament. In Acts 18:24–28, for example, we find well-spoken figures like Apollos being tutored by Priscilla and Aquila. The Apostle Paul is said to have trained Timothy (Acts 16:1–5) for a position in the church in a similar fashion. And in the second century, Irenaeus of Lyon positioned himself as a student of Polycarp of Smyrna, who (according to Irenaeus) knew the apostles. Mentorship provided an opportunity to pass down a direct line of teaching that Irenaeus understood as protecting the orthodoxy of Christianity.[3]

Outside of the official church hierarchy, independent scholars formed their own schools, known as catechetical schools, with loose connections to the church, training Christians in the basics of theology, philosophy, and apologetics. One of the best known of these scholars is Justin (ca. 100–165 CE), whose love for philosophy led him from one school of thought to another, until he eventually settled on Christianity and formed a school for Christian philosophy and theology out of his house in Rome.[4] It would be hard to make a case for any school as an official school of the church in an age when Christianity was illegal. It does appear to many scholars, however, that Justin's school had the official sanction of the church.[5]

Claiming Plato as either inspired by God in some way or having plagiarized Moses, Justin sought to place the teachings of Christianity on par with the sophisticated thinkers lauded by the Romans and Greeks. He set out to defend Christianity in an intellectual climate that ridiculed it, making his approach to education apologetical (that is, intended for the defense of religion). This would become a reoccurring motif in Christian higher education for centuries to follow.[6]

Justin's school can only be overshadowed by that of Origen (185–254), who taught at (but didn't found) a school in the cosmopolitan city of

3. Irenaeus, *Against Heresies*, 3.3.4 (*ANF* 1:416). See also C. Hill, "Polycarp *Contra* Marcion."

4. "The Martyrdom of the Holy Martyrs, Justin, Chariton, Charites, Paeon, and Liberianus, who Suffered at Rome," 2 (*ANF* 1:305).

5. For more on the nature of Justin's school as serving the church in Rome, see Lampe, *Christians at Rome*, 376, and Lampe, *Die Stadtrömischen*.

6. For a helpful overview of Justin's contributions, see J. Hill, *History of Christian Thought*, 13–21.

Alexandria. Scholars are divided on just how officially connected to the church this catechetical school was originally.[7] Origen likely took over as head at the appointment of the prominent bishop, Demetrius, who named the then eighteen-year-old theologian and apologist to the position after a wave of persecution pushed out the more seasoned leadership in the third century.[8]

From early on, Origen found that his tremendous intellect brought him significant attention and fame, which led him to travel throughout the Empire—and to become an early example of a teacher meeting controversy within the church. On a trip to Caesarea in 230 CE, he was ordained by church leaders there, sparking the ire of Bishop Demetrius, who felt Origen was contravening his authority in Alexandria, the church to which Origen officially belonged. In his dispute, Demetrius went so far as to argue that Origen was unqualified for ordination because he was a eunuch—the result of Origen's choice to self-castrate in order to thwart temptation. Demetrius prevailed, and Origen was expelled from the church in Alexandria and spent the rest of his life in Caesarea, where he a founded a school that emphasized philosophy and theology.[9] Though popular, Origen remained a controversial figure long after his death, and he was eventually condemned as a heretic by the Second Council of Constantinople (553) for his view that everyone, including the devil, would eventually find redemption.

Justin and Origen were far from the last Christian teachers to come under scrutiny. The early catechetical schools were eventually supplanted by new institutions, and unlike the early mentorships and loose associations, these monastic and cathedral schools were thoroughly ensconced in the ecclesiastical system. And as theology became more defined and authoritative, these schools, too, saw their moments of academic controversy.

---

7. Pearson, "Egypt."

8. Eusebius, *Ecclesiastical History* 6.3.3 (Loeb 2:17); Birger, "Egypt," 342. The school's official connection to the church appears to be bolstered by its organized liturgical order (much like house churches of the day) and the use of the term *presbyter*—i.e., an official church leader—to refer to Origen and his famous predecessor Clement. Origen was, however, not officially ordained until the time he arrived in the city of Caesarea. See Van den Hoek, "'Catechetical' School," 77; see also Grafton and Williams, *Origen*, 70.

9. Greer, "Introduction," 4; Eusebius, *Ecclesiastical History*, 8:1–8. The story of Origen's self-castration is not entirely undisputed, with some scholars doubting that it was done while he was an adult or that it was done at all. Others in his day were clearly under the impression that he had (see Vrettos, *Alexandria*, 182).

The Monastic and Cathedral Schools

For the nearly eight centuries between the catechetical schools and the formation of the university, the main forces behind a theological education were monasteries and cathedrals. If you were a young man during those years, this was your only shot at an education unless you were among the fortunate few who could afford to pay a tutor or attend a grammar school. The strongly organized nature of the monastery, and its connection to the service of cathedrals and local communities, provided a natural place for a Christian education. These were places of discipline and regulated living, especially with the rise of the Benedictine order.

Benedict of Nursia (ca. 480–ca. 547) is generally considered the founder of Western monasticism, having established a monastic community at Monte Casino (Italy) and written a community guide known as the *Rule*.[10] Benedict's *Rule* borrows from several sources, one of which scholars believe might be the "Two Ways" tradition of the *Didache*, and the other of which is an older and anonymous manual known as the *Rule of the Master*. Benedict's *Rule* establishes a communal system with a student-teacher relationship and an educational mission "to establish . . . a school for the Lord's service."[11] Benedict's communal system is organized around the daily offices from Lauds to Compline, leaving "free" time for well-regulated reading, studying, eating, and working; the community was a place of discipline, and this discipline is certainly part of the reason for the order's medieval success.[12]

It's fair to say that most monks trained in Christian doctrine and practice during the early Middle Ages were educated primarily in the *Rule*, but the Benedictine tradition and its *Rule* found its real success two centuries after Benedict's death, with a renaissance of education and art that occurred in the Carolingian Empire (ca. 750–900). This was not the only revitalization of its kind; the Dark Ages were not so dark as formerly thought, and scholars speak of renaissances in Ostrogothic, Vandal, and Isidorian regions as well.[13] But it's impossible to ignore the major transition that occurred in the West from the middle of the eighth century and into the

---

10. The classic text on Benedict's life is deeply hagiographical. See Gregory the Great, *Dialogues* (1959).

11. Van de Sandt and Flusser, *The Didache*, 91; de Dreuille, *The Rule*, 3; Benedict, *Saint Benedict's Rule*, 48; *Rule*, Prologue, 8.

12. White, "Introduction," unnumbered; Newman, *Boundaries*, 21.

13. Contreni, "Carolingian Renaissance," 59–60.

ninth. The Carolingian program was an organized one, supported by royal patronage and established by the enthusiasm of the church and monastery.

Among the Franks, Boniface and other missionaries established monasteries in the Benedictine tradition, attaching schools to each of them.[14] What was different about these later Benedictine schools was the expansion of the curriculum. In the edict of Emperor Charlemagne (742–814), written in 789 by the masterful scholar Alcuin (735–804), monasteries were ordered to teach chant, math, and Latin. They were also supplied with books, which—as this was prior to the printing press—required copying by hand (and therefore also required a great deal of time, plus spaces dedicated to the work).[15] Copyists took up this work with alacrity; scriptoria produced approximately 50,000 volumes in the ninth century.[16] Under Charlemagne's reforms, Benedict's *Rule* became a standard for medieval monasteries throughout the empire, and education the Benedictine hallmark.[17]

But the monastery was not the only educational game in town, as Charlemagne's revitalization efforts also extended to the cathedral schools, providing an even greater monopoly by the church. The oldest evidence for schools attached to cathedrals is from the Council of Toledo in 527, mandating that bishops educate boys under their care; that same emphasis was reiterated later under Charlemagne.[18] During the Carolingian period, an education in the monastery, cathedral, or royal court was primarily for the purpose of ecclesiastical discipline; there was a "virtually complete interchange" between monks and courtiers as "monks educated in the cloister might be called to court service and eventually made bishop; courtiers educated clerically at court might become abbots or bishops."[19]

Otto the Great (912–73) carried on as the successor of the Carolingians, implementing a more exhaustive curriculum intended to serve the church and the public interests.[20] The eleventh and twelfth centuries were the apex of cathedral education as the Third Lateran Council (1179) ordered that all churches be provided with a master—a theologian in residence—whose

14. Neuhofer, *Benedictine Tradition*, 10.

15. Colish, *Medieval Foundations*, 67–68.

16. Contreni, "Carolingian Renaissance," 711.

17. Schulman, "Benedict of Nursia," 63; Swan, *Spirituality in History*, xv.

18. Glick, "Cathedral Schools," 121–22.

19. Jaeger, *Envy of Angels*, 26. Jaeger's volume offers a thorough history of the cathedral school.

20. Ibid., 48.

job it was to train the clergy. The Fourth Lateran Council reiterated this in 1215, and schools became centers for the liberal arts. The core curriculum encompassed the *trivium* (grammar, dialectic, and rhetoric) and the *quadrivium* (arithmetic, geometry, music, and astronomy), which then led to the highest level of education with law, medicine, philosophy, and theology.

Theology was known as "the queen of the sciences," holding high prestige and great potential for advancement if one achieved that final level of education. Theologians understood their role to be that of the watchdog, noting the ideas and orthodoxy of other faculty, who were far from being equals. The arts faculty members were dubbed *artistae* by the theology faculty, a bit of a pejorative referring to those who studied the trivial (e.g., the languages). As is clear from their development, the monastic and cathedral schools were ultimately under the authority of the church, which led theologians to play a significant role in maintaining orthodoxy and stopping heresy.[21]

In some cases, accused heretics valued their positions enough to self-censure. William of Conches (ca. 1090–ca. 1154), for example, a grammarian at the school of Chartres, came under scrutiny by Cistercian theologians and self-proclaimed watchdogs William of St. Thierry and Bernard of Clairvaux. Fascinated by the atomists and natural sciences in general—or natural philosophy, as it was known then—William was accused of modalism, a heresy that sees the persons of the Trinity as manifestations of one God rather than as distinct persons, and of rejecting the story of Eve's creation from Adam's rib. William of St. Thierry said he tackled the doctrine like a philosopher and physicist, which was meant as an insult. Bernard condemned and pressured him, leading William of Conches to voluntarily redact his own work, eliminating the problematic views and allowing him to continue on in his teaching post.[22]

But not all were so compliant. The French theologian and teacher Peter Abelard (1079–1142) is a prime example of a theological punching bag. Around 1113–14, Abelard made his way to Paris armed with a reputation as a powerful teacher. He was appointed as the master of the cathedral school of Notre Dame, wrote a textbook called the *Dialectica*, and eventually was called on to tutor Heloise, the niece of Fulbert, a canon of Notre Dame Cathedral. Plenty of fiction has been written about the romance between Heloise and Abelard, but history seems to confirm that Abelard

21. Borst, *Medieval Worlds*, xi; Ginther, *Westminster*, 181.
22. See Jeauneau, *Rethinking*, 49–52.

was not only a powerful thinker but also a passionate lover. Their relationship transformed into a tragic affair, a surprise pregnancy, a secret wedding, a vicious attack arranged by Fulbert resulting in Abelard's castration, and Heloise's running away to a convent.[23]

Scandalized, Abelard fled town, eventually settling at the St. Denis monastery, where he started another school and wrote another book, *Theologia*, a tome that got him in hot water once again, as theologians felt his Trinitarianism was less than orthodox. A council held in Soissons in 1121 condemned and burned the book and sentenced the author to indefinite arrest in a monastery. Being a man of many careers, Abelard managed to secure his own release and by the next year was given a piece of land near Champagne, where he built an oratory (and with a sense of irony dedicated it "to the Holy Trinity"). He started another school and immediately drew a horde of eager students.

But Abelard's story doesn't end there. He soon found himself the target of Cistercian monastic reformers who aimed for his theology yet again, forcing him to skip town once more and move to Brittany, where he became the abbot of a monastery until returning to Paris in the 1130s to begin teaching and writing again. And, as you might predict by now, his theology again caught the attention of others, including some of the same guys who troubled William of Conches. William of St. Thierry and Bernard of Clairvaux saw Abelard as a heretic and took the issue to the council of Sens in 1140. Bernard even held a private meeting at Sens, convincing bishops to condemn Abelard, who was forced to appeal to the pope—but, unfortunately for him, Bernard beat him to Rome. The pope condemned Abelard to silence for the remainder of his life and excommunicated his followers; Abelard died shortly after.

Abelard's case is a high-profile one, but indicative of the church-school relationship in the cathedral and monastery. These were places that maintained at all costs the principle of protecting the way of truth and life. The creative minds of these institutions were under the close inspection of the church hierarchy and the self-appointed guardians of theology; to serve in these institutions was to play a role in the ecclesiastical world.

The cathedral schools carried on through the medieval period but were progressively replaced and overshadowed by another type of institution, one that received its commission directly from the pope or the emperor: the

---

23. For a general introduction to the life and thought of Peter Abelard, see Abelard, *Letters*, xiii–lii; Marenbon, *The Philosophy of Peter Abelard*; and Nielsen, "Peter Abelard."

studium generale. Later such institutions would more frequently be called *universitas* ("the whole"), providing a curriculum on everything from law to medicine to theology.

The Rise of the University

The competition for oldest university is a tight race between Bologna and Paris. Though Bologna claims it was founded in 1088, scholars debate the exact year. Bologna was a central place for trade and pilgrimage to Rome, so its location made it a natural center for gathering scholars from across the map. And in 1155, Frederick I Barbarossa turned Bologna into a friendlier place for traveling scholars. To ensure that Roman law could be used to maintain his political claims and position of power, he issued the *Authentica Habita* (also called the *Privilegium scholasticum*), which protected foreign legal scholars from abuses by local judges and provided one of the earliest safety nets offered for the academic world. The University in Bologna was, therefore, a natural place to study civil and canon law, with arts and theology faculty coming later in the mid-fourteenth century.[24]

Paris was the earliest university in northern Europe, making its appearance on the scene in the middle of the twelfth century. Unlike Bologna, the university in Paris developed out of the cathedral school there; its authority was the church and its curriculum was theological.

The Universities of Bologna and Paris are "archetypal," according to Lionel S. Lewis, in that "most aspects of the culture of the university, as it has been reproduced worldwide, can be traced back to one or the other."[25] Between 1300 and 1450, more than thirty-two universities were modeled on Paris—notably Oxford, founded later in the twelfth century, and Cambridge, in 1209. "Down to the mid-fourteenth century," writes historian David Bebbington, "only those three universities—Paris, Oxford, and Cambridge—held general European recognition for their degrees in arts and theology."[26]

---

24. Rüegg, "Themes," 1:6, 11; Rüegg, "Europe of Universities," 42; Bebbington, "Christian Higher Education," 12.

25. Lewis, introduction to Haskins, *Rise of the University,* xiii.

26. Bebbington, "Christian Higher Education," 13; Bowden, "University," 1218. Other examples of schools modeled after Paris include Montpellier (1220), Rome (1303), Florence (1321), Vienna (1365), Heidelberg (1386), and St. Andrews (1413).

And how were these universities organized? Mimicking the structure of the medieval craft guilds, professors were financially accountable to their constituency. In southern Europe, professors were often paid by city councils and elected by student guilds.[27] In the north, the relationship was one of master teacher, where scholars earned their keep by building a reputation that brought in students, whom they charged fees. While universities maintained a level of power and independence from their towns, professors ran a significant risk of losing their bread and butter if they angered their students.[28] If an instructor needed to travel, he left a good faith deposit, indicating he would not abscond with student fees.[29] To fight coercion, and to provide protection in a balance of power, professors also created their own guilds—early forms of associations and accreditation. This allowed them also to regulate student entry, admitting only those students who could pass initial examinations.[30]

Universities formed prior to colleges (*collegia*). Originally, colleges were more akin to residence halls, at times created by church authorities with the poorer student in mind. Colleges were also places where students were organized by nation. In Bologna, these national colleges were by specific country of origin; in Paris, they were based on four regions—France, Picardy, Normandy, and "the English."[31] Colleges were staffed with masters or graduate fellows who eventually became tutors in the liberal arts to undergraduates living with them in residence.[32] Colleges in England developed independently of the university and often housed divinity students whose responsibility it was to offer a mass for the soul of the benefactor.[33] Later in the early modern period, theological and arts faculty formed specific colleges that became something closer to a divinity school.[34]

Christianity dominated the universities in northern Europe, and the church held such a strong place of influence that the students were

27. Bebbington, "Christian Higher Education," 12.

28. McClellan and Dorn, *Science and Technology*, 183.

29. Haskins, *Rise of the Universities*, 15.

30. Ibid., 16–17.

31. Gieysztor, "Management and Resources," 114; Weeda, "Ethnic Stereotyping," 131, 133.

32. De Ridder-Symoens, "Management and Resources," 158–59.

33. Delbanco, *College*, 37.

34. De Ridder-Symoens, "Management and Resources," 157.

tonsured and their professors were celibate.[35] There was relative academic freedom for scholars and students, compared to the hamstringing that the laity would have experienced. In Bologna, where responsibility lay with the city councils to pay their teachers, there was more freedom. Popes and emperors established charters in order to maintain the freedom of discussion, but it would be a mistake to assume this freedom was anything close to what scholars enjoy today in the public university setting. In places like Paris, a chancellor who was appointed by the pope oversaw the interests of Rome at the university. A dance too close to general heresy could land one on the business end of disciplinary measures, usually in the form of a censure. As Alan Cobban writes, professors were often shielded from more "draconian punishments," as "academic censures were usually far less traumatic, causing only temporary embarrassment." Keeping heresy in check, however, was still of great importance, and academics had to swear not to "teach anything that was contrary to faith."[36]

John Wyclif (1328–84) is an exemplar of an academic at Oxford running up against the ecclesiastical authority. Coming from a family with the means to send him to study at Oxford, Wyclif was an eccentric who took on the role of a poor preacher, walking barefoot wherever he went. From student to teacher, he spent most of his life at Oxford, eventually becoming the master of Balliol College, a vicar, and in 1374 a special counsel to John of Gaunt, First Duke of Lancaster.[37]

Wyclif's theology challenged key doctrines of the church; his abrasiveness challenged the patience of Rome.[38] He found the idea of selling church offices repugnant, rejected what he perceived as abuses of papal power (calling the pope an antichrist), called out the increasing ignorance of priests, and rejected the doctrine of transubstantiation as recent and irrational.[39] His positions on Rome appealed to Edward of Woodstock (a.k.a. the Black Prince) and John of Gaunt, who were opposed to the extensions of papal authority and who employed him in negotiations over taxation. Wyclif had powerful friends, handy for a man who was frequently in

35. Lewis, introduction to Haskins, *Rise of the Universities*, xi; Bebbington, "Christian Higher Education," 11; Bowden, "Universities," 1218.

36. Cobban, *English University Life*, 64, 65.

37. Evans, *John Wyclif*, 88.

38. See his *De Simonia* (1380), *De Apostasia* (1380), *De Blasphemia* (1381), and *De Fide Sacramenti* (1381).

39. Lahey, *John Wyclif*, 132; Lambert, *Medieval Heresy*, 231–32.

trouble; the chancellor of Oxford, for example, rejected Pope Gregory XI's demand that the university remove him from his position.[40]

Wyclif eventually pressed his fortune too far, however, when he publicly rejected transubstantiation in 1381 and was condemned and censured by the chancellor for it.[41] The following year, the Blackfriars Council condemned him for heresy; both Wyclif and his followers were expelled from Oxford. Despite these setbacks, he remained free to write, and died after a series of strokes instead of at the stake like many apparently would have preferred. (In 1428 his bones were exhumed and burned.) Wyclif's case demonstrates that the university and public officials with an interest in the skills of their professors were able to offer some academic freedom for radicals (at least by the standards of the day).

But censure at the University of Paris in the fourteenth century was also not uncommon. In 1347, the "Medieval Hume," Nicholas of Autrecourt (ca. 1300–69), and a Cistercian called John of Mirecourt rejected Aristotle's view of knowledge and embraced skepticism, earning them condemnation as heretics.[42] Forty years later, the Dominican John of Monzón (d. 1412) was accused of denying the Immaculate Conception by the theology faculty and Pierre d'Ailly (1351–1420), who was no stranger to condemning heretics. As this was the time of the Western Schism, with popes in both Avignon and in Rome, Monzón appealed to both but was ultimately excommunicated. What is interesting about this last case is that while Monzón saw the papal authority as higher than that of the University of Paris, Pierre d'Ailly had successfully argued for the independent authority of the theology faculty from Rome in determining and handling heresy. As was the case with Wyclif, the university here served as its own court.[43]

Though the fourteenth century had its share of academic controversies, they were only a prelude to what would occur in the next two hundred years with the rise of the Renaissance and the Protestant Reformation.

40. Larsen, *School of Heretics*, 128–29.

41. The doctrine of the church that says that the substance of the bread and wine in the Eucharist is transformed into the body and blood of Christ, though the external features of the bread and wine (accidents), such as taste, smell, and color, remain the same.

42. Thijssen, *Censure and Heresy*, 73–89.

43. Shogimen, "Academic Controversies," 241.

Renaissance and Reformation

Martin Luther (1483–1546) did not start the Reformation; he only made it Protestant. Europe—and the church—were already undergoing a transformation, as the rise of Renaissance humanism brought with it a change in scholarship. *Ad fontes* ("back to the fountainhead") became the Renaissance slogan, indicating the need to recover the classic philosophers and patristic fathers, to examine the original languages, and correct the long-standing Latin translation of the Bible in the process. This led to a newly improved Greek edition of the New Testament by Erasmus of Rotterdam and provided Protestant thinkers with a source for re-evaluating the long-accepted theological conclusions of Christendom. Even the political system of Europe was turned upside down, as the rise of the merchant class helped bring about the decline of the feudal system, providing a popular voice for those without a noble heritage and influence and challenging the position of the aristocracy through capitalist gains.

A German monk, Luther was medieval in his worldview, believing that the devil was eager to torment him and that he lived in the last days before the return of Christ. As a professor of theology teaching at the University of Wittenberg, he presented a revitalized perspective of God that connected with individuals across Europe. Being made right with God was not a work of the sinner, he argued, but an outcome of the grace found in the cross of Christ. This meant that all sins were completely paid for, eliminating the need for purgatory. Additionally, all authorities (including the pope) were subject to Scripture—the only authority for truth. The *Ninety-five Theses*, his tract against the corruption of the church and the pope's doctrine of indulgences (paying for reduced time in purgatory), made him an icon and raised the ire of church leaders. Though protected by his prince, Frederick III of Saxony, his message of change led to his excommunication in 1521. Theologians followed Luther's call to reform the church, protesting doctrines and slashing away at many of its sacraments and authorities.

As the Reformation claimed territory, it also reformed universities. Wittenberg became the leader of Protestant universities, followed by Heidelberg and Cambridge.[44] And new institutions were founded by Protestants to varying success, with some, like the University of Leignitz (Poland), lasting only a short time. The Protestant emphasis in these universities was on the languages and theological training in the Bible. Though Luther was

---

44. Grendler, *Renaissance Education*, 20.

not fond of Aristotle, a pillar of medieval philosophy and theology, his younger theological confidant, Philip Melanchthon, convinced him of the benefit of Aristotelian philosophy in the curriculum.[45] Likewise, humanist philosophy became part of the educational system created by reformer John Calvin, who formed his own academy for training pastors in Geneva.

Any professors who remained at a newly Protestantized institution were required to take loyalty oaths or lose their positions. Oaths were attempts to unify the faculty of an institution, but they did not prevent divisions. At Lutheran schools, for example, chasms formed between the Philippists (named for Philip Melancthon, they called for less conservative and broader doctrinal unity) and the Gnesio-Lutherans or so-called Genuine Lutherans (who pushed for rigid doctrinal adherence). One striking casualty of this fight was Viktorin Strigel (1524–69), a Philippist ordered to sign a doctrinal statement. He refused, was placed under arrest, and several months later went to the University of Leipzig. He eventually lost his position again after he was accused of being a Calvinist. Once more he moved on, this time to the University of Heidelberg, where he spent the rest of his life. But had he lived just a few more years, he likely would have found himself unemployed once again when another loyalty oath was instituted at Heidelberg.[46]

Protestant reforms in education also led to changes for long-standing monastic schools. Luther believed that the monastic schools had been corrupted by the church's teachings. In his *To the Councilors of All German Cities That They Establish and Maintain Christian Schools* (1524), he argued that confiscated property of the monasteries should be used to create universal state-run schools, training individuals for service in the government and church. It became an opportunity to create a learned and orderly society, as Luther and Melanchthon understood it.[47] It was also an opportunity to teach Protestant theology to a broader spectrum of people.

The closing of monasteries included the closing of convents as well, prime locations for the education of women. As Protestants closed down these houses of Roman Catholic theology, they were effectively removing a significant resource for education.[48] This did not mean that Protestants removed all potential for women to be educated. Their doctrine of the

45. Marsden, *Soul of the American University*, 36.

46. Grendler, *Renaissance Education*, 21, 22.

47. Koerner, *Reformation of the Image*, 304.

48. Merrim, *Early Modern Women's Writing*, 198.

"priesthood of all believers" encouraged men and women to approach God directly, including through the reading of Scripture, previously reserved for priests. Lutherans also formed schools for girls by 1593, though as Madeleine Gray writes, "much of it [the curriculum] was geared towards inculcating the Protestant feminine ideals of humility, obedience, and devotion to housewifery."[49] Additionally, Protestants and Catholics benefited from ideals established by Renaissance humanist Juan Luis Vives (1493–1540), author of *On the Education of Christian Women* (1524). Vives encouraged the instruction of women (known as the New Learning), though it was primarily aimed at nobility; the sixth wife of Henry VIII, Katherine Parr, was a Protestant queen educated in this system.[50]

The university remained the primary place to educate men—and only men. And Protestants raised the ecclesiastical bar by demanding trained clergy; prior to the Reformation, estimates suggest that only one-fourth of the clergy were trained, opening a window for Protestants to train more clergy than Catholics. The number of men being trained as clergy in Protestant universities alarmed Rome, and their solution was to form a new type of educational institution called the "seminary," established by the Council of Trent (1545–63) as a training ground for priests. The first seminaries, therefore, were created in direct reaction to Protestant gains, and with the hope of stopping the Protestant heresy.[51]

Beginning in the seventeenth and eighteenth centuries, a new movement known as the Enlightenment began to reshape academic ideals again and led to the founding of additional universities.

The Enlightenment Ideal

The Enlightenment may not have been the first movement to challenge church dogma, but without it the modern world would not be possible. Its iconoclasts were rationalists, empiricists, scientists, and firm believers in the liberty of free inquiry unencumbered by the religious enterprise. Many of its philosophers (like David Hume) rejected what they saw as the superstition of religion in favor of skepticism, but others were not entirely irreligious, holding to a stripped-down Christianity or to the disinterested

49. Gray, *Protestant Reformation*, 130, 131.

50. See my *Katherine Parr: The Life and Thought of a Reformation Queen* for more on New Learning and its place in Henry's court.

51. Marsden, *Soul of the American University*, 38.

God of deism. Its humanistic goals and scientific enterprise were eager to improve the world, raise the quality of life, and embrace human rights; but these radical principles only went so far, as the Enlightenment project never fully embraced a truly equitable world.

For purposes of this chapter and clarifying examples found elsewhere in this book, I will limit my examination of the Enlightenment in this section, and how it changed the educational system, to two narrow points. First, its epistemological foundations turned science into a fact-gathering enterprise that did not seek permission from the church before making a truth statement about the world. If a scientific conclusion was verifiable and falsifiable, then there could be indisputable evidence for it.[52] The Enlightenment expectation of universally applicable scientific knowledge not derived from a sacred text or entangled with theology, however, is still the standard today; debates raging in religious institutions over the Big Bang or evolution versus creationism are predicated on it.

Secondly, while the Enlightenment's radical principles and emphasis on the betterment of humanity did not go far enough in embracing the full equality of all humanity, it did plant the seed for advances in the subsequent generations. In my primary examples below, what is clear is that the protection of human rights within the educational world is a move that has taken—and continues to take—time in both religious and nonreligious institutions.[53]

So how did the Enlightenment change the educational world? Following the Reformation, the university remained a central place for a Protestant education, but the Enlightenment of the seventeenth and eighteenth centuries created new institutions (e.g., the University of Göttingen) and

52. It is true that postmodernism has challenged the Enlightenment's scientific certainty, but it is far from supplanting it today. There are attempts at postmodern science, but it is not uncommon to find scientists who reel at the thought of postmodernist criticism and its demand for a plurality of narratives. Can nature (e.g., plate tectonics) have narratives and still be predictable? Could one really speak of scientific facts with a strictly postmodern approach? For a brief overview of this debate, see Grant, "Postmodernism and Science and Technology." A lengthy examination of the nuances of this discussion is beyond the scope of this book, though I would be remiss if I did not acknowledge it.

53. Here, too, the Enlightenment archetype of universal human rights has been challenged by the postmodern emphasis on the power of individual narratives. On the one hand, focusing on a plurality of perspectives can do more to build empathy and change prejudicial systems; on the other hand, are there not universal themes among these stories that lend themselves to an Enlightenment approach? There are no easy answers, but as above, I want to acknowledge the complexity of discussions on human rights.

transformed existing schools (e.g., Edinburgh) into promoters of its ideals.[54] The standards for research in the modern, non-faith-based university are indebted to the Enlightenment legacy. Conceptual arrangements of universities into distinct departments with specializations and the creation of standards for research are the product of the Enlightenment. Secularity progressively opposed the religious, and it became a fight for the metaphorical soul of the university.

In Germany, the Enlightenment ideal was exemplified in the Humboldt-University system, named after Prussian diplomat and visionary Wilhelm von Humboldt, whose own project—the University of Berlin (1810)—is considered the model for the modern university. Humboldt's ideal was influenced largely by Friedrich Schleiermacher's *Occasional Thoughts on Universities in the German Sense* (1808), which portrayed the function of the university as "not to pass on recognized and directly usable knowledge such as the schools and colleges did, but rather to demonstrate how this knowledge is discovered, in order to stimulate the idea of science in the minds of the students, to encourage them to take account of the fundamental laws of science in all their thinking."[55]

The Humboldt ideal was heralded in America with the formation of institutions like Johns Hopkins University (1876) and the University of Chicago (1892). In the United States, universities began to reflect the same changes sweeping through schools in Europe. For example, the Morrill Act of 1862 provided land grants for universities, creating institutions for the exploration of sciences and technologies, though not to the exclusion of the liberal arts. Land-grant universities were perceived as places to serve the public.[56] A new world that emphasized the scientific method and embraced an openness to explore fresh ideas, thus displacing theology as a science altogether and eschewing dogmatism, was expected to brighten the future of humanity.

There was a problem, however, in that not all of humanity was included. One might assume that a movement with a humanist emphasis would immediately shower all persons, regardless of gender or race, with opportunities for an education. And while the principles were there in seed form, the practice was still inequitable. Leading Enlightenment philosophers like

54. Carhart, *Science of Culture*, 126; Wilson, "Universities," 607.

55. Quoted in Wissema, *Third Generation University*, 13.

56. Keohane, "American Campus, 53.

Voltaire were opposed to public education and others like Rousseau saw it only as the right of upper nobility and the bourgeoisie.[57]

During the seventeenth and eighteenth centuries, women still sought meaningful educational opportunities, but such opportunities were sparse. One way to achieve an education was to correspond with well-known male philosophers, and a timeless example of this is the relationship between Lady Damaris Cudworth Masham and John Locke. Locke received many flirtatious letters from women, at times confusing some with enough intensely romantic banter that they expected a proposal at any moment. But Lady Masham's relationship with Locke was different, and far from a simple case of "fangirling," as we might call such celebrity obsession today. Locke and Masham flirted, became sparring partners, shared their writing, and fell in love. But apparently she could not get him to settle down, so she eventually married Sir Francis Masham, and Locke's shock at her marriage was probably equaled only by his obtuseness in their relationship. She continued to correspond with, and learn from, Locke, even drawing on the Masham family money to offer patronage. And though marriage was not in their future, there was one advantage of their intellectual relationship for Lady Masham: she became a philosopher in her own right.[58]

Masham entered into debate with another seventeenth-century philosopher, Mary Astell (1666–1731). Like Masham, Astell had a strong intellect and corresponded with male philosophers; unlike Masham, she had no place for romantic love or marriage. A woman married to a man became that man's slave, as Astell saw it. It was better, she argued, for women to remain single and live with one another for support. To this end, and before the idea was common for Protestants, she proposed creating a seminary for educating women, but the school never became a reality.[59]

As will be seen, the eventual rise of the Protestant seminary did provide avenues for educating women, but as radical as the Enlightenment was, the college and university classroom (religious or not) was still reserved for white males only.[60] As late as 1833, Oberlin College, for example, an

57. Fernández-Enguita, "Ethnic Groups," 261.

58. Billing, Hidden Roots, 59.

59. See my article "Mary Astell's Unlikely Feminist Revolution."

60. In America, the advancement of higher education for women came (in part) as a result of the proliferation of academies for boys and girls. Originally, academies were only for boys who were being prepared for the business of adulthood. Many were connected to churches or independent benefactors; Benjamin Franklin, for example, opened his own in Philadelphia. It was Sarah Pierce, however, who changed everything with the

evangelical institution in Ohio, became a rare, forward-thinking exception for opening its doors to women. Harvard University, which had long abandoned its evangelical roots and was considered relatively progressive, did not even allow women into the library until 1830; the first African American student was admitted in 1865, and the first female student in 1943.[61]

So while the Enlightenment brought the scientific enterprise to the forefront and transformed many expectations of the educational world, the case for full educational equality was left to the nineteenth and twentieth centuries. And as I trace the more immediate educational contexts of my own faith tradition, this narrative must eventually settle in America.

Resisting the Modern World in America

The nineteenth and twentieth centuries saw significant changes in the world of education, including the rise of the Protestant seminary and the breakdown of an educational system dominated by white males. The Protestant seminary began in a way not all that different from its Catholic counterpart; if the creation of the seminary was first a Catholic effort to counter the heresy of the Reformation, then it should be no surprise that the Protestant seminary in America got its start largely as a reaction to the Enlightenment heresy, specifically as it made its way into Harvard University.

Harvard (1636) had been founded in the new world primarily as a training ground for ministers, but when the school began taking on Arminian theology, New England Calvinists were alarmed.[62] Arminianism held to free will, rejected Calvinist notions of predestination, and was considered a gateway doctrine to Enlightenment deism. Yale College was founded in 1701 partly as a response to Harvard's changes, though Yale too became racked with controversy early on when one of its most popular rectors, Timothy Cutler, was discovered to be an Arminian.[63] With the turn of the nineteenth century, Calvinist fears of deism were eventually verified as Harvard was transformed into a Unitarian institution (1805).

---

founding of her Litchfield academy for girls in 1792. The formal Litchfield Female Academy, however, was not officially incorporated until 1827. For more, see Tolley, "Mapping the Landscape of Higher Schooling," 26.

61. Naden and Blue, *Cornel West*, 41.

62. Jeynes, *American Educational History*, 16.

63. For more on this, see my book *Becoming Divine*, 75–107.

Yet another response to this perceived heresy came in the formation of Andover Seminary (1808), the first seminary in the United States, which had a charter designed to keep it orthodox. Following soon after Andover, Princeton Theological Seminary was formed (1812), creating another conservative training ground and a proposed antidote to schools like Harvard.[64]

With each new form of perceived liberal corruption, this pattern continued. For example, the Enlightenment emphasis on scientific pursuits called for the examination of the truth-claims of the Bible as one would do with any other book, giving rise to higher critical interpretation, which looked for possible sources for the Bible from its surrounding culture (like Babylonian flood accounts). Many evangelicals had a problem with this, holding that no matter how one studied the Bible, it must not be in a way that challenged its authority and its special place as divine revelation. But others believed this was not necessarily the end result of a critical examination of the Bible. When Princeton eventually embraced higher critical interpretation, some faculty members broke away and formed Westminster Theological Seminary in 1929 as an alternative.

Changes occurred along social lines as well. Like their nonreligious counterparts, seminaries were initially male-only institutions, though sister schools, known as female seminaries (but more like intellectual finishing schools), formed right along with them (and often in close proximity). For many religious institutions, the emphasis on training males was primarily due to a reading of 2 Timothy 2:12 (about women being silent) and Ephesians 5 (about women in submission to men) as timeless social absolutes. (And while one might expect that Catholic institutions would reject the ordination of women to the priesthood, a later chapter of this book will discuss Protestant schools that—to this day—also take this conservative reading of the Bible.)

But the nineteenth and twentieth centuries did bring with them some opportunities for women about which Mary Astell could only dream. Historian Douglas A. Sweeney notes that this was a time when "women enjoyed a greater freedom to serve in missions on their own. In fact, as a rule, they worked more freely with internationals abroad than they could minister to Americans at home." This resulted in the formation of training grounds like Mount Holyoke Female Seminary, founded by Mary Lyon (1797–1849) in 1837.[65] Mount Holyoke was the sister school to Andover Seminary; among

64. Marsden, *Soul of the American University*, 182, 206.

65. Sweeney, *American Evangelical Story*, 89.

its more famous students are Emily Dickinson (who never finished) and Fidelia Fiske, who founded schools in Persia for girls abandoned by their families for financial reasons.[66]

Between 1790 and 1830, fourteen seminaries for women were formed.[67] After the American Civil War, many of these seminaries were transformed into colleges as social progress was made. However, most established colleges and universities continued to be closed to minorities.[68]

Near the end of the nineteenth century, newly formed Bible institutes were more progressive about integrating men and women. Moody Bible Institute was founded in 1889 in Chicago largely thanks to the efforts of Emma Dryer, an associate of evangelist Dwight L. Moody. Early on, many women populated the student body, earning pastoral degrees and serving as preachers and evangelists. The culture of Moody changed quickly mid-century, however, as American gender discussions drove women back into the home and turned the preaching ministry into a place for men only.[69] At the beginning of the twentieth century, Southwestern Baptist Theological Seminary allowed women to take courses, primarily to attend classes with their husbands and with the restriction that they could not enter certain male-only programs.[70] By the 1960s women in Protestant colleges and seminaries were more common, though even today many schools (including Westminster Theological Seminary) still argue that women should not be ordained for pastoral ministry.

In other words, there was never a moment when the Enlightenment vision suddenly came online in all its glory. Various social movements have pushed this ideal of human equity closer to reality, but those efforts have taken centuries and are not yet concluded. Moving into the modern world has been—and continues to be—a painful process for education as a whole.

66. Lundin, *Emily Dickinson*, 36; Story, *Five Colleges*, 46.

67. Another 158 academies for girls and seminaries for women were created between 1830 and 1860 (Kelley, *Learning to Stand and Speak*, 67).

68. Mount Holyoke, for example, became a college in 1888. Postsecondary schools were opened for African Americans, such as Wilberforce University (1854) and Howard Seminary (1866), the latter of which quickly turned into a university. Many religious schools like Southern Methodist University (SMU) allowed black students to audit their classes but not receive credit. By the 1950s, schools anticipated the Supreme Court's Brown decision in May 1956 by a few years and began desegregating between 1949 and 1950, including SMU and Southwestern Baptist Theological Seminary (Shabazz, *Advancing Democracy*, 97).

69. Ingersoll, *Evangelical Christian Women*, 117.

70. Aleman and Renn, "Southern Baptist Colleges," 53.

The Theologically Entangled

This cursory survey shows that the larger history of the Western university is inseparable from Christianity and its theological concerns. My next two chapters will look in more detail at several institutions that have pushed out professors for teaching evolution, or for seeking theologically creative ways to incorporate the best of higher critical biblical interpretation without forfeiting the authority of the Bible, or simply for being female. The long history of this complex relationship between education and religion should render these disputes unsurprising, even if unsettling (or worse), as they are far from novelties. But they are interesting case studies of the struggle for academic freedom in religious institutions.

In closing, it must be said that many modern Christian educational institutions have no quarrel with science outside of any conclusion that rejects the divine or closely foundational issues (like abortion). For these institutions, Scripture remains their authority, but they also consider it an ongoing conversation with God and are open to new perspectives. In the same way, though Paul may have said women are to be silent (1 Cor 14:34–35), many Christian schools today welcome female faculty and ordain female ministers.

But these are not the schools in which I was educated, nor are they the schools that leave the public scratching their heads.

4

The Yeshiva and Its Cultivation of Dependent Thinkers

Menachem Wecker

If one of the aims of Spartan education was to make good and loyal citizens, the goal of a yeshiva[1] education might be said to be the creation of better-informed conformists. In some ways, an uncertainty principle governs the development and proliferation of the yeshiva. Whenever one shines the light on the notion of *chidush*,[2] or innovation, within the yeshiva one necessarily loses sight of the religious mandate for homogeneity.[3] And if one focuses one's attention, instead, on the orthodoxy of Jewish study, one neglects an emphasis in Jewish texts on creativity.

In an interesting way, the acceptance of multiple, competing narratives of Jewish educational philosophy in the biblical and early rabbinic period seems to have allowed for more elasticity in the defense of dogma and greater tolerance of divergent opinions. But whatever promise for academic freedom can be gleaned from biblical and Talmudic stories has been

---

1. The Hebrew word *yeshiva*, incidentally, comes from the root ישׁב, "to sit." The yeshiva, then, is a place where people sit and study.

2. The Talmud says, for example, "It is impossible [that there be] a study [session] without a *chidush*." See *b. Chag.* 3a.

3. One such directive comes from the Mishnah, *m. Ed.* 1:3, which obligates students to repeat what they have learned from their teacher only in "the language of [their] master."

undone by a particular rabbinic slogan championed by Moses Schreiber (1762–1839): "The new is forbidden according to the Torah."[4] As I will discuss below, Schreiber's antimodern charge has shaped the culture of yeshivas today to a great extent and is at least partly responsible for modern-day yeshivas' track records when it comes to academic freedom.

But however clear are the problems plaguing yeshivas today, surveying much of the history of Jewish education can be like sifting through mountains of rumors and myths trying to locate and excavate a series of long-lost ruins, rather than charting a linear history, which involves known and established players who left behind good archival records. The quest for reliable information about rabbinical schools, in particular, throughout the ages yields many dead ends, smoke, and mirrors. Unlike at educational institutions funded across the centuries by the Catholic Church, there have not been significant communities of bearded rabbis illuminating, writing, and poring over Hebrew and Aramaic manuscripts in reading rooms—with soaring, vaulted ceilings frescoed with Old Testament scenes by renowned artists—at rabbinical colleges bankrolled by the Medici family.

By comparison to the renowned universities, such as at Paris, Bologna, Oxford, and Cambridge, described in the previous chapter, Jewish schools of every age and achievement level have been rickety, slapdash, and unceremonious, and when they have been lucky enough to own their own spaces—let alone ones whose architectural prowess and decorative elements have made them worthy of protection and preservation—those spaces tended to lie fallow or be reappropriated after the Jewish community was forced to relocate somewhere else in an almost constant ebb-and-flow of persecution, exile, and emigration.

Despite that much of what passes as Jewish educational history is unreliable or invented, there are certain dogmatic principles and approaches that have taken on lives of their own in contemporary Jewish education, and in turn have had a great impact on the discussion about academic freedom in contemporary Jewish higher education.

I will trace these in chronological fashion, starting with the forefathers.

---

4. The German rabbi, affectionately known as the Chatam Sofer based on one of his publications, was adapting a law from another context. *Chadash*, or new, also refers to new produce, which is forbidden under certain circumstances. Sofer extended it to refer to new ideas and modernity as a whole.

Where Abraham, Isaac, and Jacob Went to School

The Mishnah in *Ethics of the Fathers* (*m. Avot*) lists—in painstaking detail—the chain of the passage of Jewish teachings from master to student, allegedly dating all the way back to the Revelation at Sinai.[5] Moses taught his protégé, Joshua, who in turn taught the Elders, who passed the teachings to the Prophets, and so the chain continues: next came the Men of the Great Assembly, and among them was Simon the Just; then Antigonus of Sokho; then Jose ben Joezer of Zeredah and Jose ben Johanan of Jerusalem; then Joshua ben Perachyah and Nittai of Arbela; then Judah ben Tabbai and Simeon ben Shetach; then Sh'maya and Abtalion; then Hillel and Shammai.

But the great chain of teaching outlined in *Ethics of the Fathers* hardly represents the beginning of the Jewish religious academy, according to rabbinic tradition. Rabbinic exegesis refers to a mysterious Yeshiva of Shem and Eber—apparently maintained by Noah's eldest son, Shem, and Shem's grandson Eber.[6] The mythical theological seminary of Shem and Eber was said to be where Judah sought to have Tamar sentenced to death (burning) for adultery in Genesis 38:24,[7] one of three places where the Divine Spirit was manifest,[8] where Rebecca went to "ask of God" why her children, Jacob and Esau, were struggling in her womb,[9] where Jacob studied for fourteen years[10] while fleeing from Esau,[11] and where Joseph learned the dream interpretation techniques that served him so well as an inmate in Pharaoh's prison.[12]

5. See *m. Avot* 1:1. Online: http://www.chabad.org/library/article_cdo/aid/682498/jewish/English-Text.htm.

6. See Gen 5:32 and 10:24. Noah's three sons were Shem, Ham, and Japheth; Shem's sons were Elam, Asshur, Arpachshad, Lud, and Aram; Arpachshad's son was Shelah; and Shelah's son was Eber.

7. See *b. Av. Zara* 36b. Online: http://www.come-and-hear.com/zarah/zarah_36.html.

8. See *b. Mak.* 23b. Online: http://halakhah.com/pdf/nezikin/Makkoth.pdf.

9. See the commentary of Rashi on Genesis 25:22, who also notes that the struggles in Rebecca's womb came from Jacob trying to get out at the Yeshiva of Shem and Eber, and Esau longing to exit at "the entrance to places of idolatry." Chabad, "Bereishit," para. 46.

10. Some kabbalistic sources suggest that Abraham actually killed Isaac during the sacrifice, and that Isaac's soul was transported on the wings of angels to a "celestial academy of Shem and Eber," where it studied for three years. See Schwartz, *Tree of Souls*, 171, as well as Schwartz, "Narrative and Imagination," 196.

11. See *b. Meg.* 17a. Online: http://halakhah.com/pdf/moed/Megilah.pdf.

12. See Wineman, "Hasidic View of Dreams," 357, particularly footnote 22.

Shem and Eber's school is also invoked early and often in the inter-pretation of a variety of other biblical episodes—pretty much whenever there is a reference to learning in any kind of school in the Five Books of Moses; or when a character poses any sort of question to God, where it is unclear in what context God has been consulted on the matter; or when age-old teachings were passed down from teacher to student. One of the more succinct summaries of the academy comes from Moses Aberbach in *Encyclopaedia Judaica*, who also draws the connection between the Yeshiva of Shem and Eber and the reference to tents[13] of Shem's in Noah's curse of his son Ham and grandson Canaan:

> In line with the rabbinic concept of the pre-existence of the Torah and its institutions prior to the revelation at Sinai,[14] Shem's "tents" (Gen. 9:27) were accordingly identified as a *bet midrash*[15]—an academy with which Eber, Shem's great-grandson, subsequently became associated, and which also served as a *bet din* [court of law] (Mak. 23b; Gen. R. 36:8; 85:12; Targ. Ps.-Jon. to Gen. 9:27 and 25:22). It is said that Israel's Patriarchs studied at the academy of Shem and Eber (Targ. Ps. Jon, to Gen. 24:62 and 25:27; Gen. R. 63:10), and that students of the Law will be privileged to study in the world to come at the heavenly academy of Shem, Eber and other heroes of Israel (Song R. 6:2 no. 6; Eccles. R. 5:11 no. 5).[16]

There is no attempt in any of the discussions of the tents or school of Shem and Eber to account for why these two figures decided to cre-ate a formal school, and what, if anything, inspired them to do so. Was

13. It's worth noting, as well, that Genesis 25:27 identifies Jacob as a "tent dweller" in sharp contrast to Esau, the hunter. The Bible also makes a point of noting that Abraham is sitting at the entrance of his tent in Genesis 18:1

14. See Anderson, "Status," 1–29, for a discussion of what the patriarchs knew, and didn't know, of the Torah prior to the revelation at Sinai. See also Ruth Langer's reference to the academy of Shem and Eber as "a rabbinic-style academy and law court focusing on the study of the preexistent but as yet unrevealed Torah!" in Langer, "Response," 2, and Rubin and Kosman, "Clothing," 162–63, in which the authors observe that the rabbinic assertion that the patriarchs observed the commandments of the Torah prior to Sinai "annulled all historical development because the Torah was available to all even before its promulgation at Sinai. That thought pattern has operated throughout Jewish history ever since. Even great tragedies were unable to change this thought pattern. Everything has become a function of God's grace, even the most terrible events. No room exists, therefore, for political or any other interpretation."

15. Literally "house of teaching" or "house of learning," a distinct entity from a *beit kenesset*, or synagogue (literally "house of gathering").

16. See Aberbach, "Shem," 453.

the construction of a physical school a response to what Shem and Eber perceived as a failure of other less formal modes of instruction, perhaps homeschooling? Or maybe it was simply a logical context to bring together some of the generation's greatest minds in one place.[17]

Whether Shem and Eber cared about academic freedom in their earthly academy or the degree to which it will be valued in the academy-to-come that is spoken about, however, is impossible to say, and the details of their operation are largely unexplored. What the curriculum entailed at Shem and Eber's yeshiva, for example, is unknown, as is the structure of the school. Were there professors, and if so, how many were there? Did any have tenure? Was there a hierarchy of adjunct professors of the practice of rabbinics, associate rabbi, assistant rabbi, and senior rabbi? How many students attended, and what, if anything, was the grading scale? Was there a library of some sort, sports teams, a gift shop with Hebrew monogrammed sweatshirts? How many silver shekels did students have to shell out for tuition, and what kind of job placement rate could they expect after they graduated? Was Shem and Eber U accredited?

None of the answers to those questions is known; all that is mentioned in rabbinic literature is that this amorphous school existed, and that it was where some of the biblical characters were trained, despite an ongoing thread in the Bible of holy men and women, particularly prophets, experiencing God and deepening their spiritual understanding independently. Moses[18] and David[19] were shepherds, and before Samuel anointed him king, Saul tended his dad Kish's donkeys.[20] Shepherds spend much of their time alone in the wilderness,[21] which means they have plenty of opportunity for

17. There is a reference, for example, to a *mishneh* in 2 Kings 22:14, in which Huldah the Prophetess, the wife of Shalum the son of Tikvah the son of Charchas, sat in Jerusalem. Rashi, whose commentary can be seen in English at Chabad, "Melachim II," para. 18, cites Pseudo-Jonathan's translation of *mishneh* as "study hall" and notes that a gate in the temple court was named Huldah's Gate—which was in the south, according to the Mishnah *m. Mid.* 1:3. However others, according to Rashi, render the elusive *mishneh* as "between two walls," although Rashi allows that Huldah was still teaching in that location. This seems to suggest that there was perhaps some sort of academy in the temple. See also Weiner and Feinstein, *Woman's Voice*, 165.

18. See Exod 3:1.

19. See 1 Sam 16:19.

20. 1 Sam 9:3.

21. The Hebrew word for wilderness is *midbar*, which is often translated as "desert." There seems to be a romantic notion that desolation and the absence of human intervention is conducive to meditation and the birth and cultivation of prophets, which perhaps

self-reflection and meditation removed from the trappings and distractions of urban living and meddling people. That more "progressive" model of do-it-yourself education—a Dewey-style religious academic program—stands in stark contrast to the academy of Shem and Eber, however, where the school had walls, even if we don't know what materials those walls consisted of, or how many square feet (or *amot*, or cubits) the school measured.[22]

The school, however, symbolizes an educational philosophy in Judaism that at least purports to be contemporary with the years immediately after the flood in the time of Noah, and a stand-alone school at that, which wasn't attached to a synagogue—although invoking synagogues in the time of Abraham is an anachronism. Perhaps Shem and Eber's school is also where the many scribes in the Bible trained, such as King David's scribes Seraiah[23] and Sheva,[24] King Solomon's scribes Elichoreph and Achiyah (the sons of Shisha),[25] King Hezekiah's scribe Shevnah,[26] King Josiah's scribe Shaphan (the son of Azaliah, the son of Meshulam),[27] the families of scribes that dwelt at Yabetz,[28] Ezra the scribe, and others. Alternatively, one might assume that vocational scribal schools might have existed at the time, and perhaps the scribes mentioned above were not proud alumni of Shem and Eber's rabbinical school, or they may have studied in a program that was affiliated with the temple, such as the one where Huldah the Prophetess taught.[29] Either way, there is no indication that there was any sort of public education system at the time; the scribes would certainly have been the elite.

---

explains why so many prophets were such antisocial and controversial personalities.

22. Some artists, of course, have imagined the academy, but their depictions of the structure look suspiciously common and similar to architectural conventions of the day. See, for example, Gutmann, "Illustrated Jewish Manuscript," particularly figure 8, "Rebekah visiting the academy of Shem and Eber," from the Ashburnham Pentateuch (or Pentateuch of Tours), seventh century (Paris, Bibliotheque Nationale: Cod. nouv. acq. lat. 2334, folio 22v). See also Gutmann, "Jewish Origin," 65–66, as well as the image "Yahudah Haggadah, fol. 31v: Rebeca consulting Sem and Eber, courtesy of the Israel Museum, Jerusalem," on page 10 of the images accompanying Heller et al., "Old Testament as Inspiration."

23. See 2 Sam 8:17.

24. 2 Sam 20:25.

25. See 1 Kgs 4:3.

26. See 2 Kgs 18:18.

27. 2 Kgs 22:3.

28. See 1 Chron 2:55.

29. See note 17.

The scribal schools and Shem and Eber's school, whether they were distinct entities, almost appear to be championed as an ideal educational model in Judaism, particularly when one considers their renowned alumni. Any institution that trained Abraham, Isaac, and Jacob, all of whom communed directly with God, must have had its act together both academically and administratively. And yet the lack of clarity about how exactly the school operated in both of those regards is telling in itself. In an institution where prophets are instructing other prophets, divine truth would reign, one presumes, rather than an emphasis on diversity of opinion or academic freedom. And consider those biblical characters who voiced more populist views or perspectives that parted with the mainstream, such as Korah, Dathan, and Abiram—not only were they not embraced, but they lost their lives for their "rebellious" stances.

In Korah, Dathan, and Abiram's case, the earth beneath their feet literally consumed them. But luckily for those rooting for a more open and free Jewish academy, there has been a good deal of progress since biblical times.

The Fathers of Public Jewish Education

If the biblical period was characterized by the formal education only of scribes, priests, and those talented and lucky enough to be accepted by Shem and Eber University, the democratization of Jewish education, at least according to the Talmud, expanded a great deal in the first century CE. And unlike in biblical times, it focused on the entire Jewish population,[30] rather than just the wealthiest or the brightest students.

---

30. There is an informative passage in the *Mahzor Vitry* (late eleventh or early twelfth century) that demonstrates part of the ritual that accompanied the commencement of religious study when it was clearly more of a uniform institution rather than a home-schooling operation. According to the *Mahzor*, a prayer book that would often include special prayers and rituals for holidays, "when a person introduces his son to the study of Torah, the letters are written for him on a slate. The boy is washed and neatly dressed. Three cakes (challah) made of fine flour and honey are kneaded for him by a virgin and he is given three boiled eggs, apples, and other fruits. A scholarly and honorable man is invited to take him to school . . . The boy is given some of the cake and eggs and fruit, and the letters of the alphabet are read to him. Then the letters [on the slate] are covered with honey and he is told to lick it up . . . And in teaching him, the child is at first coaxed and finally a strap is used on his back. He begins his study with the Priestly Code and is trained to move his body back and forth as he studies." See Bortniker, "In the Middle Ages," 176.

Commenting on a separate legal manner—whether one can sue a neighbor to prevent the opening of a business in an adjoining courtyard on the grounds that the noise will prevent one from sleeping—the Talmud credits one Joshua the son of Gamala (who died in either 69 or 70 CE), who was evidently the high priest in the temple, with single-handedly saving and revolutionizing ancient Jewish education.

According to one Rabbi Judah (quoting a colleague, Rav), "The name of the man—Joshua ben Gamala—ought to be remembered for good, for, were it not for him, the Torah would have been forgotten from Israel."[31] The Talmud continues:

> For in the beginning, a child who had a father, he [the father] taught him Torah. One who did not have a father, did not learn Torah. How do we know this? [From the verse Deut 11:19] "And you shall teach them [to your children]." And "You shall teach"— [emphasizing] you. They [the rabbis] later enacted that teachers be appointed to train children in Jerusalem. What was the source [for such an institution]? [From the verse Isa 2:3] "For from Zion the Torah shall come forth." Still, someone who had a father, he [the father] took him up to Jerusalem and he was taught there. He who did not have a father, did not go up and learn. They [the rabbis] then decreed that there should be teachers in every region, and that children should begin school at sixteen or seventeen. But a student whose teacher got angry with him [and disciplined him] would drop out of school. Until Joshua ben Gamala came and commanded that teachers of children be appointed in every region and ordained that teachers of young children should be fixed in every state and every city, and that young boys begin school at age six or seven.[32]

It is difficult to know how historical this Talmudic account is supposed to be, of course. Is one to believe that prior to the high priest's educational epiphany in the first century CE that Jewish education—with the exception of Shem and Eber's rabbinical academy—essentially amounted to a father-and-son homeschooling operation? Or were there pockets of formalized educational institutions, and the rabbi united and centralized those efforts

31. See *b. B. Bat.* 21a. Online: http://www.come-and-hear.com/bababathra/baba bathra_21.html.

32. Ibid. It's unclear why age six was the cut-off, but the Talmud continues with a conversation between Rav and Rabbi Samuel ben Shelath, in which the former advised, "Do not accept students younger than six, but thereafter take them and pack them [with information] like an ox."

and made them available to all young people, regardless of their economic and social status?

The Talmudic passage continues in some detail about the nature of Joshua ben Gamala's educational reform. For example, under the new guidelines, children could be sent to school in different synagogues on different days in the same town, but it was deemed too inconvenient and trying to send them to different schools in different towns on different days. If there was a river blocking the student's path, the student might only be compelled to cross it if there was a bridge, according to Joshua ben Gamala, who called for a maximum teacher to student ratio of 1:25.

Although some of the mandates of Joshua ben Gamala's are so specific that one might be inclined to believe that they were real, there is no historical evidence that these educational reforms were actually implemented, and the majority of the Jewish population in Palestine between the third century BCE and the first century CE was rural and illiterate.[33] The reforms also are alleged to have impacted younger students, so they did not necessarily imply reformation of higher educational institutions.

The Talmudic perspective on higher education is further amplified in a variety of stories that involve some of the same players. As I mentioned in chapter 2, one Rabbi Joshua and a Rabbi Eliezer were at odds about whether a certain oven (of Akhnai) was impure, and despite the latter's marshaling a variety of miracles—including a divine voice!—to corroborate his position, Rabbi Joshua insisted that the Torah was not in the heavens, but was meant to be explored by humans on earth.

That conclusion is a victory for academic freedom, insofar as human judges are able to not only debate divine ones, but also to trump them; on the other hand, Eliezer—identified later in the narrative as Eliezer ben Hyrcanus—was excommunicated. The Talmudic passage in *b. B. Metz.* 59b, after stating that God declared Himself to have been defeated by His sons, continues:

> On that day, all of the things which Rabbi Eliezer had ruled to be pure were gathered and burnt. And they [the rabbis] voted and excommunicated[34] him. They [the rabbis] asked, "Who will alert

33. See Botticini and Eckstein, "Jewish Occupational Selection," 932. See also the ensuing discussion about the Pharisees and the Sadducees, and the impact that debate may have had on the development of Jewish education.

34. The Talmud uses the word *blessed*, but it is clear from context that this is a euphemism for excommunication. The same sort of "clean language," as it is called in rabbinic texts, surfaces when there is a reference to cursing God. The King James Version renders

him?" Rabbi Akiba told them, "I will go, lest an inappropriate person go tell him, and in so doing destroy the entire world."

What did Rabbi Akiba do? He wore black clothing and sat four hundred cubits from him [Rabbi Eliezer]. "Akiba, what has happened today," he asked. "Rabbi," he answered, "it seems to me that your colleagues have distanced themselves from you." He [Eliezer] then tore his clothing, too, removed his shoes, and sat on the ground,[35] while tears streamed forth from his eyes. A third of the world's olive crop, a third of its wheat, and a third of its barley was struck [as a result], and there were those who said that even the dough in a woman's hand was affected.

It was taught: [The impact of] that day was so great that Rabbi Eliezer burned everything that he saw with his eyes. And Rabban Gamliel was on a boat and a huge wave threatened to drown him. "It seems to me," he said, "that this must be due to Rabbi Eliezer ben Hyrcanus." He [Rabban Gamliel] then got up and said, "Master of the universe, it is clear to You that I did this for Your honor, rather than my own or that of my father's house—so that debate not proliferate in Israel." The sea then settled down.

These three players—Rabbi Eliezer ben Hyrcanus, Rabbi Joshua [ben Hananiah], and Rabban Gamliel[36]—will resurface soon, but it is important to note Rabban Gamliel's argument, which seems to earn divine acceptance, that the proliferation of argument in Israel is a matter to be avoided. If one envisions the academy as a safe place for mature and unfettered critical debate, this would seem to counterbalance the victory for academic freedom in the narrative. On the one hand, Rabbi Joshua has been permitted to debate a divine voice and has defeated it with God's blessing, but on the other hand, Eliezer's perspective gets him excommunicated.[37]

Job's wife's prescription for her husband in the predicate of Job 2:9 as "curse God, and die." The original Hebrew, however, is "*bareikh* [bless], God and die."

35. All signs of Jewish mourning.

36. I am indebted to Rabbi Eliyahu Fink of the Pacific Jewish Center in Venice, California, for helping me ascertain that these were the same figures in all of the stories.

37. The role excommunication (Hebrew *herem*) plays in Judaism is a fascinating topic in its own right. Baruch Spinoza's excommunication by the Dutch Jewish community on July 27, 1656, is perhaps the best-known example, although it was not necessarily as severe a punishment as contemporary audiences might imagine. "Although it is a convenient and common label, to call what Spinoza received in 1656 an 'excommunication' is not quite right. A religion that has no 'communion' to begin with, no formal set of obligatory sacraments and rites from which one can be excluded, cannot 'excommunicate' its members. Judaism, in its structures of power and prerogative, is not like the Catholic Church," writes Nadler (*Spinoza's Heresy*, 4).

Two of the three rabbis surface in a story somewhat earlier chrono-
logically, when Rabbis Joshua and Eliezer were younger and were students
of Rabbi Jochanan ben Zakkai, a renowned rabbi who was active during the
siege of Jerusalem leading up to the sacking of the Second Temple. As the
Talmud tells it, Jochanan managed to escape from the holy city, where Jews
were starving to death en masse, by pretending to be dead.[38] His cocon-
spirators, including Abba Sikra, his sister's son and the head of the so-called
Biryoni,[39] who advocated fighting rather than reconciling with the Romans,
placed a foul-smelling item in his coffin to convince others that he was a
decaying corpse, and only his closest students (Eliezer and Joshua) carried
the body. Only they were trusted, because, the Talmud states, a dead body
is heavier than a live one,[40] and only the most dependent disciples could be
counted upon to conceal the fact that their master was still alive.

Another telling story comes from *b. Chag.* 14b: Four rabbis—Ben Azzai and Ben
Zoma (both of whom seem so young that they are identified only by their fathers'
names), Elisha ben Abuyah (referred to in the story as Acher, or "Other," so as not to
name him, since he was to be accused of becoming a heretic), and Rabbi Akiba entered
an orchard or a garden (*pardes*), and each had a very different experience. Rabbi Akiba
told his colleagues, "When you approach pure precious stones, don't say, 'Water, water,'
for it states [in Ps 101:7] 'A speaker of lies won't be accepted before My eyes.'" Ben Azzai
looked and died, and about him the verse states [Ps 116:15], "Precious in the eyes of the
Lord is the death of his righteous men." Ben Zoma looked and was struck, and about
him the verse states [Prov 25:16], "You found honey; eat your fill, lest you overeat and
vomit." Acher (i.e., Elisha ben Abuyah) cut saplings. Rabbi Akiba left in peace. Rashi,
the eleventh-century French rabbi, notes that Ben Azzai was killed for looking at God,
which is punishable by death per Exodus 33:20, and that Ben Zoma, who was "struck," in
fact lost his mind. According to Rashi, the "orchard" the four rabbis visited was actually
a celestial abode, which they gained access to by using a divine name.

Other commentators have responded to the enigmatic story in different ways. The
Hebrew word for orchard, *pardes*, is taken by some as an acronym for four techniques
of biblical exegesis: *pshat* (simple explanation), *remez* (hinted or implied topics), *drash*
(analytical or deductive interpretations), and *sod* (secretive or kabbalistic inquiry). The
excommunication of the heretic, who is not even named in the narrative, seems even
more severe than the excommunications of Eliezer ben Hyrcanus and Spinoza.

38. See *b. Git.* 56a and 56b. Online: http://www.come-and-hear.com/gittin/gittin_
56.html.

39. See Nedava, "Biryoni," where the Biryoni are identified as a sort of robbers and
zealots. According to Nedava, the Biryoni were the parent group from which another
movement, the Sicarii, broke off.

40. See *b. Shab.* 94a. Online: http://www.come-and-hear.com/shabbath/shabbath_
94.html. The Talmud claims, "The living carries itself," which presumably accounts for
the nonscientific argument for a difference in weight.

Rabbis Eliezer and Joshua lifted the fake corpse, and when they and Abba Sikra got to the city gates, the Biryoni wanted to either pierce the corpse with a spear to be sure it was in fact a dead man, or to lift or shake it to ascertain its weight. Thinking quickly on his feet, Abba Sikra asked those guards if they wanted the Romans to say that Jews had stabbed or pushed their own master, and somehow that was good enough to persuade the would-be assailants that the rabbi was actually dead. (One also wonders why Abba Sikra, as the leader of the movement, could not just call off the guards to begin with, but apparently he could not.)

The Biryoni's surprising gullibility aside, Rabbi Jochanan ben Zakkai made a miraculous recovery when he made it to the Roman front and somehow gained an audience with Vespasian, whom he referred to as a king. The latter informed the rabbi he was deserving of death either for calling him a king—which he was not—or, in the event that he was king, for not coming to him sooner. The rabbi responded by citing Isaiah 10:34, which he construed to mean that Jerusalem would only fall to a king, and that the Biryoni prevented him from arriving sooner.

An ensuing bewildering conversation about snakes encircling honey jars aside, Vespasian, having just been informed by messenger that the emperor had died and he was the new head of state, was amid changing his boots, and was unable to remove the one he had already donned or to put the other one on. The rabbi cited Proverbs 15:30, ". . . a good report fattens the bone," and told him to call someone he disliked, for Proverbs 17:22 promised that "a damaged spirit dries up the bone." Evidently this trick worked, and the new emperor was able to arrange his footwear to his satisfaction. Impressed, Vespasian offered to grant any requests made by the rabbi as a reward. The latter asked, first, "Give me Jabneh and its wise men."

That is a roundabout way of getting to the fact that there was apparently an organized community of wise men—presumably mobilized around some sort of academy—in the city of Jabneh, a biblical city that surfaces in 2 Chronicles 26:6. Jabneh later became the seat of the Sanhedrin—the Jewish Supreme Court, of sorts—under the leadership, initially, of Rabbi Jochanan ben Zakkai.

Jabneh may also have been the place where the Jewish canon was finalized,[41] but for our purposes, it was also the place where the rabbinical

---

41. For an opposing view, see Lewis ("What Do We Mean by Jabneh?"). Citing the views that Ezra, Nehemiah, the Men of the Great Assembly, or a 90 CE meeting in Jabneh closed the canon, Lewis notes several issues, which are worth quoting at length (127): "The first problem with the gathering at Jabneh is one of terminology. In the sources the

academy was drastically altered, at least for a short period of time. In the second century, the head of the Sanhedrin (referred to as the *nasi*, or prince), Rabban Gamliel—the same one who attributed the wave that threatened to drown him to Eliezer's suspension—was temporarily removed from his post as chief justice for publicly humiliating his colleague, Rabbi Joshua—of the oven of Akhnai dispute, as well as the coffin carrying episode.

As the Talmud tells it,[42] a student asked Rabbi Joshua whether it was voluntary or required to recite the evening prayer—referred to in Hebrew as *ma'ariv* or *arvit*, both from the root *erev*, which means "evening." The latter replied that it was optional, but when the student posed the same question to Rabban Gamliel, the chief judge gave the opposite answer, saying that it was a religious mandate to pray the third prayer of the day. The student informed him that Rabbi Joshua had ruled to the contrary, so Rabban Gamliel asked him to come to the study house (*beit ha-midrash*) and wait for the sages (literally "warriors") to enter.

When they arrived, someone (perhaps the original inquisitor) posed the question again, and Rabban Gamliel repeated his answer. He asked if anyone disagreed, and Rabbi Joshua said that no one did. Gamliel challenged that and told him to stand up and let the student testify against him, to which Joshua responded that he could not counter the testimony. In obvious disrespect to the latter, Gamliel sat and taught that day's lesson while Joshua had to remain standing. This—coupled with prior insults[43]—led to

---

terms *beth din*, *methivta*, *yeshiva*, and *beth ha-midrash* are used to designate the meetings in addition to the phrase already noticed, 'in the vineyards of Jabneh.' In discussions of the Jabneh gatherings where the canon is not concerned, these terms are commonly translated 'academy,' 'court,' or 'school.' When, however, canon is under consideration, the group suddenly becomes a 'council' or 'synod.' Though these are legitimate renderings of these terms, sixteen hundred years of ecclesiastical usage and twenty-one ecumenical councils have given these latter words certain ecclesiastical connotations of officially assembled authoritative bodies of delegates which rule and settle questions. These titles are not appropriate for Judaism. One's mind immediately thinks of gatherings such as Nicea, Hippo, or Trent. It is a fallacy to superimpose such Christian concepts upon Judaism. It is proposed that the terms 'court,' 'school,' or 'assembly' would more nearly convey the true nature of the body at Jabneh than would terms like 'council' or 'synod.'"

42. See *b. Ber.* 27b–28a. Online: http://www.come-and-hear.com/berakoth/berakoth_27.html#PARTb.

43. Including Rabban Gamliel's forcing Rabbi Joshua to visit him carrying his staff and purse on the day that Rabbi Joshua thought was the Day of Atonement. Gamliel was thus insulting Joshua in the greatest possible way. Although the former did not believe the day was in fact Yom Kippur, Joshua did, so he was being forced to carry forbidden items on what he considered the holiest of days. See *b. R.H.* 25a.

a mutiny of sorts in the study hall, and there was talk of deposing Rabban Gamliel. Gamliel's colleagues decided it would be adding insult to injury to appoint Joshua the new *nasi*, so they opted instead[44] for Rabbi Eleazar ben Azariah,[45] who had a reputation for being wealthy and wise. He was also eighteen years old at the time, but after consulting with his wife and accepting the position, he miraculously sprouted eighteen rows of white beard, so that his colleagues would respect him.[46] Although his tenure was short-lived, Eleazar had a profound impact on the academy. "That day," the Talmud states,

> they removed the guards upon the entrance [to the academy], and students were given permission to enter. For Rabban Gamliel used to announce, "Any student whose interior isn't like his exterior may not enter the study hall." That day, they added many benches. Rabbi Jochanan said that Abba Joseph ben Dosthai debated the rabbis. One said that four hundred benches were added, and the other said seven hundred.[47]

This vision of Eleazar ben Azariah's, that the academy doors should be thrown open to students who were not the elite, appears to be similar to that of Joshua ben Gamala's, but the Talmudic passage continues by attempting to undermine Eleazar's populism. Rabban Gamliel, evidently, worried when he saw the new benches that his restrictive vision had slowed the study of Torah in Israel, but he was shown a vision in a dream of white caskets soiled on the inside—presumably in support of his insistence that students' souls be in line with their deeds. However the Talmud also suggests, further complicating matters, that the dream was only shown to Gamliel to make him feel better, and that every law which had previously befuddled the rabbis was resolved on that momentous day.

The day may also have been a good one for proponents of academic freedom if viewed from the perspective of Joshua's controversial views ultimately being recognized despite their opposition to the academy's official position on the interpretation of the law. But however victorious that day was, Rabban Gamliel was soon reinstated—with Eleazar promoted, or

44. After rejecting Rabbi Akiba, whose pedigree they thought Gamliel would attack, since he was a convert.

45. A different character from Eliezer ben Hyrcanus.

46. Incidentally, he is mentioned in the Passover Haggadah as saying, "Behold I am as if I was 70 years old," which is consistent with this story.

47. See *b. Ber.* 28a.

demoted, to a different role—and the notion that every prior theological controversy was resolved on that day is quite unbelievable.

This episode would capture the imagination of many subsequent Jewish educators and educational theorists, but there is no historical evidence that this Talmudic academic revolution ever occurred, or that it directly affected the subsequent development of the Jewish academy in the second century.

Regressing from the Middle Ages to the Dark Ages

Rabbis have produced dizzying amounts of biblical scholarship and religious responsa (legal rulings issued in response to practical questions and quandaries), to be sure—some of which I studied in my eighteen years of Jewish education—and students who attend Jewish schools today often study the Five Books of Moses verse by verse, simultaneously examining nearly half a dozen commentators juxtaposed on each page with the biblical passages. In one type of bible, called *mikraot gedolot* (or "great/large readings"), the appended commentaries include the eleventh-century French rabbi Rashi (Shlomo Yitzhaki), the thirteenth-century Spanish sage Nachmanides (Moshe ben Nachman), Onkelos (largely active in the late first and early second centuries CE), the twelfth-century Spanish commentator Abraham ibn Ezra, and others. But it is difficult to chart the larger scholarly contexts in which some of these commentaries were produced, even though we know the names of some of the institutions: from the Talmudic academies at Sura and Pumbedita to the yeshivas at Worms and Mainz where Rashi studied.

In Sicily, for example, perhaps the "most memorable episode in the Jewish intellectual life in the island," as Cecil Roth observed,[48] was King John II of Aragon's decision in 1466 to allow the Jewish community to open its own university with faculties of law and medicine, "with the right to engage teachers, to conduct courses, and to confer degrees." Religious schools and academies with copies of the Talmud furnished by Samuel ibn Nagdela of Granada existed in the eleventh century, and in the fifteenth century there was a rabbinical college, which had a building and "a number of scholastic books," but the school was cl osed in 1476, "on the pretext that its object was illegitimate: for the Sicilian Jews had been guilty not

---

48. See Roth, "Jewish Intellectual Life," 330.

only of studying the Talmud, which the Popes had condemned, but also of diffusing other literature in which Christianity was blasphemed."[49]

The university that King John II permitted in 1466 had similar luck, as the Jews were expelled from Sicily in 1492, and, as Roth observes,

> Unfortunately, we do not know anything about the organization or the curriculum of this institution, nor even whether it actually came into being. But it is to be imagined that its principal object was to have been the opening of a medical faculty, in view of the difficulty experienced by Jews at this time in obtaining training as physicians in the normal manner.[50]

There are other isolated examples of Jewish intellectuals landing spots on the faculties of certain universities in the Middle Ages, but those are the exceptions to the rule rather than the norm, and those professors studied and taught at Christian, rather than Jewish, schools.

On January 9, 1555, Pope Julius III ordered the University of Padua to consider Simon Vitale, a Jewish student, for a doctorate, despite a 1434 Council of Basle ban on bestowing degrees upon Jews.[51] "The pope's motivation was neither religious tolerance nor academic freedom," William W. Brickman notes, "but rather the hope that conversion of the candidate and, consequently, of other Jews would be facilitated."[52]

Some of the educational philosophies that developed along the way are important to note for their continued impact today. The notion of a transmitted *mesorah*, or theological tradition, passed down from master to student—as articulated in the quote from *Ethics of the Fathers* above—comes with two contrasting principles. On the one hand, there is a notion of "generations increasingly shrinking"[53]—that as each generation becomes more and more removed from Sinai, that individuals' connection to the holiness implied in that revelation diminishes. This is manifest in the Talmud, where rabbis of certain generations cannot argue with rabbis of prior

49. Ibid., 329.

50. Ibid., 330.

51. See Brickman, "Universities," 407.

52. Ibid.

53. Or "nitkatnu ha-dorot," articulated, for example, in *b. Shab.* 112b: "Rabbi Zera said in the name of Rabba bar [son of] Zimuna, 'If early scholars were sons of angels, we are the sons of men, and if the early scholars were sons of men, we are donkeys." For some reason, the Talmud finds it necessary to clarify, adding, "and not like the donkey of Rabbi Hanina ben Dosa and of Rabbi Pinchas ben Yair, but like other donkeys." See also Deutsch, "Forbidden Fork," 4 n. 2.

generations, although they can side with a predecessor in a dispute with another predecessor. On the other hand, there is a notion that contemporary rabbis are in a better position to weigh new scientific developments when they issue their legal responsa, so there is ground, in certain instances, to prioritize the current rabbinate over its predecessors.

This often inverse relationship between living rabbis and ancient commentators is further complicated by the notion of *Daat Torah* (or *Daas Torah*, depending upon one's pronunciation)—the idea that present-day rabbis are quasi-prophets, whose *halakhic* (legal) rulings are somewhat divinely inspired. The term has come to mean "a 'pronouncement of the halakhists *ex cathedra*,' made binding upon religious Jewry and with its authority based simply upon the general prestige conferred upon the halakhists," notes Jacob Katz,[54] who connects the development of the concept with the slogan of Moses Schreiber (the Chatam Sofer), "The new is forbidden according to the Torah."

As Rabbi Tzvi Hersh Weinreb, the executive vice president emeritus of the Orthodox Union, wrote in the Jewish organization's publication, *Jewish Action*, the Chatam Sofer coined his motto in response to the "growing strength of the Reform movement."[55] Weinreb's article betrays his admiration and that of other Orthodox Jews' for the Chatam Sofer, who was, Weinreb writes,

> faced with those who demanded relatively minor modifications in religious observance, as well as those who were ready to abandon much more essential Jewish practices. His strategy in preserving the mesorah was a simple one: no compromise whatsoever. Borrowing a phrase from a specific halachic context, he asserted,

---

54. See Katz, "Da'at Torah." See also Kaplan, "Rabbi," 245–47. Kaplan writes in part, "I believe that Orthodox Jews who are not adherents of Agudat Israel and its philosophy should be wary of the entire concept of *Daat Torah* and its all too casual use, both in the pages of *The Jewish Observer* and on the part of Agudah spokesmen in general. Rabbi Bernard Weinberger, in an important article in an early issue of *The Jewish Observer* ('The Role of the Gedolim,' October 1963), defines *Daat Torah* as 'a special endowment or capacity to penetrate objective reality, recognize the facts as they really are and apply the pertinent halakhic principles. It is a form of *Ruah Hakodesh* [prophecy; literally "holy spirit"], as it were, which borders, if only remotely, on the periphery of prophecy.'" Kaplan later wonders aloud, "should we dispense with all questions and simply accept the notion of *Daat Torah* on the basis of *Daat Torah*?" See also Lederhendler, *Who Owns Judaism?*, 30 n. 20.

55. See Weinreb, "Preserving Our Mesorah."

"Chadash assur min haTorah; All that is new is prohibited." He opposed modernization in all its forms.

The Chatam Sofer's approach reflected his deep mistrust of the historical developments of his time that originated in non-Jewish sources. To him, all values had to stem from impeccably Jewish origins. Every deviation, no matter how slight, was to be vigorously opposed. Every proposed innovation, however innocuous it might seem, had idolatrous roots and would lead to serious transgressions.

For the Chatam Sofer, not one iota of mesorah [tradition] could be sacrificed. He used to say, "Let one thousand of my opponents be lost, but let not one jot or tittle of Jewish custom be dislodged from its place," and, "Anyone who questions our norms and customs is suspect [of heresy]."

Weinreb goes on to discuss Rabbi Avraham Yitzchak HaKohen Kook, Israel's first chief rabbi, whom he contrasts to Sofer, but he notes that the two rabbis were more complicated than they might seem. Weinreb concludes with a plea to readers to "cope with attempts to 'improve' or 'advance' our mesorah."

This development, which I have traced from the mysterious biblical academy of Shem and Eber and the incredibly open-minded Talmudic debates—albeit with a troubling propensity to excommunicate—to what are often more rigid approaches to theological differences of opinion in the modern yeshiva, is certainly only a part of the story. But it suggests, I hope, a trajectory that will set the stage for some of the approaches to academic freedom and open debate that prevail at Yeshiva University, the modern Orthodox flagship institution.

One must of course be careful about comparing apples and oranges, however, and the observations of Yiddish writer Asher Penn about the rabbinical academy Beth Medrash Govoha in Lakewood, New Jersey, in 1958 still hold true. The "large study hall" is a great deal to the right of Yeshiva University, but Penn's reflections underscore another important aspect of Orthodox Jewish study, which cannot be underestimated: the all-encompassing and perpetual mandate to study Jewish texts both for the sake of one's education and to better understand the law. "I had lengthy discussions with a great many students. They were almost unanimous in demonstrating to me the fact that 'here in Beth Midrash Govoha' everyone learns solely to deepen himself in Torah. One does not come to the Beth Midrash Govoha to acquire rabbinic ordination. They are not occupied with such 'trivialities,'" he writes. "They go here exclusively to study, and actually do so from morning until late at night. And one need not worry how long he studies. If they do tell me 'how long,' they mean it not in terms of days, weeks, or months; they have come here to study for years."[56]

Today's yeshivas are surely very unique sorts of communities—where the notion of learning for the sake of learning (*Torah l'shma*) governs, and where time can seem to slow down. But however comforting those insular communities might be, and however appealing they are to those who inhabit them, it is important to be honest—another Jewish value—about how exactly they operate and how open they truly are. I will get to some of that in my next chapter.

56. See Penn, "Advanced Talmudic Academies."

PART THREE

Our Limitations

5

The Outrageous Idea of Christian Academic Freedom

Brandon G. Withrow

In 2002, Sheri Klouda accepted a position as theology professor at South-western Baptist Theological Seminary (SWBTS) in Fort Worth, Texas. Little did she know, the seminary of the Southern Baptist Convention was experiencing a "momentary lax of . . . parameters" by hiring her, according to Paige Patterson. When Patterson became president of the seminary in 2003, he was determined to return the school to its "traditional, confessional and biblical position." In other words, he may as well have posted a "No Girls Allowed" sign in the faculty lounge.

Klouda was denied tenure in 2006 because of her gender; both sides of the dispute agree on this point. According to Klouda, Patterson made several patriarchal statements about women prior to his joining SWBTS, and this worried her. She did what any tenure-track professor might be reluctant to do—she asked him about it. Who would want to invest in tenure at an institution that would never grant it to you? According to Klouda, Patterson assured her that she had nothing to worry about, but she recalls discovering through the grapevine that he had no plans to support her tenure.[1]

Paul's words in 1 Timothy 2:12—"I permit no woman to teach or to have authority over a man; she is to keep silent"—are interpreted by many

---

1. Associated Press, "Professor: Seminary Ousted Her over Gender," para. 17.

in the Southern Baptist Convention as applying only to the local church. But for Patterson, and the larger tradition of Southern Baptists, Paul's command—and that's how they take it, as a universal command—also applies to the seminary. The institutional narrative in the Klouda situation, therefore, is that of returning not only to a more conservative Baptist heritage but also to a theological command to silence women.

Klouda opted not to be silent and challenged that narrative in the court system as a violation of equal opportunity laws. She lost. The judge in her case dismissed it as a religious matter, upholding the seminary's decision—and adding insult to injury by ordering her to pay the school's court costs.[2]

In chapter 3, we saw the evolution of religious higher education and how prominent a role theology has played in it historically. Klouda's story, like those in the pages ahead, demonstrates that this is not a thing of the past. In this chapter, I will examine the ongoing conflict between academic freedom and the theological narrative(s) of a Christian educational institution. My purpose is to ask why academic freedom looks different in religious institutions, and (in part) whether academic freedom in Christian institutions is possible.

I've already noted that controversies such as these are often far more complicated than we realize. But I intend to show that they are primarily about control, and that theology is often the justifying narrative for gaining or maintaining that control. Whatever the other interpersonal issues involved—bias, ambition, faculty hobbyhorses, pressure from donors, or the unquestioned will of a leader—the theological is most likely the rallying point. This is not to say that theology is a diversion or that it is immaterial to a school's identity, especially a religious school, but that academic freedom in religious institutions, by nature, will always be limited and shaped by theological identity. This identity can also unfortunately become a tool for drawing lines between so-called good or bad individuals. Maybe this theological limitation imposed on faculty is understandably shocking to those outside of religious higher education, but for insiders it shouldn't be.

A closer look at three disputes, which occurred at Shorter University, Westminster Theological Seminary, and Cedarville University, will demonstrate the relationship between theology and control. The extensive public

2. Barrick, "Judge Dismisses Gender Discrimination Suit," para. 13. Klouda was offered a chance to remain on for a couple of years in a different, non-teaching position, until she found another job, which she eventually did at Taylor University.

discussion of all three situations helps bring out the theological agendas, personal tragedies, and power struggles. These stories are also examples of institutions with tightly drawn religious identities, as (in my experience, at least) is often the case within conservative schools.[3] The fact that many conservative theologians often criticize liberal theologians for being too theologically open or pluralistic is a point that can only be made if conservatives are advocating a theology that is narrow and exclusive. (In a later chapter, I will also bring in examples of the reverse within an institution, that is, conservative faculty members pushed out for holding something offensive to their liberal academic communities.) For some of the people involved, these situations are battles between right and wrong—even heaven and hell—and which side a faculty member or institution is on depends on where the viewer is standing.

Shorter University

For years, Shorter University in Rome, Georgia, had identified itself as a Christian school, though it was broadly welcoming of those from different backgrounds. But in 2011, Shorter found itself in the middle of a complete upheaval.

It had all started a decade earlier when the Georgia Baptist Convention (GBC), which had provided financial support for years, decided to abandon the school's proposed nominee list for new trustees and began unilaterally appointing conservative Baptists. Initially, the faculty and administration did not want the convention to have full oversight of the school, at least partly because of fears that becoming a conservative Baptist school would lead to problems with accreditation. Seeking to sever the relationship completely, Shorter's board of trustees attempted to turn control of the school over to its nonprofit foundation, which led to a court battle in 2005. The board was told that they were not free to end the relationship with the GBC. They sought an appeal, but the Georgia Supreme Court refused to reconsider the ruling. To assuage the faculty's accreditation fears, the GBC assured them that they were seeking full accreditation and that their tradition of welcoming diverse Baptist perspectives would continue.[4]

---

3. It may be said, however, that even many of the individuals pushed out of these conservative institutions explored in this chapter are still likely to be considered conservative by many standards.

4. Jaschik, "Conceding Defeat at Shorter," para. 13.

But, probably to no one's surprise, things began to shift as the Baptist convention added new trustees. And in 2008, they joined the conservative evangelical organization The Council for Christian Colleges and Universities, signaling a new direction.

In 2011, Shorter's faculty consulted with The American Association of University Professors about the board's fall approval—without faculty consultation—of four key documents. These documents included a "Faith Statement" and a "Personal Lifestyle Statement"; failure to sign both would result in termination. The AAUP was concerned that forcing existing faculty to accept the new faith statement was a violation of academic freedom. The statements proved problematic for many faculty and were viewed as tools for a fundamentalist takeover. Signatories gave their assent to the doctrines of an "inerrant and infallible" Bible, the "everlasting punishment" of all non-Christians, and creationism, and the lifestyle statement condemned homosexuality and public drinking, among other practices.[5] For the school's new president, Donald Dowless, the priority was to ensure that all faculty members were "Bible-believing Christians," implying that those who disagreed did not believe the Bible.[6]

Faculty and students reacted strongly, leading to a mass exodus, public protests, and websites critical of the school. Many members of the community felt that the Shorter University they once knew was no longer. They felt blindsided, and were confused about how to apply the new statements in their various roles. A new biology professor, for example, had been assured at her interview that teaching evolution would not be a problem, but a few months later was forced to resign when the new faith statement required her to teach (and believe) creationism. It also took the school's tenured librarian, Michael Wilson, by surprise, when he discovered that the community that had welcomed him for over fourteen years suddenly condemned him for being gay. All in all, according to *Inside Higher Ed*, eighty-three of Shorter's faculty, staff, and administration resigned, which included thirty-five of its ninety-four full-time faculty members, four deans, and a vice president.[7]

---

5. Nelson, "Refusing to Sign," para. 10; the Shorter University statements may be found online: https://web.archive.org/web/20130907075140/http://shorter.edu/about/news/2011/10_25_11_logo_statements.htm. See also the American Association of University Professors, "Letter to President Donald Dowless," para. 5.

6. Nelson, "Banned," para. 17.

7. Sloan, "Shorter Librarian Prepares to Leave," para. 1; Nelson, "Shorter's Exodus, a Year Later," para. 10.

Shorter's evolution was more of a revolution. It was a Christian school that went from broader acceptance of diverse theological opinions to an enforcement of one theological narrative, the rejection of which condemned members of the community as non-Bible-believing Christians. Those who left saw the move as a crude takeover of fundamentalists from the outside.

The website Save Our Shorter (saveourshorter.com) responded to the crisis by publishing the resignation letters of faculty who agreed to make them public. In one instance, a Pentecostal biology professor, Richard Pirkle, expressed his disappointment "with being forced to teach Creationism or Intelligent Design (both of which are philosophical and religious beliefs) in addition to being forced to teach evolution as 'just a theory.'" He challenged the element of fear spread by the administration. "The process of weeding out non-compliant faculty has created an environment where those that could leave (like myself) has [*sic*] uprooted their family and moved on," wrote Pirkle. "Those that couldn't, whether they agree with the statement of faith or not, will sign it to keep their jobs."[8] His comment captures the complexity of faculty and staff caught in the middle of an administrative overhaul like the one at Shorter. Pirkle was fortunate enough to find another position where he could teach according to the standards of his field and his conscience, but others were forced to choose between being honest about their personal convictions and putting food on the table. Depending upon one's position and contract, the grace period varied before effective termination; tenured librarian Michael Wilson was given until the end of the school year, but others may not have been so fortunate.[9]

There were no easy solutions in a complicated situation in which a narrow theological agenda was given priority over the considerations of what a community owes to its members who have made their homes there. For many former Shorter members, the university's turnover is about misplaced Christian priorities, that is, a missing empathy for fellow Christians due to a priority placed on a doctrinal identity.

Unfortunately, Shorter University is far from being an isolated example.

8. Pirkle, "Letter," paras. 7, 8.

9. Nelson, "Shorter's Exodus, a Year Later," paras. 53–54.

Westminster Theological Seminary

As seen briefly in chapter 1, when Peter Enns wrote his *Inspiration and Incarnation: Evangelicals and the Problem of the Old Testament* (2005), he was immediately immersed in controversy at Westminster Theological Seminary in Philadelphia. Enns was accused of violating his faculty oath, which required him to adhere to the Westminster Confession of Faith.[10] Enns went on the record as saying that the conclusions drawn in his book did not negate his commitment to the confession. The parallels between Westminster and Shorter are not in the numbers—Westminster is a much smaller institution than Shorter and lost fewer faculty and staff in its controversy—but the theological narratives of the revolutionaries followed a very similar doctrinal emphasis.

Much of the ink spilled over the Enns controversy addresses the theological concerns thoroughly, and a detailed review is unnecessary here. But it is helpful to summarize a few points to get at the role theology played in the situation. It could be said that the problem begins with a debate over the nature of the Bible and the question of inerrancy.

Scholars agree that the Bible reflects the surrounding cultures of its day in characteristics like literary genre. Many Evangelicals are uncomfortable, however, with saying that a divine book like the Bible borrows from local cultures in any way that appears to downplay its unique revelatory nature, that it is mythical in its creation account, or that it could have an error in its recorded history.[11] To them, this makes the Bible far too human.

Rather than reject this very human side to the Bible, Enns applies what he calls an "incarnational analogy," which is not as complicated as it may sound. In the Christian tradition, the Son of God is incarnated, meaning that he joined humanity on earth through a human birth, becoming a single, fully divine and yet fully human person. As to his humanity, Christ slept, ate, and possessed limited knowledge; but as to his divinity, Christ is perfectly flawless, infinite, and all-powerful. He expresses these attributes

---

10. The Westminster Confession of Faith was written by the Westminster Assembly in 1646 during the English Civil War. It is the standard of faith for Presbyterians worldwide.

11. For an example of this, see the well-known evangelical "Chicago Statement on Biblical Inerrancy." Article XII states, "We affirm that Scripture in its entirety is inerrant, being free from all falsehood, fraud, or deceit. . . . We further deny that scientific hypotheses about earth history may properly be used to overturn the teaching of Scripture on creation and the flood" (International Council on Biblical Inerrancy, "Chicago Statement on Biblical Inerrancy").

of both natures (human and divine) as one person and without a schizo-phrenic struggle of identity.

If this incarnational perspective becomes an analogy for the Bible, one might say that the very human elements of Scripture, such as the use of mythology or inaccurate historical accounts, are the expressions of human authors. God accommodates his message to the limitations of humanity, as ancient peoples are not likely to understand the Big Bang or evolution. The authority, message of redemption, and other theological truth claims of the Bible are expressions of its divine author. The analogy means that the human authors and the divine author come together to write one book that represents them all, much as the human and divine natures are expressed in the single person of Christ.

Opponents of Enns were not pleased with his incarnational analogy, as they believed it damaged a strong biblical inerrancy.[12] They asserted that his view of Christ's incarnation was not orthodox because it implied that the divine nature was not in control of the human in the person of Christ. This meant that by applying the incarnation to the Bible, Enns was also giv-ing too much control to the human authors, allowing for error in the Bible as well. In other words, Christ may have been human, but the divine nature was always top dog, and while the Bible may have had human authors, the divine author ultimately protected it from error.[13]

---

12. Five separate points were made by the response of the Historical and Theologi-cal Committee in an official document released by Westminster Theological Seminary: "1) a doctrine of Scripture that diverges from the classic Reformation doctrine, in par-ticular the tradition of Old Princeton and Westminster and specifically, the Westminster Confession of Faith (WCF), chapter 1; (2) a reductionistic Incarnational model; (3) a Post-Conservative Evangelical (PCE) approach to the discipline of theology; (4) a lack of clarity; (5) the appearance of speaking for the entire faculty." The focus was on points 1 through 3, with point 3 as another point based on the inerrancy and authority of Scripture, connecting *Inspiration and Incarnation* to a perceived postmodern relativism (Westminster, "Official Documents," 10).

13. In a meeting to address student concerns, the seminary president, Peter Lillback, noted that the issues "revolve around the doctrine of Scripture, the first chapter of the [Westminster] Confession." This means that even if Enns was not unorthodox in the broader Christian tradition, he was heterodox (as some faculty saw it) when it came to his "faithfulness" to the Westminster Confession of Faith (in the unofficial, unpublished, and anonymous "Transcript of the Report on the March 26, 2008 Westminster Theologi-cal Seminary Special Board Meeting," 3). One could argue, however, that the seminary's emphasis on the divinity falls nearly into the realm of Apollinarian Christology, a Chris-tology that essentially replaces the human mind of Christ with the logos. I've also written on an analogy similar to Enns's made by Reformed theologian Jonathan Edwards; see my book *Becoming Divine*, 157–67.

Enns repeatedly affirmed that his theological solution is only "analogous" (a helpful metaphor) borrowed from the incarnation of Christ, but not "identical" to it. This analogy meant that the problematic human elements did not need to be relegated "to the sidelines"; rather, they were honest representations of human authors.[14] Enns's opponents disagreed, arguing that the divine nature must preserve the Bible and that these human elements, particularly the "extrabiblical" materials from surrounding cultures, were "important" but ultimately "irrelevant."[15] The Bible cannot include error or anything historically untrue (e.g., ancient myths).

The battle over which theological narrative would tell the story of events at Westminster made its way into the public. From one point of view, the seminary was fighting for the truth and saving the Bible from liberals; from the other, the seminary was targeting the academic freedom of an honest and orthodox faculty member who did not suggest anything contrary to his Reformed and Presbyterian tradition. For those supporting Enns, it was not about rejecting conservative ideas for liberal ones, but about rejecting fundamentalism. In other words, one could keep the authority and inerrancy of the Bible and not have to resort to the heavy controlling hand of fundamentalism.

During the height of the controversy, Westminster students launched a petition called "Save our Seminary" in support of faculty like Enns, arguing that the administration was acting un-Christian and taking a fundamentalist direction. Later, Westminster administrators launched the "Full Confidence Tour" and the "Westminster Conference on Science and Faith," in which they touted their place as promoters of the absolute authority, reliability, and inerrancy of Scripture.[16]

Internally, the story was a mess and involved many potential, though not disconnected, narratives vying for prominence. A different take on the controversial era could be the story of its presidency. Then-president of the school (and my dissertation chair) Samuel T. Logan transitioned to chancellor, and then professor emeritus, amid faculty division, challenges to his leadership, and his support of Enns. Alternatively, one could follow the less

14. Enns, "Authority of Scripture," paras. 7, 9.

15. Westminster, "Official Documents," 15, 22. Enns was effectively accused of the heresy of "kenoticism," that is, the idea that Christ gave up his divinity to be human rather than maintaining both full divinity and humanity.

16. See examples at "Full Confidence Tour," http://www.wts.edu/stayinformed/view.html?id=855, and "Westminster Conferences on Science and Faith," http://www.wts.edu/stayinformed/view.html?id=855.

public fears that employees had expressed of losing their positions when the new president, Peter A. Lillback, joined the school in 2005. But in my experience, no recent faculty dispute at a theological school met the level of media attention, production of published literature, creation of conferences, and fiery student reaction than the narrower issue of what to do about Peter Enns.

When Lillback took the reins, he initiated two committees to address the issue of Enns's book—one consisted mostly of Enns's opponents, and the other his allies, which led to a faculty debate over the book that lasted for two years. When the committees were done, two professors (William Edgar and Michael Kelly) led a motion for faculty to affirm that Enns upheld his oath; it passed in December 2007.[17] Being a faculty-run school, the twelve to eight vote represented a significant rift in the faculty over which type of school Westminster would be: one restricting opinions to maintain a certain interpretation of the Westminster Confession, or one preserving academic freedom and broader faculty opinions.

As a faculty-run school, the vote also should have ended the question (though not the rift), as the faculty had spoken. But it didn't. President Lillback pushed the matter to the board of trustees, a move that called into question what seemed obvious; suddenly it was unclear who really controlled the school, the faculty or the board. The answer came quickly when, by a majority vote on March 26, 2008, the board suspended Enns. Nine board members resigned over the decision and the Internet exploded with posts by angry students.

On April 1, 2008, Lillback assured students at a campus Q and A that he had attempted to maintain impartiality to heal the rift and had not taken a side until three months earlier, when the board asked him to do so. Students found this claim of fairness hard to accept. One student blog noted that by April 3, a book in honor of a retiring faculty member was already in its final layout stages, including a chapter by Lillback highly critical of Enns's work; the implication was that the chapter must have been underway and reviewed by others months earlier. This left students wondering just how impartial Lillback was in his dealings if he was already writing against Enns long before his stated impartiality.[18] A few months after that campus

17. Westminster, "Official Documents," 115.

18. Anonymous, "Transcript of the Report," 10. For an example of a student response and the first to note the timetable discrepancy, see Moore, "Continuing Our Series," paras. 3–4.

meeting, Enns and Westminster parted ways. The deeply conservative faction had wrested control from the faculty and returned the school to its more fundamentalist beginnings.

One Westminster faculty member, and the second reader for my dissertation, Carl R. Trueman, publicly bragged that Westminster "organized and prepared for every eventuality, putting into place safety nets and multiple 'Plan Bs', they identified the places where influence could be wielded, mastered procedure, fought like the blazes when they had to, stood strong and immovable in the face of violent opposition, and outmanoeuvred their opponents by continual attention to meeting agendas, points of order, procedural matters, and long-term coordinated strategy." They "did not waste time and energy on irrelevant sideshows like rhetorical petitions," such as the student-run Save our Seminary, since "angry but sincere petitioners generally lose, while sincere but canny parliamentarians generally win."[19]

Perhaps Trueman's rhetoric should be surprising, but it is a frank display of what goes on in the background of these disputes. It would be a mistake to assume that in situations like these, a ruthless stratagem for control is nonexistent. Such a calculated approach might be understood as necessary and the lesser of two evils for preserving a theological position or for keeping what is perceived as the better party in control. And while it would be a mistake to assume that every participant on either side of a complex issue has malevolent intentions, it is also hard to imagine there is no ego involved among those at the top of these power struggles.

The fact is that the theology of a narrative is a powerful thing, and in my own conversations with those committed to removing Enns, several saw it as a terrible necessity for remaining orthodox and defending the Bible. When the victory is final in situations like this, a professor like Enns can only pick up the pieces, redirect his career, and find like-minded communities that are free to engage theology openly.

Cedarville University

Some schools have trouble settling on an identity. The case of Cedarville University is less about conservative versus liberal than it is about shades of theological conservatism.

A conservative Baptist school near Dayton, Ohio, founded in 1887, Cedarville was originally part of the General Synod of the Reformed

19. Trueman, "Being Presbyterian," para. 11.

Presbyterian Church of North America. For several decades, Cedarville struggled to remain financially sound. During the controversy between fundamentalists and modernists in the 1920s, the seeming solution to Cedarville's stability was to open its doors to a broader base of prospective students, especially those in the Presbyterian Church USA. So, in 1928, they obtained a release from their denomination.[20]

The solution failed, however, and after two more decades of struggle and a presidential scandal, the school was brought to the point of near closure in 1943. This time their salvation came in the form of a merger with the Baptist Bible Institute of Cleveland, and eventually coming under the control of the fundamentalist General Association of Regular Baptist Churches (GARBC), a denomination that only a decade earlier separated from the Northern Baptist Convention over the NBC's growing liberalism.[21]

Cedarville thrived and in September 2000 became a university, representing forty-one denominations. In his history of Cedarville, Murray Murdoch praises the school "as a marvelous testimony to what can be accomplished when an institution is faithful to its mission," noting that it "entered the twenty-first century committed to the same values that were the foundation of the institution well over a century ago." Despite this praise, given in 2003, Cedarville has spent a significant portion of the first decade of the new millennium embroiled in controversies.

In 2002, Cedarville's growing relationship with the conservative Southern Baptist Convention prompted the GARBC to question its orthodoxy, particularly since the very conservative SBC, according to the GARBC, is not conservative enough in its affirmation of the inerrancy of the Bible; its members are "inclusivists" who "permit the presence and ministry of liberals within the convention."[22] Actual liberals would not share this perception, which signifies just how far to the right the GARBC actually is. In 2006, the University and the GARBC severed their ties.[23]

Amid these concerns over inerrancy and truth, a committee was established in 2005 to discuss the issue of certainty of truth and the "degree to

20. Murdoch, "Cedarville University," 111.

21. Ibid., 112.

22. Moll, "Two Degrees of Separation," para. 2. The GARBC practices what is called second-degree separationism, that is, separating from those who have a connection to individuals or organizations that tolerate policies, practices, or beliefs that the GARBC cannot tolerate.

23. Roach, "GARBC Severs Ties," para. 1.

which one may know that truth."[24] Cedarville's official doctrinal statement on Scripture reads, "We believe the Old and New Testaments as verbally inspired by God and inerrant in the original writings, embracing all matters which the biblical authors address, and believe that they are of supreme and final authority in faith and life."[25] In 2006, the addition of the "Truth and Certainty" statement to this doctrinal statement became the sparking point for controversy, since Cedarville faculty members are expected to endorse not only the doctrinal statements of the school, but also any accompanying position statements. In the following year, Bible professors David Hoffeditz and David Mappes lost their faculty positions when they argued that the "Truth and Certainty" statement downplayed the assurance of truth that can be found in Scripture.

The addition of the "Truth and Certainty" statement resulted in what Hoffeditz and Mappes considered too much postmodern openness.[26] "*Believers do possess an inner conviction and assurance concerning the truths taught in the Scripture,*" says that statement, but the emphasis fell on the human limitations for fully grasping those truths.[27] "Christians can be assured that their beliefs are warranted," it continues, "even if their understanding is not comprehensive or perfect in every instance. This certainty is to be held with humility and love."[28] Traditionalists like Hoffeditz and Mappes understood this language as a capitulation to postmodern relativism, a concern that Scripture had lost its authority to subjective human interpretation and incipient liberalism. It should be noted, however, that the school's required affirmation of its statement of faith, which hails the Bible as inerrant and the "supreme and final authority," had not changed. The fear appears to be more in the idea of a slippery slope.

The rift within faculty and between faculty and administration took on a life of its own. Much like the Enns situation, blogs exploded with rumors and concerns that the school was tolerating liberals or that professors, like Hoffeditz, were being targeted by the university administration without cause or recourse.

Despite what was a veritable fifty shades of conservativism that undoubtedly confused many outsiders and actual liberals, the end result for

24. Cedarville, "Accreditation," 54.

25. Cedarville, "Doctrinal Statement," point 1.

26. Pulliam, "Cedarville's Tenure Tremor," para. 2.

27. Cedarville, "Truth and Certainty," 3. Emphasis in original.

28. Ibid.

professors like Hoffeditz evolved beyond a mere doctrinal disagreement. He was terminated shortly after signing a new contract in 2007 and cited as disruptive to the community.[29] Hoffeditz argued that he was targeted by the administration and not given a fair hearing on the issue. Students sent in letters of protest, one providing a secret recording of the university president admitting that "we did not want to take these actions before our accreditation . . . Because we felt . . . if everybody's stirred up, there's going to be this problem with accreditation." With months of advance knowledge of impending firings, the priority was given to preservation of accreditation rather than allowing professors sufficient time to find an amicable departure.[30]

The American Association of University Professors investigated and found in favor of Hoffeditz, arguing that Cedarville lacked "meaningful shared governance" and failed to provide a fair hearing. But with their only sphere of influence extending to recommendations, official statements of findings, censure, and potential evidence for a civil suit, the final report of the AAUP had little effect.[31] The university dismissed the AAUP report as "fatally flawed" and "designed to preserve pre-determined conclusions consistent with the AAUP's historical bias against religious schools."[32]

In the end, Hoffeditz took Cedarville to court, but the case was dismissed as a religious matter, with the court concluding that "it could not pass judgment on the personnel decision without unconstitutionally intruding into the Baptist college's religious affairs."[33]

While the "Truth and Certainty" dispute lasted well into 2009, it is far from being the latest. As I write this chapter in 2013, another controversy continues within Cedarville faculty. Professor of theological studies Michael Pahl lost his position at the school, a move that was quickly followed

29. According to an FAQ sheet posted on Cedarville's website: "These personnel actions relate to how we as a family of professional colleagues serve together in ways that honor a fellow believer and uphold the University's clear guidelines on academic freedom and professional ethics" (Cedarville, "FAQ: Recent Personnel Actions," para. 1).

30. Grovois, "University Timed Firing," para. 1.

31. The final American Association of University Professors report, "Academic Freedom and Tenure: Cedarville University," may be found online: http://www.aaup.org/report/academic-freedom-and-tenure-cedarville-university.

32. Jaschik, "Faith, Science and Academic Freedom," para. 18; Bartlett, "Cedarville U. Board," para. 1.

33. Schmidt, "Court Dismisses Wrongful-Termination Claim," para. 1.

by the resignation of the president and a vice president.[34] The very quiet nature of their departures returned the school to controversy and became the speculation of blog posts and newspaper articles online.

The new issue at stake concerned the idea of an original Adam in Genesis 1–3. While both Pahl and Cedarville faculty agreed that there was an original, literal Adam, they arrived at their conclusions by different means. Pahl's book *The Beginning and the End: Rereading Genesis's Stories and Revelation's Visions* (2011) became the center of that controversy. As Pahl tells *Christianity Today*, "I hold to a historical Adam and Eve, though not on exegetical grounds. . . . My reasons are more theological in nature."[35] Reaching the same final conclusion was not enough; Cedarville was ultimately unhappy with how Pahl got there. By way of analogy, if the debate was plotted in Google Maps, it would not be enough for both the institution and Pahl to arrive on time at the same location; they must also take the same route.

The problem? As Pahl reads the creation stories of Genesis, they are "ancient Israelite cosmogonies" resembling "ancient Mesopotamian and Egyptian stories of origins" and not to be taken as history in the modern sense.[36] For Cedarville, the rejection of Genesis as history in the modern sense must lead to a rejection of the literal Adam. Pahl, however, found plenty of theological reasons for believing in a literal Adam—such as appealing to the genealogical and theological statements elsewhere in the Bible—and he even accepted Cedarville's doctrinal statement that emphasizes a literal six-day account of creation.[37] Cedarville concluded, nevertheless, that he "is unable to concur fully with each and every position," something Pahl noted was an unstated exegetical matter and never mandated.[38] In this case, one might expect the school to see Pahl as being unfaithful to Scripture, amplifying the reason for his termination, but that is not what happened. Instead, they affirmed that his "orthodoxy and commitment to the gospel are not in question, nor is his commitment to Scripture's inspiration, authority and infallibility."[39] Many evangelical schools that could state this about their faculty would be satisfied enough, but not Cedarville.

---

34. Nelson, "Campus in Turmoil," para.1

35. Steffan, "Crisis of Faith Statements," para. 4.

36. Pahl, *Beginning and the End*, 11, 12.

37. Schneider and Steele, "On the Firing of Dr. Pahl," para. 2; Cedarville, "Doctrinal Statement," para. 4.

38. Steffan, "Crisis of Faith Statements," 5.

39. Pahl, "It's True," para. 4.

Much like the newly hired biology professor at Shorter University, Pahl's time at Cedarville was less than a year. His book came out in June 2011 and he moved from Alberta, Canada, to begin teaching at Cedarville in the 2011–12 school year. By September, the trustees issued their "Doctrinal White Paper,"[40] which emphasized the school's adherence to creationism and a historical Adam, and by October 2011 Pahl's dismissal was official and he was relieved of his teaching duties.

This time around, the controversy also took with it other high-profile figures at Cedarville, including the president, William Brown, in 2012 and Vice President for Student Life Carl Ruby in 2013. The reasons for the timing of their resignations were kept quiet, but a former trustee divulged to the *New York Times* that they "were considered problematic by the faction of trustees fearful of what they perceive as a creeping liberalism." Ruby, for example, believed that the Bible condemns homosexuality, but he encouraged and provided opportunities for students to learn how to act "gracefully" with those with whom they disagree. According to many, it was this social conscience that contributed significantly to his resignation.[41] This was followed by the 2013 departure of Professor T. C. Ham in the Old Testament department over the poor treatment of Pahl.

Two dominant and competing theological narratives appeared to drive the Cedarville case. On the one side, many students and alumni viewed these events as indicative of an anti-intellectual and fundamentalist overhaul. This suspicion was reinforced when Cedarville announced it was terminating the philosophy department. The move was officially for financial reasons, though it was asserted by some that it might also have something to do with an editorial written by philosophy professors Shawn Graves and David Mills titled "Why I Am Not Voting for Romney."[42] At the time of writing this chapter, the philosophy department is set to close and Graves has taken a position at the University of Findlay (Findlay, Ohio), leaving little hope that Cedarville will offer a philosophy major in the future.

In addition, several new appointments to the faculty, administration, and board of people with connections to Southwestern Baptist Theological Seminary amplified fundamentalist fears. The first was the reappointment of Southwestern Seminary President Page Patterson to Cedarville's board

40. For the text of the white paper, see http://storify.com/fiatlux125/cedarville-2012-2013/.

41. Oppenheimer, "Ohio Christian College Struggles," paras. 8, 13.

42. Ibid., para. 5. See Graves and Mills, "Why I Am Not Voting for Romney."

of trustees in 2013; Patterson had previously served from 2003 to 2011. Cedarville's new president, Thomas White, also raised eyebrows, as he was the former vice president for student services and communications, as well as former associate professor of systematic theology, at Southwestern. And another apparent signal of change was the hiring of former historical theology professor and chair of Southwestern's church history department, Jason Lee, as dean of Cedarville's new school of biblical and ministry studies.[43] This last appointment has suggested to alumni and students that Cedarville might be looking to transform itself into a Southern Baptist school, much as the GARBC accused them of doing over ten years earlier, and following the pattern set by Paige Patterson at Southwestern at the time of the termination of Sheri Klouda.

On the other side of the Cedarville story is a narrative of returning the school to its biblical foundation; it is about fidelity to its tradition. Cedarville's academic vice president, Thomas Cornman, referred to changes during the Pahl incident as not being about squelching academic freedom but about establishing the boundaries of the school's identity as a confessional institution.[44] The new president, Thomas White, whom Patterson lauds as a "humble, courageous, brilliant prophet of God," sees his place at the school as leading it "down the familiar path of standing faithfully for the Word of God and the testimony of Jesus Christ." Doctrinal fidelity, even that which appears to be splitting hairs by those outside of the institution or by faculty and alumni who perceived the changes as a threat to Christian diversity and academic freedom, is considered key to the survival of the school and its biblical mission. Like the situations at Shorter and Westminster, the defenders of what has occurred at Cedarville see themselves as leading the best, necessary response for their institutions to remain communities approved by God.

Is the Idea of Christian Academic Freedom Outrageous?

These incidents at Shorter University, Westminster Theological Seminary, and Cedarville University have produced broadly documented, widely

43. *Baptist Press*, "Cedarville calls SWBTS' White as President," paras. 1, 11. Steffan, "Turbulent Year," para. 1.

44. Thomas Cornman's response was originally posted on his blog but then removed. Copies were retained online at a blog covering the Cedarville controversy at http://fiatlux125.wordpress.com/old-ltbl/articlesetc/trustees-white-papers-and-christ-centered-higher-education/.

discussed controversies that influenced significant change within their institutions. In each case, one theological narrative eventually trumped all other contrary narratives. And also in each case, a question often raised was the complex relationship between faith commitments and academic freedom. Is it possible for a Christian professor to exercise true freedom in research and teaching?

When many individuals explain academic freedom, their descriptions often echo the Enlightenment concept of education as the pursuit of truth, a journey unhindered by religious oversight and intended to benefit humanity. Since this perspective helped lay the foundation for the modern university, and recognizes the need to maintain the standards of specialization, it should be no surprise that the spirit of the Enlightenment can be found in the oft-adopted 1940 statement on academic freedom by the American Association of University Professors (AAUP). This document states that "teachers are entitled to full freedom in research and in the publication of the results, subject to the adequate performance of their other academic duties," and that "institutions of higher education are conducted for the common good and not to further the interest of either the individual teacher or the institution as a whole." This "common good depends upon the free search for truth and its free exposition."[45]

The AAUP recognizes that there are limitations in communities in general and especially in religious organizations. "College and university teachers are citizens, members of a learned profession, and officers of an educational institution," the AAUP points out. "When they speak or write as citizens, they should be free from institutional censorship or discipline." At the same time, the AAUP reminds professors that what they say may affect their institutions publicly, and therefore they should show restraint when necessary. And since these restrictions may be far more detailed in religious institutions, the AAUP suggests that these restrictions be "clearly stated in writing at the time of the appointment."[46] However, not every case of theological disagreement between a faculty member and his or her institution—especially when restrictions were *not* stated in writing at the time of the appointment—warrants removal. Instituting new theological demands on existing faculty members for the purposes of transforming a university's faith priorities does not fit these restrictions. In the case of

---

45. American Association of University Professors, "1940 Statement," paras. 6, 3.

46. Ibid., para. 8.

Shorter University, the AAUP saw the actions of the school as violating the tenure appointments and academic freedom of existing faculty.

Religious schools begin with a different set of priorities. Two individuals may apply for a faculty position, and if one individual has significantly better credentials but does not endorse the faith statement (or is perceived as not endorsing it), credentials will not win the day. This means that the individual with the less impressive *curriculum vitae* but stronger adherence to the statement of faith will be given priority. The practical outcome of this is that faith commitment *is* a credential, and one that on its own outranks the combined demonstrable credentials of education, teaching experience, research specialization, and publication record.

While this reality often befuddles journalists and other members of the public, it's a long-standing approach to education in Christian schools, as we saw in chapter 3. Cedarville's Thomas Cornman referenced this approach as a standard one when he wrote that "Cedarville has been a confessional school since the beginning of its existence . . . faculty have been required to sign their agreement with and adherence to the Cedarville University doctrinal statement. This is not a new requirement." Nor is it a "draconian policy of recent invention." On this point he is right; it is an *old* draconian policy. While certain levels of academic freedom were established at the medieval University of Paris, for example, ultimately faith limitations were always imposed; thus modern religious educational institutions are doing nothing new. The Queen of the Sciences has ruled the land of religious education, and the more constrained an institution is in its theology, the more that constraint will be evident in the institution's treatment of its community.[47]

For this reason, statements on academic freedom in religious schools attempt to acknowledge the expectation of doctrinal adherence. Cedarville's statement on academic freedom, for example, affirms that they are "committed to the pursuit of truth," but believes that pursuit must remain "within the framework of Scripture." This means that faculty members are "free to examine and discuss with students different points of view relative to the subject matter involved, but in the teaching role" they "may not advocate a position contrary to the University's doctrinal statement or standards of conduct which are annually affirmed."[48]

47. Cornman, "Trustees," para. 2.

48. Cedarville, "Academic Freedom," para. 1.

Similarly, Shorter University's statement on academic freedom—which borrows language from the 1940 statement of the AAUP—recognizes that academic freedom is "fundamental for the protection of the rights of the teacher in teaching and of the student to freedom in learning," but reminds the professor that he or she is bound to "adhere to and perform under" his or her contract.[49] As faculty and staff discovered, this contractual agreement could be amended at anytime to include the unanticipated signing of new faith and lifestyle statements.

Westminster Theological Seminary is no different. "Progress is constantly being made, as it has been made in the past, in the discovery, the exposition, and the expression of the great body of divine truth set forth in the Scriptures," declares the faculty manual.[50] Faculty are encouraged to contribute to that progress, and "should be (within reasonable and stated restraints) free to propose and discuss conclusions." But in the end, they are limited not in their questions, but in their answers, as their faculty pledge restricts their pursuits to the Westminster Confession of Faith and Catechisms "as a summary and just exhibition of that system of doctrine and religious belief, which is contained in Holy Scripture, and therein revealed by God to man for his salvation."[51]

In some cases, like that of Cedarville's Pahl or Westminster's Enns, professors may feel they can affirm the doctrinal statements as they read them, but still be forced out as if they did not. How? Because the theological narrative is not limited to what is stated but includes how those statements are interpreted. The fight is ultimately over who gets to control that interpretation and, therefore, control the future of the school.

So is the idea of Christian academic freedom outrageous? If one's expectation of academic freedom in religious schools is closer to that of the freethinking Enlightenment, then academic freedom is certainly outrageous. Limitations are unavoidable when education and religion meet, even at a liberal school, and for that reason, settling on a universal definition of academic freedom is impossible. But that does not mean that professors and institution should ignore best practices, especially if they want to avoid the media nightmares of Shorter, Westminster, and Cedarville. That's the discussion I'll turn to in chapter 7.

---

49. Shorter, "Faculty Handbook, 2012–2013," 75.
50. Westminster, "Précis," 6.
51. Westminster, "Faculty Pledge," para. 2.

6

A Lack of Kosher Venues to Study Nonkosher Ideas

Menachem Wecker

I have long wanted to curate an art exhibit about sin, which would allow visitors to experience all of the biblical sins—the seven deadly and otherwise—in a "kosher" way in a gallery setting. Like the midrashic accounts of Abraham and Jacob miraculously thwarting strategic ceilings in Abimelech's and Pharaoh's palaces designed to force visitors to bow to idols, the exhibit might feature a low doorframe with an idol on the other side. A kid might cook in its mother's milk in one corner, and another might feature an artistic interpretation of "Thou shalt not kill." There would also need to be a delicate way of depicting the incestuous prohibitions from Leviticus, and a creative way of making some of the more tedious sins—such as mixing wool and linen—more exciting. The idea would be to afford visitors the unprecedented experience of sin in a non-sinful manner, although of course it would invite the question of whether experiencing sin in such a manner is in itself sinful.

In many ways, religious higher education holds the promise of being just such a crucible; its hallowed halls furnish a comfortable and safe environment in which dangerous, sinful thoughts can be tested, tossed around, debated, and figured out with caution, of course, but without repercussion. The tools one developed while handling such potentially lethal concepts in the academic laboratory could then, the hope would be, serve graduates when they left those protective walls.

I'm sure I wasn't the only student headed to Yeshiva University expecting to find an open environment in which religious and secular concepts alike—and particularly controversies—could be batted and tossed around. To be sure, there are some brilliant and amazing faculty members at Yeshiva, and I can still remember many of the classes I attended and conversations I had as being open and unfettered. But that's not the way things always are or always have been at Yeshiva, where academic freedom is selectively invoked when convenient but blatantly disregarded and abandoned when it collides with the institution's central and deep-seated orthodoxy.

Stepping onto the Yeshiva University campus in the Washington Heights neighborhood of northern Manhattan—named for the Revolutionary War stronghold Fort Washington—can feel like an experience out of the *Twilight Zone*, although the landscape is a study in dull browns and grays, rather than black and white. The campus, which is home to the university's undergraduate men, rabbinical school, high school, and graduate school of social work, surrounds the main administrative buildings on Amsterdam Avenue and 185th Street. Recent renovations have contributed a minor modern architectural flavor to the otherwise outdated feel, but in many ways, the campus is a bubble that hasn't changed all that much since a 1999 *New York Times* article referred to it as a "carefully tended Jewish enclave in a largely Hispanic neighborhood."[1]

Walking among the bizarre academic buildings and dormitories on campus, one encounters Zysman Hall, a particular blend of scary called Moorish Revival, which would look like the Central Synagogue some 130 blocks south on Lexington Avenue and 55th Street if the latter was allowed to fall into disrepair. The hall, the oldest building on campus (it dates to the 1920s), is home to the main study hall (*beit midrash*), Yeshiva's high school, and the college dormitories; and as I remember from living in the adjacent Muss Hall in my first year on campus, the building is a labyrinth of hallways and staircases without elevator access to much of the building. Whether there is a Minotaur within the maze I don't recall, although the floor in the entrance to Zysman features a compass with a representation of the zodiac signs. If memory serves, the zodiac wheel was often covered with a carpet, which was rumored to be a concession to those on campus who felt the

1. See Arenson, "Yeshiva," 15.

illustrations violated the second commandment and its prohibition against representing celestial objects.[2]

However much of an eyesore it is, the architecture isn't the most striking part of navigating the Yeshiva campus. On most college campuses, one is likely to see students wearing informal college uniforms, the staples of which include jeans, shorts, T-shirts, short skirts, and baseball caps. At Yeshiva, passersby encounter an unusually high percentage of bearded rabbis wearing fedoras, suits, and ties; students wearing *yarmulkes* (skullcaps) and *tzitzit* (ritual fringes); and very modestly dressed women. With separate campuses for men and women, the gender diversity on the campus in the Heights skews in favor of the former, and it is not uncommon to see men engaged in nuanced debates of Jewish texts and ideas spill out of the library or the campus's many synagogues and study halls and onto the street at all hours of the day and well into the night.

A few blocks away, however, one can find *raspado* (flavored ice) and a variety of decidedly nonkosher street food, as well as a high concentration of barber shops, convenience stores selling Presidente beer, and cheap clothing, luggage, and electronics stores. Needless to say, the Yeshiva "ghetto" and the larger Latino population mix like oil and water, or matzo balls and pork carnitas.

In one sense, Yeshiva is more like the thirty-five hundred or so other colleges and universities in the country than it is unlike them. It has dormitories and classrooms; although the cafeteria serves only kosher food, the cuisine gives rise to as many complaints as at other institutions; and there are offices for academic advising, career development, and all the other services one would expect at a higher education institution. The overwhelming majority of the professors who teach at Yeshiva have superior academic credentials,[3] and the few classes that I actually attended regularly continue to stick out in my mind as great learning experiences.

But in other ways, Yeshiva is very different from other colleges and universities. For one thing, students are required to observe the Sabbath,

2. Talking to several former classmates, I wasn't able to get to the bottom of the rumors. Some remembered, as I do, that the mosaic was always covered; others thought only when it was raining outside; and others weren't too sure. It's worth noting, however, that zodiac signs do appear in several important and historical synagogues, such as the sixth-century Beit Alpha. See for example Zanger, "Jewish Worship, Pagan Symbols," and Fine, *Sacred Realm*.

3. Yeshiva College's dean, for example, holds a PhD from the University of Pennsylvania, where, prior to his Yeshiva appointment, he taught Assyriology for forty years.

celebrated from around nightfall every Friday night until about nightfall on Saturday night. "Shabbat offers a unique opportunity to enjoy the bonding that drives YU's special brand of community," according to a Yeshiva webpage for women's housing,[4] and part of preserving that special sense of community, evidently, necessitates threats:

> Observance of Shabbat is a prerequisite for living in university housing. It is your responsibility and that of any guests you invite for Shabbat to abide by the residence regulations. Students' and guests' behavior and dress should be appropriate for Shabbat. . . . No radios, TVs, microwave ovens, etc., are permitted to be used on Shabbat even if set to go on and off automatically. Such appliances will be confiscated immediately if this rule is violated, and the student(s) involved will be subject to disciplinary action. The use of computers and the Internet is prohibited on Shabbat.

Although the nature of that disciplinary action isn't spelled out, its phrasing is sufficiently ominous—even if the reference to radios is outdated.

The Yeshiva curriculum is also quite different from those at other schools. Like many students on the Washington Heights campus, I took about forty-five credit hours a semester, between my Talmud classes—which ran from 9 A.M. to 3 P.M. every day, not for credit—and courses in biblical Hebrew, Old Testament, and Jewish history, which does not include the regular course load in the humanities, sciences, and the like.

Yet despite Yeshiva's mandated Sabbath observance, as well as requirements that students study biblical Hebrew and Old Testament and attend prayer services multiple times a day, when the university files its paperwork with *U.S. News & World Report* (my former employer), Yeshiva—for reasons that continue to baffle me—self-identifies as a secular institution. That self-declared secular institution operates as a carefully choreographed atmosphere, where the ideas, like the food, require stamps of kosher certification from the rabbinate.

Jewish history is chock-full of theological disputes about everything under the sun, but even at an institution like Yeshiva—which presents itself in a somewhat contradictory fashion as both modern and orthodox—the orthodoxy of belief is a good deal more pronounced than the tolerance for a broad range of perspectives. That's the sort of uniformity that one would expect at the many rabbinical schools to the right of Yeshiva University, but despite its comparatively open-minded mission, Yeshiva worships at

4. See Yeshiva University, "Shabbat," paras. 1, 5.

two competing altars; perhaps because its obedience to its secular master isn't questioned nearly as often as its submission to its religious mandate, it tends to prioritize the latter over the former.

Despite its self-identification as secular at heart, Yeshiva acts in a manner that demonstrates that, at least at the highest levels, it envisions itself as a religious community, one that impersonates a regular university insofar as that doesn't compromise its religious identity.

Yeshiva's Bewildering Secular Self-Identification

One of the first things I did when I started my job as the education reporter at *U.S. News & World Report*[5] (of the Best Colleges survey fame) in Washington DC, was to get my hands on a copy of the responses Yeshiva sends to the *U.S. News* questionnaire.[6] In the document submitted in 2011,[7] Ariel Fishman, the director of institutional research and an assistant professor of management, left the response to question 9 blank. The question reads, "Religious Affiliation (*please specify, if no religious affiliation, leave blank*)"; Fishman's leaving the answer blank signified that Yeshiva has no religious affiliation whatsoever. That's why people who visit the webpage for Yeshiva's undergraduate programs on the *U.S. News* website[8] will see, under the "General Information" heading, "Religious affiliation: N/A."

In an email, Bob Morse, the director of data research for *U.S. News & World Report* who is known for typically letting the rankings speak for themselves, told me, "Basically on religious issues we leave it up to the school and don't challenge a school's response. The better question is why does Yeshiva answer it that way?" I posed that question to Richard Joel, the president of Yeshiva, and I will get to his responses below.

The other references to religious affiliation—or lack thereof—in the paperwork submitted for the rankings is equally informative and surprising.

---

5. I worked at *U.S. News* from September 2011 until December 2012.

6. It may surprise many readers of the *U.S. News & World Report* Best Colleges and Best Graduate Schools rankings that the data is all self-reported by the schools, either directly to *U.S. News* or to the government. That has been a source of controversy, particularly when schools admit to, or are exposed for, doctoring their statistics to improve their *U.S. News* rankings.

7. The *U.S. News* timeline can be a bit confusing. Schools fill out questionnaires in 2011, with data from 2010, for the 2012 rankings, for example.

8. See *U.S. News & World Report*, "Yeshiva," para. 7.

Later on in the survey Yeshiva submitted to *U.S. News*, the university was asked to rate (on a scale that included the following options: very important, important, considered, or not considered) several academic and nonacademic factors in admission decisions for first-time, first-year, degree-seeking freshmen. In answering question 143, under "Religious affiliation/commitment," Yeshiva staff checked the box for "not considered."

In answering questions further on in the survey, Yeshiva confirmed that Jewish studies coursework is required for graduation (question 360) and that "religion/theology" is required for graduation (question 364). Question 471 asks Yeshiva to list religious organizations, and officials wrote, "Student Organization of Yeshiva University (SOY)" and "Torah Activities Council." Evidently, the university isn't religious, but its general student organization is somehow religious. (Imagine the main Princeton student association being a religious group; it's not the sort of thing one imagines in a secular institution.)

Indeed, in its answer to question 475 (which asks for "Religious preference: Estimated religious preference percentage of fall 2010 enrolled undergraduate students"), Yeshiva notes that 100 percent of undergraduates are Jewish, and no students are Catholic, Protestant, Muslim, Hindu, Buddhist, "claim no religious preference," "don't know," or are "other." Finally, in question 601, Yeshiva—the nonreligious institution—checks a box noting that it offers religious counseling services.

Question 322 of the survey, which asks Yeshiva for its take on its own mission, yields a noteworthy response:

> Yeshiva University is a major national research university with the guiding vision that the best of the heritage of contemporary civilization and knowledge is compatible with the ancient traditions of Jewish law and life. On the undergraduate level this is embodied in the dual curriculum under which students pursue a full program of liberal arts, the sciences, and business *while taking a full core of Jewish studies*. On the graduate level the University's mission is embodied in the emphasis on the *moral dimensions of the search for knowledge and the Jewish ethical values and principles* that govern professional practitioners [emphases mine].

Needless to say, that's a pretty religiously slanted mission for a nonreligious institution, and it's at the heart of the question of what kind of environment Yeshiva administrators are trying to dictate. In addition to its religiously mandated student life code, Yeshiva has also acted in a manner that more closely resembles institutions like Brigham Young University and Oral Roberts University than secular peer institutions.

All the News that the Censors Permit to Print

At first, it was the shot heard on a few street corners in certain administrative buildings in Washington Heights. But the censorship of a Yeshiva University student publication would later make national and international headlines and spark a fierce debate on topics as significant as the First Amendment and the moral implications of premarital sex. It also raises questions about what kind of an institution Yeshiva University really is.

The fiasco began on December 5, 2011, when a publication known at the time as the *YU Beacon* published an anonymous first-person essay titled "How Do I Even Begin to Explain This."[9] The article appeared in the online, student-run publication's Written Word section, which, according to its website, celebrates "student literary expression with both fictional and nonfictional content." This particular story was told from the perspective of a narrator who purported to be a twenty-year-old undergraduate student at Yeshiva's Stern College for Women, which is based in midtown Manhattan.

As scandalous as the piece later proved to be, it began relatively innocuously, and the article's allegiance to ritualistic terminology and the faith tradition that bore it will strike many readers as ironic given the subsequent commotion. The anonymous author, for example, notes in the first sentence that she has just left a "melave malka,"[10] a Hebrew reference to the meal on Saturday night when the Sabbath is departing, which, to many rabbis, invokes the notion of accompanying the anthropomorphized Shabbat "queen" as she leaves for her weekly hibernation.

Having departed this weekly, sacred meal, the *Beacon* author, with "new Longchamp bag" in tow, checks into a Manhattan hotel, proud of her anonymity in the city of millions of people. "I can't look at my reflection in the mirror on the nightstand. I'm not ready for that yet. Peeling off my Stern-girl exterior I slip on my lace and spray my newly liberated skin with a noticeable amount of floral perfume," she writes. "My transformation from Occasionally-Cute-Modern-Orthodox-Girl into

9. See Anonymous, "How."

10. See *b. Shab.* 119b. Online: http://www.come-and-hear.com/shabbath/shabbath_119.html#PARTb.

Sexually-Appealing-Secular-Woman: complete. I had managed to startle myself so much that I rush to cover myself in my peacoat."

Even as she sheds her Yeshiva identity like snakeskin, the author notes her "Hadaya necklace," referencing a Jerusalem-based jewelry designer whose wares often feature Stars of David, Hebrew epigraphy, and Israeli cityscapes. The designer offers a line of what it calls "Yeshiva girls" jewelry.

But the narrator of the *Beacon* article has designs of her own: being un-Yeshivish. And so it goes; her male caller arrives with Stella Artois, and "shut[ting] off my conscience," she plays drunker than she really is. "After all of our secret rendezvous, I'm still not used to seeing him without his *yarmulke* [skullcap] on, but this time it's somewhat of a comfort," she writes, noting his bare head. A few drinks, some frolicking, and a night's sleep later, she has learned for the first time how to march the walk of shame.

If the piece sounds tame, well, it is. "Yeshiva University Is in an Uproar Over a Not-Very-Saucy Sex Column" read the headline to Adam Clark Estes's December 9, 2011 article in the *Atlantic*, for example.[11] Writing in the *New York Times*, Sharon Otterman notes that the *Beacon* article was "the kind of first-person tell-all that would probably pass without much mention at the average secular university."[12]

The *Beacon* piece is more 1950s television–style suggestive prose than *Playboy*. At the essay's most erotic moment, the narrator mentions a bra coming off, some kissing, and "the fumbling, the pain, the pleasure." But that was enough to get the publication's coeditors-in-chief, Simi Lampert and Toviah Moldwin, a less-than-enthusiastic email from a senior administrator, who was involved with the *Beacon* both before and after the episode in question.[13]

"I am already getting calls from rabbis and folks within the administration about the 'where do I begin' piece that was just posted," the administrator wrote. "It is certainly not news reporting and mot [*sic*] sure it is a

---

11. See Estes, "Yeshiva."

12. See Otterman, "Orthodox Jewish Student's Tale," para. 1. Otterman adds, "As an Orthodox Jewish institution that teaches both Jewish and secular subjects, the university attracts many religious students who consider premarital sex—not just the act but even talking openly about it—well beyond the acceptable bounds of modesty. But it also enrolls students willing to push those limits" (para. 4). It's worth noting that the *Times* article makes two points that I will reveal to be fiction: (1) that it was the student council that first requested that the piece be removed from the *Beacon* site, and (2) that university administrators were not involved in the controversy.

13. The person or persons who shared the emails with me asked that I not mention the administrator by name as a condition of publishing the contents of the emails.

feature. I fear it will likely run you afoul of the student councils and put you in a position of losing support—which means you will not be able to use yu [*sic*] email and the like. Is there any way this piece can be taken down?"

It's worth noting a few points about this email up front, as they will become contentious later on in this chapter. First, the administrator notes that the complaints are coming from rabbis—i.e., faculty—and administrators, although members of the student council will likely be opposed in the future. One might fairly assume that the student council had not yet voiced its opposition. Also, the senior administrator references losing support, which, as one might guess, is a threat of funding cuts.

Politely declining to back down, Moldwin and Lampert responded several hours later in an email that Moldwin sent and that he and Lampert signed. The two explained that the Written Word section features "student literary pieces, usually fictional." They elaborated:

> This particular piece is a stirring account of a sexually active student from a community that looks down heavily upon premarital sexual activity, the conflicting emotions experienced by the student during the act itself, and her guilt afterwards. The piece obviously has literary value; I know I was moved by it, and judging by the number of [Facebook] "likes" the post received, it would seem that many other students did as well. Whether this story was fact or fiction, it undoubtedly represents something that does happen in the YU community, whether we like it or not. The piece's worth is not to be taken in a vacuum; the very reaction of the deans, rabbis and students is precisely why the piece is so valuable—it's something that happens, but no one wants to talk about it, because it is a taboo discussion topic despite its importance.

And then the email from Lampert and Moldwin gets even more interesting. Rather than accepting the religiously motivated criticism of the anonymous "rabbis and folks within the administration" that the senior administrator has cited, the two students rolled up their sleeves and dug into the theological and social implications of the piece they had published. After all, the two noted, sexual content surfaces not only in many of the greatest works of secular literature, but also in many that are required reading on syllabi in Yeshiva courses.

Does it make sense, they wondered aloud, for a student publication to be barred from publishing the sorts of things that Yeshiva students must read in their English classes if they want to get passing grades?

"If this type of writing is offensive to the university's sensibilities, a great deal of changes would need to be made to both the literature and art departments at YU, as both departments offer many courses that present material much more erotic than that contained within the article under discussion," Lampert and Moldwin wrote, employing a *reductio ad absurdum* strategy. "Furthermore," they continued,

> the sexual content in the piece is no more explicit than works that are written by prominent rabbis from our tradition. The Jews (even rabbis) of medieval Spain wrote erotic poetry that surpasses the vividness of the article in question. One need only look at the poems of Rabbi Moshe ibn Ezra to see that erotic writing has strong antecedents in the rabbinic tradition (to say nothing of the biblical tradition, with reference to *Shir Hashirim* [Song of Songs] and various passages in the later prophets).
>
> It is thus difficult to see why this piece should be perceived as troublesome to the university. We are aware that our agreement when we received YU funding was to come forward with any articles we thought might be problematic; however, given that we reached an agreement with both you and [Stern Assistant] Dean [of Students Beth] Hait that sex is a topic which would not be considered off-limits, we didn't see any reason to pass this article by you before posting. Nevertheless, if the university still finds this piece objectionable and wishes to silence a student who wishes to speak about an important subject in a maturely written work of fiction, we at *The Beacon* are willing to give up our funding and the convenience offered by the YU email list to protect students' right to be heard, but we hope it won't come to that.

Again, Moldwin and Lampert referenced the penalty of the censorship—the loss of funding—in a manner that suggests that it was a statement of fact.

About two and a half hours later (after 10 P.M.) there was a response, and it did not contest the matter of the funding being in jeopardy. "I appreciate your detailed and thoughtful response," the senior administrator wrote, adding,

> While there is much merit in what you say, the one issue I have to take exception to is the comment that Dean Hait and I gave you free reign to present matters of a sexual nature. I think what we have tried to convey is that sexual topics are not on their face out of bounds; but these are precisely the kinds of issues that we have hoped and expected you'd bring to us for discussion before

publication. Obviously these issues raise all kinds of concerns for the administration and while there is certainly precedent in both Jewish literature and other literary traditions for this kind of material, there is a difference between material either clearly delineated as fiction or presented as poetic or metaphorical imagery and an essay which leaves its status somewhat more vague—as this article does. In any case, I've conveyed your comments to the concerned administrators and will get back to you as soon as I've received a response from them. That said, there are quite a few interesting articles posted on your site.

Interesting articles, apparently, only when they don't collide with the administration's vision of the university. And in a subsequent email, the senior administrator told Moldwin and Lampert, "this journalism is a tricky business." Tricky indeed, particularly when it is censored while trying to speak truth to power.

In this email, additionally, the administrator again reiterates that the complaints are coming from the administration—not from the student council—and the administrator unabashedly refers to the intricacies of the agreement brokered between the university and the publication as a precondition for publication.[14] Needless to say, many journalistic enterprises, both student and professional, would never agree to an arrangement that institutionalized censorship, even if it is innocuously described as being brought "for discussion."

The University's Version of the Story

After trying in vain to schedule an interview with Yeshiva's president, Richard Joel, for months, I finally had a chance to chat with him by phone. Asked about Yeshiva's self-identification in its *U.S. News* survey, Joel tells me, "Legally, we're not a religious institution. Legally, we're a secular

14. It's worth noting that this kind of agreement is the exact opposite of what the Society of Professional Journalists advocates for in its Campus Media Statement, which is accessible on its website. "Student media are designated public forums and free from censorship and advance approval of content," the society states emphatically. "Because content and funding are unrelated, and because the role of adviser does not include advance review of content, student media are free to develop editorial policies and news coverage with the understanding that students and student organizations speak only for themselves. Administrators, faculty, staff or other agents shall not consider the student media's content when making decisions regarding the media's funding or faculty adviser." See Society of Professional Journalists, "Resources for Students," para. 1.

university." That is why, Joel says, Yeshiva's rabbinical college, RIETS—the Rabbi Isaac Elchanan Theological Seminary—is "separately chartered and incorporated as a religious corporation." Yeshiva University, alternatively, is chartered as a secular institution. "It has some implications in terms of funding, in terms of state dormitory funds," he says.

That may be inside baseball for many people, though, for whom it does not make sense for there to be a rabbinical college, which is obviously a religious institution rather than an academically oriented school of divinity, within a larger secular university.

"I believe if you look at Fordham or St. John's, they're also not religious universities," Joel says. When I tell him that the Jesuit schools Fordham University, Boston College, and Georgetown University, as well as the Mormon school Brigham Young University, all self-identify in their filings to *U.S. News & World Report* as religious institutions,[15] Joel downplays the significance of the reporting.

"There's no inside story to that," he says. "I can't discriminate on accepting someone to Yeshiva College, because they're not Jewish."

But, Joel admits, there haven't been non-Jewish students at Yeshiva yet, and if a gentile wanted to attend, she or he would have to have a functional grasp of Hebrew (including biblical Hebrew), be willing to spend half the day studying the Torah (typically not for credit), and agree to abide by a student code of public Sabbath observance, among other rituals. "You might have to be *meshuganah* [Yiddish, "crazy"] to come as an Orthodox Jew," he jokes, although it's a sobering thought to a Yeshiva alumnus such as me.

Just as Joel sticks to his story about Yeshiva being a secular institution, he also insists that his administration did not pressure the *Beacon* at all. Asked about the press coverage of the story in question in the *Beacon*, Joel says, "I shouldn't [have to] tell you that you shouldn't believe everything you see in the press."

"The administration had zero to do with the *Beacon*—it was a student group. Students were outraged at the manner in which they did this," he adds:

15. See the following online reports:
http://colleges.usnews.rankingsandreviews.com/best-colleges/fordham-university-2722
http://colleges.usnews.rankingsandreviews.com/best-colleges/boston-college-2128
http://colleges.usnews.rankingsandreviews.com/best-colleges/georgetown-university-1445
http://colleges.usnews.rankingsandreviews.com/best-colleges/brigham-young-university-provo-3670.

Frankly, a couple of the editors of the *Beacon* resigned over it. It was someone who wanted a career in journalism,[16] and found a way to have a career in journalism. And [student leaders] said, "That's not a student group anymore. We defunded them." They took their $250 away. If you want to ask me the question of: "Had they not acted, would I have found myself on the horns of a dilemma?" I haven't thought that through. But I would tell you that . . . *Yeshiva as a private Jewish institution with a culture of Torah U'mada, particularly at the undergraduate level, our greatest value is not completely unfettered expression* [emphasis mine]. Our greatest value is being an environment where we try to live a life of Torah U'mada and have full expression within that.

Many people would no doubt expect an academic institution to act like one, but Yeshiva, according to Joel, is about building a community, so unfettered expression is less important than religious concerns such as *Lashon Hara* (literally "evil tongue") and *Rechilus* (gossiping).

If the *Beacon* had published an article attacking him as the university president, Joel would have considered that par for the course, as he did when the undergraduate men's newspaper, the *Commentator*, published a letter by three anonymous faculty members "saying that everything is going to hell in a handbasket," he says. "I knew that was going to be published; I didn't make any effort not to publish it."

The article in question, titled "Polishing the Jewel That Is Yeshiva University before It Is Too Late,"[17] begins,

After the recent State of the University address by President Joel, reasonable people might conclude that all is okay at Yeshiva University. We think that this conclusion is deeply flawed and we are very worried about the future of YU. We see six central challenges confronting Yeshiva, and we think that if each and every one of them is not confronted and examined closely, the very existence of Yeshiva is in danger.

Who are we to write such a bold opening paragraph? We are three Yeshiva faculty members: one of us is a Rosh Yeshiva [a "head of the rabbinical academy," a term reserved for senior

16. Lampert, who had previously published in *New Voices* (the Jewish Student Press Service), has since published more frequently in national media outlets, so one assumes she is the one whom Joel is referencing.

17. Rabbi A., Dr. B., and Mrs. C., "Polishing the Jewel That Is Yeshiva University before It Is Too Late," *The Commentator*, October 30, 2012, http://www.yucommentator.org/2012/10/polishing-the-jewel-that-is-yeshiva-university-before-it-is-too-late/.

rabbinic faculty and administration], one of us is a college faculty member, and one of us works at Stern.

The authors, who claim to have more than a century of Yeshiva involvement between them (and nearly three hundred years if one counts their parents' and children's involvement), explain that they are writing the letter anonymously, "exactly because if we have learned anything over the years, it is that this institution rarely responds well to criticism, and we have seen many people driven out of their jobs for lesser offenses than we are going to discuss in this column."

The six institutional challenges that the authors identify stem from "terrible mismanagement of the endowment over the last decade" and a lack of balance between the university's religious and secular arms—which the authors say the university president has not been able to manage effectively—among other institutional decisions.

After explaining that Yeshiva's discretionary endowment is nearly zero and that the "overall endowment has not only plummeted in value, but has plummeted in relative value," the authors refer to a religious crisis at the school, which, they say, is "equally as scary." The charge is worth quoting at length:

> President Joel has utterly failed to balance the Torah and the Maddah [science] better at Yeshiva. At the time of his appointment, all of us were afraid that he would prove incapable of leading the Roshei Yeshiva ["heads of Yeshiva"] specifically or Jewish life generally. Now we are not afraid, as we know such is completely true. One is hard-pressed to see a single point of contention between the Roshei Yeshiva and the President about Jewish life or law resolved in his favor, from the trivial to the important. . . . In his early years as president, Richard Joel used to refer to one of the powerful Roshei Yeshiva by the nickname "Torquemada," and we were all sitting one day for lunch with one of that [rabbi's] students and he remarked to us how surprising it is that notwithstanding the rhetoric, "Torquemada and his talmidim [students] still rule." Rabbi Reiss, brought in with a stellar Yale education and with high hopes to modernize RIETS, seems to spend his time working on pornography filters for the dorm rooms.

Needless to say, filtering students' on-campus Internet access to prevent them from viewing pornographic content and websites isn't the sort of thing that colleges are typically in the business of doing.[18]

But Richard Joel responds to the anonymous criticism of his faculty members as he does to the article in the *Beacon*—by focusing on the secrecy of the writers. Over the phone, Joel explains that he doesn't respond to anonymous comments, and he thinks it is poor journalistic practice to deal with unidentified sources.

"There's a difference between whether [student journalists] have the right to voice unpopular views or opinions, which I think they do, as opposed to whether the kind of literature they're publishing goes over the bounds of *tzniut* [modesty] and *rechilut* [gossip]," he says. "If they want to talk about premarital sex at Yeshiva, it's completely within bounds; if they want to write a piece about how this woman felt when she was in a hotel room, and the guy came in, and the *yarmulke* came off, I think there is a collective culture that people buy into. . . . It's out of bounds."

But out of whose bounds, exactly? Who determines the boundaries of what is acceptable and what is too provocative? Asked about the contours of academic freedom at Yeshiva—specifically which body is convened to decide whether a faculty member has crossed some kind of line—Joel says that he's a one-man show when it comes to defining academic freedom.

"Probably, I'm the body that's convened," he says. "One of the issues about Yeshiva University, because of the peculiarity of our constituency: Are we a university? Are we a Yeshiva? [We are] closer to being a college-town college. Every conversation is not limited to an academic conversation, but to a campus conversation."

18. It's worth noting, however, that a Yeshiva administrator did dismiss one filter that was considered "creepy" and too much like "big brother," although the creepiness factor seems to have been amplified, for him, by the fact that the filter was a product created by a "right-wing Christian organization." See Abramowitz, "Rabbi Yona Reiss Unveils Plan." See also Levi, "New Internet Filters," paras. 7, 9, which notes the range of faculty and student responses to the filter. "One student, speaking anonymously, stated: 'I'm upset about it. As much as this is a yeshiva, it's foremost a university,'" writes Levi, who suggests that "Yeshiva University joins a number of other national universities that conduct filtration." The article names only one such institution, however—Brigham Young University. For an opposing student view, an op-ed in which the author argues that the university's filtering the Internet doesn't amount to censorship, see Hyman, "Internet Filtration."

Every conversation at Yeshiva, according to Joel, is somehow a statement about policy for the Jewish people.[19] "I kind of draw lines in the following ways," Joel says:

> I think that people who are members of the faculty—whether it's rabbinic faculty, whether it's faculty involved in the wisdom of the world [i.e., secular studies]—are entitled to the same academic freedom that they have anywhere else, and their speech has to be protected. They're saying unpopular things has to be protected, as long as it's repeated again and again that only the president speaks for the university.

Deans, however, become management, and they are not free to say what they please, Joel says. "They speak for their schools," he adds:

> A *Ra"m* [acronym for a rabbi who teaches a class], or professor, has a right to voice his or her views and opinions in all kinds of venues, and freedom of expression does not mean freedom from criticism. Therefore, if they say something that institutionally is damaging or is against the mores of the institution, so we reserve the right to criticize that person. Now, if someone engages in anything that contravenes the law, if there's hate speech, if there's inflammatory speech that jeopardizes the public good, then I think it's stopped. But I don't think there is an *a priori* sense of censorship.

Whether the rest of the Yeshiva community agrees with Joel that the university—particularly the undergraduate schools—has a sense of "collective common good" remains to be seen. Joel cites as his "proof text" the fact that the two undergraduate student newspapers at Yeshiva, the *Commentator* and the *Observer*, have faculty advisors, but he likes the fact that the faculty advisor isn't a faculty censor.

"In the last decade, there has been nothing except support for the student newspapers expressing themselves in an unfettered way and free of censorship," he says.[20]

But that doesn't mean Joel thinks academic freedom applies to students in the same way, as evidenced by his thoughts on the *Beacon*. Asked whether students enjoy the same protections under academic freedom as

19. Although Yeshiva maintains an institute called the Center for the Jewish Future (as if there's a singular Jewish future), many Jews both to the right and to the left would no doubt question its self-endowed central role in Jewish policy and practice.

20. Although perhaps Joel is correct about the last decade, the university does have a history of censoring the student newspaper, the *Commentator*. See Arenson, "Yeshiva."

professors do, Joel says, "The student, in some way, submits to being in an environment of control, and an academic—there's a difference between, perhaps, what an academic would teach in class and what an academic would choose to publish."

The same goes for student groups when they invite speakers, according to Joel, who maintains that students can go off campus to listen to any speaker they choose, but that not everyone has the appropriate values and perspectives to speak on campus. The university would not host a speaker lecturing on being Orthodox and egalitarian, he says. "They can go somewhere else for that. We stand for *Torah U'mada.*" But if an egalitarian Orthodox Jew wants to give a speech about fifteenth-century medieval history, that person should be welcomed with open arms, he says.

When the *Cardozo Journal of Conflict Resolution*, a student group at Yeshiva's law school, the Benjamin N. Cardozo School of Law, recently invited former President Jimmy Carter to speak on campus, many members of the Yeshiva community, who feel that President Carter is anti-Israel, if not anti-Semitic, were outraged. Joel balks at the suggestion that his hands were tied, even though he claims he reluctantly allowed the event to take place. "By the way, it's not an issue of free speech," he says:

> Because the truth is that if a student group invited a former president of the United States, who is a latent or blatant anti-Semite, and he said "Yes," and then the dean and the president find out about it, I have no problem saying "Too bad. Un-invite him, or go down to Plains, Georgia, to give him his award." I thought it was about—once a student group invited him in innocence and he already said "Yes," and he's not Ahmadinejad, and no Israeli has died on the border of Egypt for 35 years because of him, I think he's not a hero. I wouldn't give him any award. I wouldn't show up for any award. But the lesson was not to say, "We are now going to shame you, student groups, and we are going to shame the past president of the United States."

A group that called itself the Coalition of Concerned Cardozo Alumni surfaced and criticized the invitation extended to President Carter, whom the alumni group accused of "an ignominious history of anti-Israel bigotry."

Even as Joel didn't yield to the alumni group, he posted a statement on an official Yeshiva blog in which he wrote, in part, "While he has been properly lauded for his role in the Camp David Accords of 1978, I strongly disagree with many of President Carter's statements and actions in recent years which have mischaracterized the Middle East conflict and have served to alienate those of us who care about Israel."[21]

The former president's appearance on campus, according to Joel, "in no way represents a university position on his views, nor does it indicate the slightest change in our steadfastly pro-Israel stance."

The Rest of the *Beacon* Story

Sitting in a lobby of one of the academic buildings at Stern College, Simi Lampert, the former coeditor of the *Beacon*, discussed the controversy and her broader experiences at Yeshiva University, after having just come out of what she described as a "very fluffy, right-wingy" course on Jewish views on marriage.

She spends much of her time in the class criticizing what the professor says, but her classmates "eat it up," she explains. "It's very like 'You cover your hair for spiritual reasons,' when the basic *halakhah* [Jewish law] is very clearly not spiritual."

Lampert also studies with Joy Ladin, the David and Ruth Gottesman professor of English at Yeshiva and director of the Beren Writing Center. Ladin found herself in the spotlight when she transitioned from Jay to Joy Ladin after having earned tenure at the college.

"Being in a class like that, I don't feel like the university really restricts what their teachers say, although that could be because she has tenure," Lampert says. "If President Joel were taken into a separate room, he might say, 'Yeah, I agree that gays should marry.' But I think that if he were standing at the YU Chanukah [Hanukkah] dinner, he would say, 'YU believes this is against halakhah, therefore we should not support it legally.'" Lampert also allows that Ladin's courses are probably classes that certain segments of the Stern College student population tend to avoid.

"I've overheard girls saying things like, 'Oh, I would never take her class,' or like, 'I'm uncomfortable just by her being in the building.' You could say that that's the right-wing reaction, but it's definitely a certain type of reaction in the Stern student body," she says.

But that's nothing compared to what her male friends uptown tell her about Yeshiva's uptown campus, where rabbis are always watching. That's when the conversation turns to the so-called Censorship Committee[22]—

---

21. See Yeshiva University, "President Carter at Cardozo," para. 3.

22. See Liss, "Censorship," para. 5. "While the committee is charged with regulating

or more formally, the Yeshiva University Events Committee—a panel of faculty and administrators that determines who can and cannot speak on campus. "The administration is not subtle about trying to shut down things that disagree with them," Lampert says.

The *Beacon* was started to provide a voice for the population of students at Yeshiva who wanted change. "I would say we number in the hundreds, which in a small school like YU, that's a big number," Lampert says, describing Yeshiva as a place where many students are too respectful to fight back even when they oppose aspects of the way the school is administered. "People are kind of accepting of the status quo," she says.

Asked if the *Beacon* and the community organized around it amounts to an Occupy Yeshiva movement, Lampert is cautious. "I think that's a very optimistic and flattering view of what happened," she says, and she isn't convinced that the actions she and some of her classmates are taking are actually likely to change the institution.

"If I were to one day become fabulously wealthy, YU would not be my preferred place of donation," she says, "because of their complete ignorance, or decision to ignore a huge segment of the student body for their own purposes."

Lampert decided to cofound the *Beacon* after being disappointed as a reporter at the *Observer* by the ways the editor censored stories and sought to mold the publication into a "newspaper that promoted the virtues of YU." A colleague proposed an article for the *Observer* about alcohol consumption at Yeshiva, she remembers, and *Observer* editors rejected the pitch because they feared it would reflect poorly on the university. So Lampert and a few other *Observer* staffers defected and founded the *Beacon*. The new publication was founded as an official Yeshiva newspaper, she says, and she and her colleagues were told by university officials that anything that might cause a "disturbance" should be run by the administrators prior to publication.

The *Beacon*'s budget, as an online paper, consisted simply of a few dollars here and there for the domain name and the hosting, and Lampert and two colleagues chipped in to cover costs out of their own pockets. As an official Yeshiva University club, they were given a "microscopic" budget, which they used for "ridiculous things like making T-shirts," she says.

___

student events, it does not have a defined procedure for canceling events and appealing cancellations, nor written standards explaining what mandates censorship. Students whose events are cancelled by the committee often do not know until it is too late," Liss writes.

Although she knew the *Beacon* was taking risks, the "How Do I Even Begin to Explain This" article fiasco caught her off-guard. "I definitely didn't expect what came. I don't think I was surprised when I first got emailed from YU saying 'Please remove this article that's come to our attention,' but I also didn't think that it would blow up to the proportion that it did," she says.

"Honestly, I didn't think this article was controversial at all, so I didn't send it to them," she says of the Yeshiva administrators who were supposed to preview prospective disturbances. But that wasn't unusual, Lampert says, because she and her colleagues had not sent any articles to the administrators prior to that point.

Although she characterizes the tone of the emails from the senior administrator as demanding that the article be removed, Lampert notes that "they later retracted and said that it was the student council who was asking us to take it down." She adds, "That in itself became a small little controversy within a larger one."

Lampert and her colleagues were called into a meeting with the student council and several Yeshiva deans, and they were told that if they didn't take the article down, the *Beacon* would lose its funding and its official club status. "Our biggest loss was our access to the ystud-sstud system [Yeshiva University's email listservs], to send mass emails. That gave us mass publicity," she says.

At that point, a *Wall Street Journal* reporter and former editor of the *Observer* learned about what was happening at the *Beacon* from her sister, who was a Stern student. That reporter tipped colleagues off, and soon Lampert and Moldwin were being contacted by a *Journal* reporter. They shared that information with the Yeshiva deans and asked if they could forward the emails from the senior administrator to the *Journal*. (They were told not to.) "So YU knew that something big was coming," Lampert says. "I think they handled it PR-wise very stupidly."

At the meeting with student council members and Yeshiva administrators, *Beacon* staffers couldn't convince the other meeting attendees to back down on their demands that the article be removed, but the latter group was willing to compromise. They were okay with Lampert and Moldwin attaching verbiage to the top of the article identifying it as a fictional account, but Moldwin and Lampert refused to do so, Lampert says, because the article was based on true events. "I knew that it was a true story, because the author's friend is my friend," Lampert says, "but I didn't feel like it was necessary to make it clear one way or another."

"We went into the meeting fairly certain that we weren't going to come to any agreement and that we were going to lose our club funding, which we had agreed before we were OK with," she adds. "The thing that YU was so scared of was people realizing that this sort of thing actually happens at the perfect flagship of modern Orthodoxy.[23] So if that sort of thing happens, you don't know what else could happen. So to make it fiction would be to wipe away any possibility of tainting YU's name."

The deans and student council members seemed upset that no agreement could be arrived at, Lampert remembers. "It was their choice in the end."

Soon Lampert was hearing from Yeshiva's legal department, which asked that the publication name be changed. In an email signed by the assistant general counsel and university director of compliance in Yeshiva University's Office of the General Counsel, Lampert was told to take steps to protect Yeshiva's trademarks. Particularly, Yeshiva's counsel wrote:

> . . . please delete "YU" and "Yeshiva University" from the name (it should not be "YU Beacon") and tag line of your paper (it should not be "A Voice of Yeshiva University Students"). In addition, please cease using YU in your domain name (www.yubeacon.com) and in Facebook and Twitter. (As I noted, it doesn't make any difference if YU is being used as a different acronym.) Lastly, you should include a disclaimer on your site (and on Facebook and Twitter) disclaiming any affiliation, sponsorship or endorsement of the paper by YU. You mentioned it's in your mission statement, but a disclaimer on the bottom of the page next to the copyright notice would be a better place for it.
>
> Feel free to call/contact me if you have any questions. I would appreciate your prompt attention to this matter.

---

23. A survey of readers on the webpage of the original *Beacon* article (accessed in early June 2013) yielded the following responses: "Are you a past or present student of YC/Stern?" [2,072 answered, 29 skipped; 875 yes (42.2 percent), 1,197 no (57.8 percent)]; "Have you ever violated the laws of shomer negiah [refraining from touching members of the opposite sex pre-marriage] in any way while in a romantic relationship?" [2,071 answered, 30 skipped; 1,327 yes (64.1 percent), 744 no (35.9 percent)]; "Have you engaged in premarital sex?" [2,064 answered, 37 skipped; 611 yes (29.6 percent), 1,453 no (70.4 percent)]; "Do you know of others who have?" [2,055 answered, 46 skipped; 1,539 yes (74.9 percent), 516 no (25.1 percent)]; and "Do you agree that premarital sex is more common in YU/Stern than people tend to think?" [2,017 answered, 84 skipped; 1,449 yes (71.8 percent), 568 no (28.2 percent)].

The *Beacon* complied, but Lampert still doesn't understand why the Yeshiva references had to be removed. "There are plenty of things called YU-what-ever-you-want-it-to be," she says. "They don't own 'YU.'"

YU's "Gay Panel" and Other Discontents

Although the *Beacon* debacle serves as a microcosm for a lot of the identity issues that plague Yeshiva, it is by no means an isolated story. On December 22, 2009, Yeshiva hosted an event titled "Being Gay in the Modern Orthodox World," which drew an estimated six hundred to eight hundred attendees.[24]

Speakers on the panel included university administrators and gay alumni and a student, and the discussion "focused on the participants' personal stories rather than halachic or psychological issues regarding homosexual behavior," the *New York Jewish Week* reported. The event seems, the article continued,

> to have widened a schism at the university between liberal and conservative elements, reflecting a division over homosexuality in the general Modern Orthodox community as to how much attention to give it and whether to cast it in a softer or harsher light.
>
> Separate statements issued by President Richard Joel,[25] and by leading members of the rabbinical school's Talmudic faculty, distanced themselves from the event while not outright condemning it.[26]

The statement by six prominent rabbis on the Yeshiva faculty does more than just distance itself from the event. "The Torah," according to the statement,

> requires that we relate with sensitivity to a discreet individual who feels that he/she has a homosexual orientation, but abstains from any and all homosexual activity. Such sensitivity, however, can not be allowed to erode the Torah's unequivocal condemnation of homosexual activity. The Torah's *mitzvos* [commandments] and judgments are eternally true and binding. Homosexual activity constitutes an abomination. As such, publicizing or seeking legitimization even for the homosexual orientation one feels runs

24. See Lipman, "Gay YU Panel Broadens Discussion, Debate."
25. The YU president's statement appears in full in Frohlich, "President."
26 Lipman, "Gay YU Panel," paras. 5–6.

contrary to Torah. In any forum or on an occasion when appropriate sympathy for such discreet individuals is being discussed, these basic truths regarding homosexual feelings and activity must be emphatically re-affirmed.[27]

Although Richard Joel's statement was not nearly as blunt as the rabbis' comments, it was clear that he was not as enthusiastic about the event as were the (then) newly founded student group YU Tolerance Club and the university's graduate school, the Wurzweiler School of Social Work.[28]

In an interview, Rabbi Josh Yuter of the Stanton Street Synagogue in Manhattan, a 2003 graduate of Yeshiva's Rabbi Isaac Elchanan Theological Seminary,[29] suggested that Yeshiva's problem with academic freedom is epidemic.

Even if Yeshiva's academic freedom extends to professors having the ability to speak their minds, it has a dismal track record when it comes to inviting speakers with views that are in opposition to those that the institution presents.

"Rav [Rabbi] Hershel Schachter has made a lot of, shall we say, controversial statements. And YU has routinely supported him by saying, 'We believe in academic freedom.' And that was their way of basically saying, 'Well we're not going to censor any faculty member of ours,'" Yuter says. "On the other hand, when they had the gay conference, Richard Joel came out with a criticism of it."

To say that Schachter is one of the most prominent rabbinic voices at Yeshiva is an understatement. According to an official biography[30] on the Yeshiva website, Schachter joined the faculty in 1967, when, at age twenty-six, he was the youngest Rosh Yeshiva (senior rabbi) at the rabbinical school. Further, according to the site,

In addition to his teaching duties, Rabbi Schachter lectures, writes, and serves as a world-renowned decisor [legal scholar] of Jewish Law. A prolific author, he has written more than 100 articles, in Hebrew and English. . . . At age 22, Rabbi Schachter was appointed

27. See N., "Yeshiva University Rabbis," and Solomont, "YU Holds Discussion."

28. See also Kleinman, "Joel," para. 3, for responses from law students at Yeshiva, who confronted administrators at the law school to "confirm that President Joel's statement does not reflect a change in Cardozo's policy toward its lesbian, gay, bisexual, transgender and queer (LGBTQ) students."

29. Yuter also holds bachelor's and master's degrees from Yeshiva.

30. See Yeshiva University, "Rabbi Hershel Schachter"

assistant to the renowned Rabbi Joseph B. Soloveitchik zt"l ["May the righteous man's memory be a blessing"]. Rabbi Schachter earned his B.A. from Yeshiva College, an M.A. in Hebrew Literature from the Bernard Revel Graduate School in 1967, and was ordained that same year.

Due to his reputation at Yeshiva and in the larger Modern Orthodox community, Schachter often finds himself speaking to large audiences. He often takes those opportunities—whether intentionally or otherwise—to share controversial opinions, to say the least.

Speaking in London in February 2013, Schachter questioned whether allegations that rabbis sexually abused children—a rampant problem in the Orthodox Jewish community, as it is in the Catholic world—should be presented to the police. One of his reasons was that "American state prisons are dangerous for Jews because they could be locked up 'with a *shvartze*,[31] in a cell with a Muslim, a black Muslim who wants to kill all the Jews.'"[32] As the *Jewish Daily Forward* reported at the time, Schachter—"regarded as one of America's most influential Modern Orthodox rabbis"—has previously caused problems for Yeshiva's public relations shop, which has often changed its tune in its invocation of academic freedom. According to the article,

> Y.U. sought to distance itself from Schachter's remarks, citing its faculty's "freedom of speech and expression." But one day later, under pressure from the Anti-Defamation League, Y.U. condemned Schachter's use of the word *shvartze*.
>
> "The recent use of a derogatory racial term and negative characterizations of African Americans and Muslims by a member of the faculty are inappropriate, offensive, and do not represent the values and mission of Yeshiva University," a Y.U. spokesman told the ADL, which, in turn, passed on the statement to the Forward.
>
> . . . Schachter's statements have caused uproar before. In 2004 the rabbi invoked a common talmudic idiom about monkeys to explain why any Jew, even a woman, may publicly read out a Jewish marriage contract, or *ketubah*, as part of a wedding ceremony.
>
> In 2008 he was forced to cut short a trip to Israel and to issue an apology for suggesting that the Israeli prime minister should be shot if he ceded control of Jerusalem.

---

31. A derogatory Yiddish word for African Americans that literally means "black."

32. P. Berger, "Yeshiva Rabbi Hersel Schachter Stirs Hornet's Nest," para. 3.

> At the time, Schachter and Y.U. President Richard Joel said
> in separate statements that Schachter's words did "not represent
> [Schachter's] views."[33]

Some other colorful views of Schachter's include suggesting that rabbis who engage in dialogue with the Catholic Church in Israel are guilty of idolatry,[34] that women can be compared to animals,[35] and that non-Jews "have different genes, DNA and instincts."[36]

In the phone interview, Yuter, the rabbi and Yeshiva alumnus, refers to Yeshiva "whitewashing" Schachter's controversial comments. In a March 12, 2008, post on his blog, YUTOPIA, Yuter observed that Yeshiva rabbis' "cloistered life" leads them to commit naïve errors in judgment, particularly because it is considered disrespectful for students to ever challenge their rabbinic teachers.

"In the ebony tower of the Yeshiva, Roshei Yeshiva are particularly susceptible to hubris," Yuter writes. "Roshei Yeshiva have no obligation to defend their assumptions or positions, but rather it is the responsibility of the student to absorb and regurgitate as if the words came from Sinai itself." Rabbis, who are humans like the rest of us, are no less prone to errors as the general public, Yuter notes, so they shouldn't be venerated as anything greater than human.

"You can split hairs and say, YU respects the academic freedom of everyone that they're already filtered and given permission to teach here," he adds, "but if you want to bring in an outside person, we're not going to extend that same academic freedom. It is inconsistent."

In other words, it's only kosher at Yeshiva to voice opinions that are already deemed to be kosher—sort of having your kosher cake and eating it too. Couching censorship in softer terms and rebranding it as community building trivializes the fundamental difference between Yeshiva and peer

33. See ibid. Berger's article is worth reading in full for the context it offers on "an outpouring of claims of emotional, physical and sexual abuse against former employees of Yeshiva University High School for Boys between 1970 and 1995."

34. See Rosenblatt, "YU's Schachter Accused of Obsolete Views," para. 24, who notes that "Rabbi Schachter has been known to make blunt, politically incorrect statements in the past."

35. See Rosenblatt, "Rabbinically Incorrect," para. 21, who notes, "Richard Joel, the president of Yeshiva University, was unavailable for comment. In the past he has cited academic freedom as a reason for not publicly criticizing faculty."

36. See Yuter, "Unmaking of a Gadol," para. 5.

institutions that truly encourage and respect the value of open dialogue and communication rather than paying lip service to it.

Yeshiva, of course, is well within its rights—particularly as a private institution—to place whatever parameters it wants on its classroom discussions, but it ought to place signage on its marketing materials that flag those restrictions for prospective students and their parents. But Yeshiva does the exact opposite when it reports to *U.S. News*, whose rankings figure into countless students' higher education decisions, that it is a secular institution.

It is also at odds with public comments that Richard Joel makes about the institution. "YU tries to hug the middle, to be a kind of Harvard on the Heights that integrates halachic rabbinic authority into the classic American undergraduate experience of a liberal arts education on a leafy campus," reports the *New York Jewish Week*,[37] which quotes Joel—with "characteristic enthusiasm"—as saying, "There's no place that can offer what this place can offer. . . . If you're in our honors program, you're with students of the same caliber or better than the Ivy League. You're writing a thesis, and you're at YU and you're growing as a Jew."

But to even come remotely close to truly competing with the Ivy Leagues, Yeshiva would have to make a great many changes, particularly when it comes to its track record on academic freedom.

37. See Chernikoff, "Pressure on YU," para. 11.

PART FOUR

Our Solutions

7

Academic Freedom and the Religion Cause

Brandon G. Withrow

Nothing posted on the Internet is truly private. Exposure is only a screenshot away, as William Crenshaw, a tenured English professor and thirty-five-year veteran of South Carolina's Erskine College, discovered in 2011. When asked by alumni in a Facebook group "what qualities he would like to see at the college," he put the spotlight on the importance of "real science" as the "litmus test" for education. In fact, he continued, "any college that lets theology trump fact is not a college; it is an institution of indoctrination. It teaches lies."[1] That's when the "Queen of the Sciences" (theology) walloped him with her scepter.

Crenshaw was not a theologian, but his outspokenness did not help him at Erskine, the school affiliated with the very conservative Associate Reformed Presbyterian Church (ARP). The school had already been immersed in controversy over which theological direction it was heading, and Crenshaw's comments confirmed to some their fears of liberalism. The ARP newsletter said Erskine had been "betrayed" by Crenshaw and called him an "infidel." He was originally offered a severance for silence, according to an interview, but he declined, as he didn't want to take a "bribe." Erskine eventually terminated him for allegedly dissuading students from

1. Jaschik, "Dissenter Is Fired," para. 7.

enrolling, a claim that Crenshaw and the American Association of University Professors (AAUP) reject.[2]

Perhaps an English professor should not expect to lose his or her position over a theological opinion offered outside of the classroom, no matter how strongly worded, but at a school with deep roots in Reformed theology, it should go without saying that accusations of indoctrination and lies in connection to an institution's theology are not likely to end well.

When it comes to academic freedom, there is no universal rulebook to which all adhere, though there are themes. Casual conversation easily brings out diverse opinions, from the check-your-personal-agenda-at-the-door perspective to the professor dead set on starting a revolution. As a professor, I admit that my initial response to stories of colleagues being terminated over an opinion is one of sympathy. Maybe it's the fact that I was raised within a theological world where having a publicly held opinion (educated or not) about a host of issues was expected of me. While I'm more directly working in religious studies and I am not a theologian—nor do I want to be—I still cannot ignore that drive to formulate an (hopefully educated) opinion on most things. It is, as the prophet Jeremiah might say, "a burning fire shut up in my bones; I am weary with holding it in, and I cannot" (Jer 20:9)—a sense of conviction that what is important cannot be silenced.

Herein lies the dilemma. Every professor has his or her ideal of academic freedom. It may resemble the AAUP's 1940 Statement of Principles on Academic Freedom and Tenure. It may even be thought of as a universal human right that should never be challenged. But the ideal is not the reality; and the reality is that though the AAUP statement is used by many schools, these schools do not agree on its interpretation. Is academic freedom a human right like freedom of speech? Is it the freedom of the professor? The student? Or does it reside with the institution alone? These questions are complex and messy.

The goal of this chapter is not to laud a singular ideal of academic freedom wherein professors have the right to say anything and avoid all consequences. Neither is it to articulate a final definition on academic freedom to end all definitions. Instead, I seek to frankly identify the reality as it touches on the traditions within which I have experience and which I have been exploring in this book. This reality is full of difficulties for the

2. Jaschik, "Battle of Wills," para. 3; Wilson, "Vision for Erskine," para. 10; Wilson, "Interview with Bill Crenshaw," para. 6.

institution, the professor, and the student. In identifying this reality, I hope to provide a realistic, pragmatic perspective on academic freedom.

The Triumvirate of Academic Freedom

Modern affirmations of academic freedom developed out of Enlightenment Germany's Humboldt system. Academic freedom (*akademische freiheit*) consists of the freedom to learn (*lernfreiheit*), the freedom to teach (*lehrfreiheit*), and the freedom of the university for self-governance (*freiheit der wissenschaft*).[3] Inherent in each of these is the intention to protect the pursuit of knowledge from undue coercion by the state, or in the case of the medieval system, the pope. These are the *sine qua non* of successful higher education affirmed in the American system, especially the first two. It took some time before these ideas were articulated in official forms, as has been most notably produced by the American Association of University Professors.

None of the above three aspects of academic freedom should be considered independent of the others. The 1967 Joint Statement on Rights and Freedoms of Students states that freedom in the classroom means that "the professor in the classroom and in conference should encourage free discussion, inquiry, and expression. Student performance should be evaluated solely on an academic basis, not on opinions or conduct in matters unrelated to academic standards." This allows for "reasoned exception to the data or views offered in any course of study." They are still required to "learn the content of any course of study for which they are enrolled," but they should be protected against "prejudiced or capricious academic evaluation." This freedom includes off-campus activities protected by the U.S. Constitution, such as the freedom of speech and the right to assembly.[4]

In its 1915 Declaration of Principles on Academic Freedom and Academic Tenure, the AAUP took on the question of academic freedom for the professor. It goes without saying that anyone with a gun to the head—that is, anyone who fears reprisal—cannot produce research for the betterment of humanity. As the Declaration indicates, no one "can be a successful

---

3. De Ridder-Symoens, "Intellectual Heritage," 86; Nelson, *No University Is an Island*, 1; Metzger, "Profession and Constitution," 1269.

4. AAUP, "Joint Statement," paras. 8, 9, 29. This statement was produced by several groups, of which the AAUP was only one, but for purposes of simplifying citation, when a document was accessed from the AAUP, it will be designated that way.

teacher unless he enjoys the respect of his students, and their confidence in his intellectual integrity . . . this confidence will be impaired if there is suspicion on the part of the student that the teacher is not expressing himself fully or frankly, or that college and university teachers in general are a repressed and intimidated class who dare not speak with that candor and courage which youth always demands in those whom it is to esteem."[5]

Academic freedom for the professor, says the report, "comprises three elements: freedom of inquiry and research; freedom of teaching within the university or college; and freedom of extramural utterance and action." While faculties have obligations to their institutions and communities, they are, according the statement, "appointees, but not in any proper sense the employees."[6] An appointment is the recognition of a professor's specialization and "professional functions to perform in which the appointing authorities have neither competency nor moral right to intervene." Other qualified professionals, such as peers on the faculty senate and the professional organizations to which they belong, judge professors. They are, as the 1940 Statement of Principles says, "entitled to full freedom in research and in the publication of the results, subject to the adequate performance of their other academic duties."[7] The freedom to teach is not, however, a license for a professor to say anything he or she wishes or to ignore the subject matter of a class, to harass, to falsify research, or to ignore the standards of one's profession.[8]

Academic freedom is the professor's right to research, to practice his or her own pedagogical strategy, and to freely express her or his views in speech and writing, the latter two of which have consistently tied academic freedom to the First Amendment. During the 1950 McCarthy witch-hunt, the relationship of academic freedom to free speech took front and center. Ever since that chaotic search for subversive groups, the courts addressing the rights of professors repeatedly connected the two ideas of First Amendment protections and academic freedom.[9]

5. AAUP, "1915 Declaration of Principles on Academic Freedom and Academic Tenure," 25.

6. Ibid., 21.

7. AAUP, "1940 Statement of Principles on Academic Freedom and Tenure," para. 6.

8. Cary Nelson's article "Defining Academic Freedom" offers several helpful points on what academic freedom is and is not.

9. Kaplin and Lee, Law of Higher Education, 1:738.

The legal case that still influences this conversation today is the 1954 *Sweezy v. New Hampshire* decision, where economist and professor Paul Sweezy came under investigation in New Hampshire's search for "subversive persons," after a guest lecture he gave led to suspicions of Marxism. When questioned in court, Sweezy refused to answer and was held in contempt. The U.S. Supreme Court overturned the conviction in support of faculty freedoms.[10] Chief Justice Warren's opinion centers the decision around the role of education in democracy:

> The essentiality of freedom in the community of American universities is almost self-evident. No one should underestimate the vital role in a democracy that is played by those who guide and train our youth. To impose any strait jacket upon the intellectual leaders in our colleges and universities would imperil the future of our Nation. No field of education is so thoroughly comprehended by man that new discoveries cannot yet be made. Particularly is that true in the social sciences, where few, if any, principles are accepted as absolutes. Scholarship cannot flourish in an atmosphere of suspicion and distrust. Teachers and students must always remain free to inquire, to study and to evaluate, to gain new maturity and understanding; otherwise our civilization will stagnate and die.[11]

The essence of a thriving democracy, then, is bound up in our educational system, one that requires a libertarian approach to knowledge for success.

The equation of academic freedom with freedom of speech in the Sweezy case has protected many scholars over the years in public institutions. Whether a case of violating one's free speech makes it to court or not, the expectation is that this connection to the First Amendment is a strong defense. For example, when Kenneth Howell, an adjunct professor at the University of Illinois at Champaign-Urbana (a public institution), taught "Introduction to Catholicism," he ran into trouble when he accurately explained the church's position on homosexuality as a violation of natural law. His explanation of the Catholic position (also his own) was followed up by an email to his students, resulting in a student complaint of hate speech and Howell's termination. The language of the email does lend itself to that possibility, but Howell and the Alliance Defense Fund saw his termination as a violation of his First Amendment rights. Rather than contest this in the courts, the university rehired him, though they ended a long-standing

---

10. Poskanzer, *Higher Education Law*, 69.

11. U.S. Supreme Court, *Sweezy v. New Hampshire*, 354 U.S. 234 (1957), para. 49; U.S. Supreme Court, *Garcetti et al. v. Ceballos*, 547 U.S. 410 (2006), 1.

relationship with a Catholic center that had nominated him and paid the salaries of professors teaching this course, and they decided to keep the issue under investigation.[12]

Professors of religious institutions have made similar appeals to free speech, but as David Hoffeditz (see chapter 5) discovered, the courts were unwilling even to rule on religious matters. First Amendment rights only go so far within private institutions. For example, Jamal-Dominique Hopkins, a former New Testament professor at the Interdenominational Theological Center (a consortium of seminaries), was fired for passing out an antigay book. This termination was called a violation of his First Amendment rights. Hopkins also claims that the ITC changed the grades of students in the wake of his firing. Though he filed a complaint with the U.S. Equal Employment Opportunity Commission, Hopkins has yet to take the case to court, where (like Hoffeditz) the likely decision is that a ruling on his rights cannot happen without interfering with religion.[13]

As much as professors of religious institutions may want the same protections of academic freedom found in public universities, this may be short-sighted, as it appears that the law is permanently changing the way public institutions themselves need to address these issues. In 2006, *Garcetti et al. v. Ceballos* put the question of free speech and academic freedom back on the table. When Los Angles County deputy district attorney Richard Ceballos wrote a memo to his supervisors that was critical of the sheriff's department, he found himself demoted and transferred. Ceballos claimed that the retaliation was a violation of his First Amendment rights. Initially, his case was dismissed as not being "protected speech," only to be overturned by the Ninth Circuit as applying to First Amendment protections. In an appeal, the U.S. Supreme Court reversed this decision, saying that "when public employees make statements pursuant to their official duties, they are not speaking as citizens for First Amendment purposes, and the Constitution does not insulate their communications from employer discipline."[14]

Justice Souter immediately recognized a potential problem: does this not also affect academic freedom? The result was the far less clear "Garcetti Reservation," which states that in relationship to academic freedom there were "additional constitutional interests that are not fully accounted for by

---

12. See Jaschik, "A Separation and a Return," and Heckel, "E-mail that Prompted Complaint."

13. Berrett, "Fired Professor," paras. 4, 9.

14. Long, "July 2012 AAUP Summer Institute," 2.

this Court's customary employee-speech jurisprudence. We need not, and for that reason do not, decide whether the analysis we conduct today would apply in the same manner to a case involving speech related to scholarship or teaching."[15] While the final say on how this decision on work-related speech affected academic speech was not resolved, the potential for issues was felt in subsequent cases that appeared to ignore the reservation, leaving schools and the AAUP to scramble for potential solutions to protect the rights of faculty.

As seen above, prior statements by the AAUP indicate that professors are not properly employees.[16] The Garcetti case, however, leaves that question open for further study. So is this a problem for academic freedom? Writing in *The Chronicle of Higher Education*, Joan DelFattore argues that it might be a good thing. "Rather than focusing on the First Amendment," she writes, "public institutions would do better to expand, update, and revitalize campus policies in recognition of their crucial role in defining and protecting academic freedom. Indeed, *Garcetti* itself encourages government-run institutions to establish their own free-speech regulations."[17] As DelFattore writes, *Garcetti* is "far from being a catastrophe," as it might "boost" the world of academic freedom by forcing institutions to write effective policies to protect professors and enabling them to hold court internally through well-defined manuals and contracts. This puts academic freedom at public and private institutions closer to being on the same level.

Professors with tenure may find more protection than others, though tenure has never been foolproof, as cause for termination may still exist. Religious schools have the ability to terminate professors with far more ease than do public institutions, often by invoking religious matters protected under the Constitution. The AAUP's 1915 statement acknowledges this reality, arguing that "if a church or religious denomination establishes a college to be governed by a board of trustees, with the express understanding that the college will be used as an instrument of propaganda in the interests of the religious faith professed by the church or denomination creating it, the trustees have a right to demand that everything be subordinated to that end."[18] In order to protect the academic freedom of religious professors, the 1940 statement called for clear policies and contracts: "Limitations of academic freedom because of religious or other aims of the institution

---

15. U.S. Supreme Court, *Garcetti et al. v. Ceballos*, 547 U.S. 410 (2006), 13.

16. See AAUP, "Protecting an Independent Faculty Voice."

17. DelFattore, "To Protect Academic Freedom," paras. 14, 18.

18. AAUP, "1915 Declaration," para. 12.

should be clearly stated in writing at the time of the appointment."[19] Now, post-*Garcetti*, this concept has been seen as a better road for public institutions as well. "A promising alternative to the First Amendment approach," writes DelFatorre in the AAUP magazine *Academe*, "is to follow the example of private universities in defining academic freedom as a professional standard embodied in university policies."[20]

As will be seen, the implementation of better policies and contracts may seem like bureaucratic red tape, but it is more likely to foster a just and flourishing community.

The Religion Cause

The best hope of protection an individual might have at an evangelical institution is that of tenure; without it, any theological change that raises an eyebrow leaves a professor's position at risk. Many schools, however, rely on breakable contracts in place of tenure, and this practice cannot foster trust. In 2000, for example, Alex Bolyanatz, then an assistant professor of anthropology at Wheaton College—sometimes dubbed the "evangelical Harvard"—was terminated. Popular with students, a recipient of great evaluations and recommendations by faculty, he expected to have a renewed contract, only to be told he had "failed to develop the necessary basic competence in the integration of Faith and Learning, particularly in the classroom setting." According to Bolyanatz, it was his approach to creationism that set things off. An evolutionist, he attempted to walk a safe line, indicating that faith and evolution can coexist, but the provost, who sat in on Bolyanatz's lectures, felt he discouraged "thoughtful engagement of theology," and despite the support of faculty and students he was fired.[21]

Just a few years later (2005), Wheaton philosophy professor Joshua Hochschild also lost his contract. His conversion to Roman Catholicism did not seem to him to be a barrier to teaching at the school, and he felt that the doctrinal statement demanded nothing that he could not continue to agree to. But Wheaton administrators disagreed, arguing that he could not be Catholic and sign their statement in good faith.[22] Since Title VII

19. AAUP, "1940 Statement," para. 7.

20. DelFattore, "Defending Academic Freedom," para. 19.

21. Today he's at the College of DuPage (Glen Ellyn, Illinois). McMurthrie, "Do Professors Lose Academic Freedom," paras. 2–3.

22. Golden, "Test of Faith," para. 1; Jaschik, "Tests of Faith," para. 7.

of the 1964 Civil Rights act allows religious institutions to discriminate in hiring by giving employment preference to those who share their faith, Hochschild was terminated.[23] He's now Dean of the College of Liberal Arts at Mount St. Mary's University. (Ironically, well-known evangelical historian Mark Noll left Wheaton the same year of Hochschild's firing to replace departing historian George M. Marsden at the Catholic University of Notre Dame, which apparently has no problem with hiring evangelicals.)[24]

Faculty contracts are often short in duration, rolling, and easy to break. Tenured positions are harder to end, though at many religious institutions they often end in severance arrangements that indicate that neither party is interested in protracted legal situations. In 2011 religion professor John Schneider lost his position at Calvin College (Grand Rapids, Michigan) when he and another religion professor, Dan Harlow, were invited to speak at The American Scientific Affiliation and publish their papers on whether an original biblical Adam existed in light of current scientific evidence.[25] Schneider and Harlow both agreed that common ancestry does not seem to leave room for a literal and traditional Adam and that this requires consideration of other potential approaches (e.g., literary) for understanding the biblical Adam and Eve. What generally concerns theologians when it comes to the denial of a literal first pair of humans in the garden is twofold. First, a nonhistorical Adam seems to run contrary to the depiction of Adam's historicity by the Apostle Paul (Romans 5). This is considered a problem for the inerrancy of Scripture, since if Paul was wrong, so was the Bible. But this also raises the question of original sin. If there is no original Adam, then how did sin enter into the world? How is Adam's posterity guilty?[26]

It is clear that both Schneider and Harlow were attempting to find a potential solution that met the standards of their traditions in a school that already accepted evolution as true.[27] Both articles were vetted and followed procedures at Calvin for greenlighting publication, which should have meant that Schneider and Harlow would face no repercussions. The problem seems to be that the school's president was on sabbatical during the vetting of the papers, and it was he who disagreed with their positions,

23. U.S. Civil Rights Act of 1964 (Sec. 702, 703.3.e); U.S. Equal Employment Opportunity Commission, "Questions and Answers," para. 13.

24. Moll, "Mark Noll Leaving," para. 1.

25. Harlow, "After Adam"; Schneider, "Recent Genetic Science."

26. For a discussion on this see, Enns, *The Evolution of Adam.*

27. Calvin College Biology Department, "Perspectives on Evolution," 1.

according to Harlow. The president opened Pandora's box during a faculty senate when he accused the professors of violating their responsibility to uphold the school's confession of faith. The end result was an investigation, threats of lawsuits, a negotiated severance, and the eventual departure of Schneider to Notre Dame as a fellow, where strong literalism does not prevail. Harlow stayed, fought, and remained on as a professor, but took to the public to challenge Calvin's narrative of the situation, which treated Schneider's departure as amicable; Harlow argued that Schneider was forcibly pushed out.[28]

Another tenure case in which academic freedom was at stake involved Christopher Rollston, the tenured professor of Old Testament and Semitic Studies at Emmanuel Christian Seminary. In 2012, Rollston wrote a controversial piece for *The Huffington Post* titled "The Marginalization of Women: A Biblical Value We Don't Like to Talk About." Rollston drew attention to the Bible's dominant message about women being one of marginalization, citing passages that authorize treating women as property (Gen 34:12) or requiring them to marry their rapists (Deut 22:28–29). He was careful to note that "some biblical authors . . . pushed back against the marginalization of women," but "these voices were the exception not the rule."[29] As he writes,

> People today often wish to turn to sacred literature for timeless trues [*sic*] about social norms. This impulse is certainly understandable. But that impulse can be fraught with certain difficulties. After all, to embrace the dominant biblical view of women would be to embrace the marginalization of women. And sacralizing patriarchy is just wrong. Gender equality may not have been the norm two or three millennia ago, but it is essential. So, the next time someone refers to "biblical values," it's worth mentioning to them that the Bible often marginalized women and that's not something anyone should value.[30]

Reactions to Rollston's article ran the gamut. Emmanuel Christian Seminary president Michael Sweeney argued that Rollston was "at odds with the purpose and goals of the school" and "exacerbated" the school's "financial

---

28. Jaschik, "Fall from Grace," 23–24; Nazworth, "Calvin," 3. Calvin College and John Schneider, "Joint Statement," 1; Calvin College, "FAQ," questions 1–3; Van Farowe, "Calvin Profs," para. 8; Matheson, "Silence Camouflages," para. 4.

29. Rollston, "Marginalization of Women," para. 6.

30. Ibid., para. 7.

problems." In effect, a significant donor of the school refused to give, citing as a rationale that Rollston was "detrimental to students." It was a case of "Tenure vs. Donors," as *Inside Higher Ed* reported. Across the blogosphere support came for Rollston, leaving academics wondering about Emmanuel's commitment to academic freedom.[31]

As James F. McGrath, the Clarence L. Goodwin Chair in New Testament Language and Literature at Butler University, wrote on his blog, Emmanuel had "failed to communicate to its students, some of its faculty members, and its board of trustees how to disagree constructively as Christians," and thus they "have failed to live up to their identity as a Christian institution." What seemed apparent is that Emmanuel's problems were far from being about a single professor and a single donor. By December, Rollston and Emmanuel came to an agreement and he left voluntarily. By the spring semester of 2013 he began a new post at George Washington University, and Emmanuel, which was no longer financially stable, announced plans to merge with Milligan College.[32]

Religious institutions have a lot of wiggle room when it comes to enforcing the belief standards of their schools, and the law is not increasing protections for employees. The Supreme Court's June 2013 opinion issued on *Vance v. Ball State University* narrows Title VII, making it even more difficult for employees to sue over perceived retaliation by an employer.[33] Even tenure is on the decline. According to a survey by Gallup for *Inside Higher Ed*, "70 percent of provosts at public and private four-year institutions" say that tenure is "important and viable" at their schools. But when asked whether they "favored or opposed a system of long-term contracts for faculty over the existing system of tenure in higher education," 64 percent said they did. On whether they agreed with the statement "Future generations of faculty in this country should not expect tenure to be a factor in their employment at higher education institutions," 58 percent of provosts at public institutions and 53 percent at private institutions said they agreed or strongly agreed.[34]

31. L. Nelson, "Tenure vs. Donors," para. 11.

32. McGrath, "In Support of Christopher Rollston," 4. A call for letters of support went out from Robert Cargill, assistant professor of Classics and Religious Studies at the University of Iowa. Cargill, "Call for Letters," chart; Cargill, "Winners and Losers," 4.

33. See *SCOTUSblog*, "Vance V. Ball State University," paras. 1–2, and U.S. Supreme Court, *Vance v. Ball State University* (No. 11–556, 2013 BL 167357, 118 FEP Cases 1481); AAUP, "Supreme Court Issues New Rulings," para. 6.

34. Jaschik, "Skepticism about Tenure," paras. 10–14.

What does this mean for religious higher education and evangelical institutions in particular? How can professors and institutions protect one another?

Universitas et Communitas

The solutions that need to be recognized are not simple, easily implemented, or perfect. And though they are flawed, they are necessary and urgent for principled institutions—which all religious institutions should be, by their very nature. The *universitas* is "the whole body" and all educational institutions are *communitas*. In universities, colleges, and seminaries, there is a responsibility of the members to the whole, and of the whole to its members. The functioning interplay of the whole and the parts is destroyed by unilateral, top-down leadership. While the church has always had its leaders, the church has never existed for its leaders; it has existed as a body.

Like public institutions in a post-*Garcetti* America, private religious institutions would do well to improve their policies and structure. Clear policies on the rights, expectations, and judicial recourse of a faculty member must be spelled out. This includes faith statements that are precise not only in what is affirmed, but also in what is denied. The AAUP has never been unclear about its dislike of faith statements, given their regular use to curtail academic freedom, but this seems to be less about what is stated and more about what is not stated. As Jordan E. Kurland, Associate General Secretary of the AAUP, once told *The Chronicle of Higher Education*, "We said early on that if an institution is going to place limits on academic freedom, they should state what those limits are . . . that's been the AAUP's main scrape with these institutions over the past few decades. [These professors] didn't know what they were not supposed to say until they said it." And this remains a tremendous problem, as many of the professors discussed in this book were not terminated for their outright rejection of a school's faith statement, but for trespassing in a territory where no "no trespassing" sign could be found.[35]

Professors trespass for many reasons. Some enjoy interdisciplinary work, and so they are invited to explore new territory as it relates to the discipline in which they are specialists. Others may research and opine about things for which they have no expertise, which rarely goes over well with those who do. When it comes to the theological, trespassing is often the

35. McMurthrie, "Do Professors Lose Academic Freedom," paras. 10–11.

result of stating a perspective that is verboten, though it was never explicitly identified as such.

Some professors attempt to take the safer route of limiting their personal transparency in the classroom. In his *Save the World on Your Own Time*, Stanley Fish advocates for a classroom without advocates for moral and ideological causes.

> College and university teachers can (legitimately) do two things: (1) introduce students to bodies of knowledge and traditions of inquiry that had not previously been part of their experience; and (2) equip those same students with the analytical skills—of argument, statistical modeling, laboratory procedure—that will enable them to move confidently within those traditions and to engage in independent research after a course is over.
>
> If you think about it, that's a lot to ask. It's at least a full-time job and it wouldn't seem to leave much room for taking on a bunch of other jobs.[36]

My appreciation for his snarkiness aside, there is little in this approach that will permit the existence of a religious institution. If the history in chapter 3 shows anything, it is that religious institutions advocate for beliefs, moral positions, and societal change. There is often an expectation by students that professors will enter the classroom and represent every and all positions evenly, and while professors should present opinions that are relevant, they are not, however, automatons who lovelessly engage subjects as if there is no better opinion worth advocating. They cannot empty themselves of the passion that drove them to their disciplines and perhaps shaped their perspective on the world morally and ethically.

This reality is the point that Cary Nelson makes when confronting Fish in *No University Is an Island*. Nelson teaches poetry, which inevitably leads to discussions of race, gender, and war. But Fish sees poetry differently. "The exploration of problems, not their solution, and certainly not a program of political action, is what poetry offers," says Fish. "Poems don't ask you to do anything except read them and be responsive to the intricacies of their unfolding."[37] Nelson is incredulous at the thought that poetry is so bereft of moral positioning. "But thousands of poems literally urge us to go to war," writes Nelson, "just as thousands urge the reverse. Poems

---

36. Fish, *Save the World*, 12–13.

37. Ibid., 52.

promote racial equality and debunk it." Poems capture our attention because they demand that we think and act as humans.[38]

Like poetry, Christianity seeks to address the meaning of life and the nature of a life well lived. It is, as seen previously, a call to the path of life and a warning against the way of death. A religious institution is one that not only looks at the diverse positions and solutions to life's problems but also advocates for a theological solution. It should be no surprise that this is the heart of a religious education and the main differentiator from a secular education.

In his critique of Fish, Stanley Hauerwas writes that "Christians should know what their universities are for. They are to shape people in the love of God. Christians should know who their universities serve. They serve a people who must recognize that the university, at its best the kind of university Stanley Fish is willing to defend, is not the kind of university we should want. If Christians are a people with an alternative history of judgments about what is true and good they cannot help but produce an alternative university."[39] In my experience in the evangelical world, the expectation of a Christian education is one in which all departments meet at the intersection of a discipline known as theology. All departments are expected to engage in spiritual formation, which requires strong opinions and advocacy of moral and ethical positions.

And this combination of missing "no trespassing" signs while expecting faculty to take public stands on moral and ethical issues leads to the high concentration of academic freedom disputes in Christian institutions. It is harder (though not entirely impossible) to step into the classroom and *not* take a moral position on something. The administration expects it of their faculty, your peers expect it of you, and your students demand it in every class period. Thus there are simply more opportunities to step over the (often vague or invisible) line. Religious institutions must acknowledge this reality and provide appropriate structures for protecting faculty who either unknowingly step over the line or, while staying within the lines, step close enough that they upset another faculty member, administrator, donor, student, or parent.

Of course, making faith statements *more* detailed might feel to many like a straitjacket. But the results might be worth it. Professors who are considering a long-term relationship with an institution (or even short-term

38. Nelson, *No University Is an Island*, 183.
39. Hauerwas, *State of the University*, 91.

adjuncting) will know what is expected of them ahead of time. Theologians talk about the mysteries of the faith, but there should be no mysteries of the faith statement. And frankly, if the statement or confession or supporting faith documents do not state something explicitly, it should be left open for professors to disagree. If a community did not take the time to clearly lay out a limitation or constraint on beliefs, then that same community needs to own that decision and not retroactively punish faculty for bringing the omission to their attention. New discussions may merit the development of additional statements, but these should never be used to rush existing faculty out the door for the sake of a successful revolution, as such behavior does irreparable harm to individual members of the community and to the community's reputation as a whole.

Institutional challenges will occur, and no system is perfect, but unlike the situation at Calvin College where a president single-handedly bypassed institutional processes for his own agenda, judgment must be made in community. To that end, Cary Nelson proposes what he calls the "three-legged stool": academic freedom, shared governance, and tenure, which "together support the higher education system we have had in place for over half a century." Shared governance acknowledges the roles everyone has in a school's success. It opens the door for faculty to understand administration and vice versa. Across many institutions, faculty and administration offices are in separate locations and that gap can feel, to use a biblical metaphor, as large as the chasm between Abraham's bosom and paradise (Luke 16:26). "Academic freedom is an empty concept, or at least an effectively diminished one," writes Nelson, "if the faculty does not control its enforcement through shared governance."[40]

As in the case of Rollston, where it became evident that donors were largely in control of employment decisions, shared governance can offer protections from outside intrusion.[41] This would have been beneficial to biologist Richard G. Colling, author of the 2004 book *Random Designer: Created from Chaos to Connect with the Creator,* which sought to reconcile Christianity with evolution by arguing that science is not antireligion. Colling discovered that his community at Olivet Nazarene University (Bourbonnais, Illinois) did not appreciate his perspective. Conservative denominational members were upset to learn that Colling was teaching evolution in his biology class and rejecting the historicity of the Genesis creation account. Thanks to their interference, the school banned him

40. Nelson, *No University Is an Island*, 183, 32.

41. Ibid., 34.

from teaching the course, which Colling and the American Association of University Professors saw as a violation of his academic freedom. The final result was an agreement between Colling and the university that led to his departure in 2009.[42]

In the case of Peter Enns at Westminster Theological Seminary, shared governance would have involved less strong-arming by "canny" Presbyterian "parliamentarians" all too eager for a replay of the English Civil War. Shared governance would have prevented the board from stepping in and removing him when the faculty vote didn't go the way the administration desired. Shared governance also protects faculty in one department from bullying faculty in other departments; theology professors or church historians, for example, would not have authority over Old Testament professors, and vice versa, and would lean on the expertise of peers for such things. As Larry Gerber writes for the *Journal of Academic Freedom*,

> The faculty, however, are not one undifferentiated mass. Shared governance taps into their many overlapping communities of expertise by giving primary responsibility for different academic issues to the appropriate group. Shared governance does not mean giving all physics faculty an equal vote with English faculty in judging the qualifications of professors of literature; nor does it mean allowing the history faculty to determine what classes should be required of a chemistry major. But many academic issues cut across disciplinary boundaries, and on these all faculty should have an equal voice.[43]

There is no single approach to shared governance, and each institution will develop its own system for its own context; but without shared governance, there is too great a risk of power being in the hands of only one arm of an institution, and not necessarily among those who have the credentials to judge or plan appropriately.

> Shared governance cannot install full democracy in a university. It is a negotiated strategy for sharing and adjudicating power and its application and effects. Shared governance exists when boards of trustees agree to cede authority over areas—such as curriculum development and faculty hiring—where the faculty have greater expertise. It has nothing to do with democracy. Rather, it

---

42. AAUP, "Academic Freedom and Tenure: Olivet Nazarene University (Illinois)," 44; Jaschik, "Academic Freedom and Evolution," para. 3.

43. Gerber, "Professionalization," 18.

recognizes that governing boards do not have the requisite competence to make these decisions.[44]

When a university, college, or seminary offers clear policies, supports academic freedom in areas not explicitly limited by faith statements, embraces shared governance by enlisting stakeholders with requisite expertise, and preserves tenure as a demonstrable show of commitment to its faculty, the likelihood of offenses decreases—and both academic development and the health of the community increase.

In the Meantime

Until the day comes when one's school has implemented just policies and procedures, one needs to be smart about his or her work. Faculty members must face the fact that disputes over theology will continue to occur at evangelical seminaries and colleges and other religious institutions so as long as there are unjust systems in place. How might a faculty member avoid the common ending of many of the stories in this book?

First, be proactive. I've met faculty who know very little about the institutions they are engaging and the expectations of the community they are joining. Prospective faculty should do their research on the schools they apply to and ask the appropriate questions in interviews. It is better to know what you are getting into than to jump at any position that opens up. Be aware of not just the institutional issues, but what your future colleagues have written or taken positions on and what (if any) denominational disputes are potentially in play. Just because it's only a denominational issue at the moment does not mean it won't become an institutional one in the future.

While institutions, especially seminaries, should be explicit about faith expectations in position postings, don't assume that's the case. Due diligence may save you from wasting not only the time (and money) of the hiring institution but also your own. Transplanting a family to another state or country is not easily undone. This is not foolproof, since, as we've seen, it's not beyond some institutions to revise their faith expectations in an *ad hoc* manner, but it is one helpful tool among many in determining whether a school is a good match for you. In my experience on hiring committees at both a seminary and a university, the cover letters and CVs of

---

44. Nelson, *No University Is an Island*, 37. See also Heaney, "Democracy, Shared Governance, and the University."

potential candidates often belie the fact that they have not done the initial legwork, which at a minimum means paying attention to the details of a posting, reviewing a school's website, and knowing who may be in the hiring department.

Second, be careful about playing in another's sandbox. If you want to be a biologist who accepts conclusions based solely on the evidence, regardless of how it affects a theological interpretation or reading of the Bible, then a conservative institution is not for you. Period. In faith-based institutions, theologians are expected to have an educated opinion about the relationship between science and theology, and it is likely that a biologist (such as the aforementioned Richard Colling) is supposed to have an educated opinion about how his or her field would relate to theology. Classrooms are expected to be places of spiritual formation, even those that are not called "Spiritual Formation." The legitimacy of that learning outcome for biology, physics, or mathematics aside, the reality of other disciplines assessing theological claims provides more opportunities for theological disputes. Scientists must adhere to the professional standards of their fields, which include sound methodologies and peer review, and this may not mix well with a theological perspective that requires a literal reading of Genesis 1. Know your playground and its rules; and if you can't play by those rules, find a playground that suits you better.

Third, don't borrow trouble. If a school has unstated positions, but it is clear that there are potential minefields, don't rush to trigger an explosion. I've known faculty who are constantly trying on new ideas for size and others who think and act at a snail's pace. If you are the type of person who's confident about your theological views and don't expect to have any paradigm-shifting moments, then by all means join the religious community that fits your perspective. But if you are adventurous, love the theological imagination, and are open not only to the questions but also to new answers, then choose an academic environment that allows for such growth.

And as passionate as you may be about a subject, it may be appropriate to reserve your opinions for the sake of *communitas* as well as gainful employment. The fundamentalist who has to have the last word on all subjects might see this as deceptive, but contrary to the cliché, just because a mountain is there doesn't mean one has to climb it. There is integrity in providing food, shelter, and health insurance for your family. Though it may mean a less satisfying job experience and not a long-term solution, it may be an appropriate survival mechanism. This is closer—though not the same thing—to what Stanley Fish advocates. If you can be a scientist and not advocate a theological position contrary to the standards of your field, then try to toe that line. Obviously, this will not always be possible, as a biologist who ignores evolution or an astrophysicist who holds to a six-thousand-year-old universe is unlikely to be successful in his or her field.

When it comes to religion, however, there may be another way to approach potential problems. I teach religious studies at a university with my specialization in religious history, and from a professional standpoint, I do not see my job as advocating for a religion. Both religious studies and history engage similar sources and methodologies, and I use these. There is an attempt in both fields to analyze the subjects of study rather than advocate a theological position. While not properly sciences, they can (or should) take the position that steps into a metaphorical laboratory. As K. L. Noll writes,

> The religion researcher is related to the theologian as the biologist is related to the frog in her lab. Theologians try to invigorate their own religion, perpetuate it, expound it, defend it, or explain its relationship to other religions. Religion researchers select sample religions, slice them open, and poke around inside, which tends to "kill" the religion, or at least to kill the romantic or magical aspects of the religion and focus instead on how that religion actually works.[45]

According to Noll, this means that "religious study attempts to advance knowledge by advancing our understanding about why and how humans are religious, what religion actually does, and how religion has evolved historically."[46] This clinical approach may be viable in some seminaries and is, as Fish says, a full-time job all by itself, without the advocacy component.

My approach in both the seminary and the university is to maintain a classroom more attuned to religious studies' methodologies.[47] I choose textbooks that deliver discussions of comparative religions that let the various adherents speak for themselves. And I require assignments that enlarge students' perspectives and keep them from acting simply as theologians.

My point is that there may be more than one approach to take. Consider what your community requires you to say in the classroom. If you can

45. Noll, "Ethics of Being a Theologian," para. 6.

46. Ibid., para. 13.

47. Withrow, "Finding Empathy."

approach your subject leaving the advocacy to others, it may be appropriate to do so for the sake of community.

Lastly, own up to the possibility that it may be time to leave. This last move is tough but potentially necessary. The academic job hunt takes time and involves many risks. And the frog-in-the-kettle experience and life circumstances make it harder to realize when you've reached the point of needing to leave. One theological change may be inconsequential; a second change might be just be a minor inconvenience; but if you're on the path to controversy, don't let it catch you unawares.

In 2010, Bruce Waltke, an Old Testament professor at Reformed Theological Seminary, gave an interview to Biologos, an evangelical organization interested in the conversation between science and theology. In the interview, Waltke endorsed evolution in a way that some interpreted as eliminating the need for an original Adam and Eve, a point he never intended to make. That he endorsed evolution at all became a significant issue, but not clarifying his position only made it worse. Rather than turning the seminary into a battleground, Waltke did two things: first, he wrote a clarifying letter about what he affirmed and denied in the relationship between science and religion, and second, he resigned. His resignation was accepted and he eventually took a post at Knox Theological Seminary in Florida.[48]

Perhaps a new belief does not warrant leaving a community. But it is possible that when the total problem is examined, one will discover just how much of an outsider one has become. It may be that for the sake of one's sanity and the community, it is time to take a cue from Bruce Waltke and make a gracious exit.

When in Rome, Do Better than the Romans

The extant letter of an early anonymous Christian apologist known as the *Epistle to Diognetus*, likely written in the second century, has an interesting take on the place of Christians in society. The author attempts to defend Christianity, noting many characteristics of the young religion worthy of commendation. "For the distinction between Christians and other men, is neither in country nor language nor customs," says the author. The language is fairly lofty, as "every foreign country is their fatherland, and every fatherland is a foreign country." But there's one line that stands out to me

48. Weber, "Bruce Waltke Headed to Knox Theological Seminary?"

every time I read it: "They obey the appointed laws, and they surpass the laws in their own lives."[49]

After *Garcetti*, public universities can no longer rely simply on the Constitution to protect their communities. They need to borrow a page from many private schools and begin to craft just policies and contracts that protect schools and community members. These contracts, like the second-century Christians who impressed the writer of the letter to Diognetus, excel the law, making up for where it lacks.

Why should religious institutions hold to the bare minimum of the law, hiding behind the Religion Clause, and avoid paying into unemployment or balk at providing health insurance and other standard benefits? Should they not instead excel the law and public expectations, offering tangible demonstrations of their faith principles and their commitments to integrity and community? Why not work harder to create and maintain a truly just community that treats its members with dignity, whether they are just joining it or on their way out for whatever reason?

Preserving academic freedom through clear statements of faith and institutional policies, engaging in shared governance, and writing tenure contracts that offer real safety for faculty are just a few considerations, but they would go a long way in demonstrating that when in Rome, Christians do better than the Romans.

49. *Epistle to Diognetus* 5:1, 5, 13, 10.

8

Dogma by Its Own Name
May Smell Less Foul

Menachem Wecker

Throughout the interviews I conducted for this book, a common refrain that I encountered, which is relevant to a discussion about how to find solutions to some of the limitations of yeshivas with respect to academic freedom, was that Yeshiva University operates in a different arena than its peers. I was told early and often that the yeshiva represents some kind of moral oasis in the higher education desert of immorality, temptation, and other horrors, where religious students can have their (kosher) academic cake and eat it too—mature dialogue and intense, high-level study without all of the mistakes college coeds regret the morning after in their quest to "find themselves." Why, the argument goes, should an Orthodox Jewish student have to endure ideas and behavior that she or he finds theologically troubling or repugnant in a classroom setting[1] and in the dormitory? Surely biology can be taught without giving a platform to evolution, the argument maintains, and the Bible can be examined from a respectful vantage point that recognizes its divine authorship, rather than adopting a critical

---

1. After all, the Talmud states, "Cursed be the man who raises pigs and cursed be the man who trains his son in Grecian wisdom." See *b. B. Kam.* 82b. Online: http://www .come-and-hear.com/babakamma/babakamma_82.html.

approach that wastes everyone's time with questions about when the book was really written, and by whom exactly.

Although yeshiva students are likelier to know the texts they study by heart than their peers in Jewish studies courses at secular institutions, and the former no doubt spend countless more hours grappling with primary sources than do their colleagues at nonreligious universities, there is a fundamental difference between academic and theoretical analysis of the text in secular classrooms on the one hand, and the sort of spirited yet comparatively narrow and polemical inquiry that takes place in yeshiva study halls.

In this chapter, I will examine some potential solutions that Yeshiva University could employ to improve academic freedom on campus. First, YU needs to be more transparent in its mission statement and marketing materials so that prospective students and parents know what they are getting themselves into. If indeed the senior staff is more concerned with creating a dogmatic, traditional environment than encouraging free dialogue, the university's communications office must go back to the drawing board. If YU does choose to rethink its academic identity—and the time is ripe for such introspection, as the university is currently grappling with other challenges—it could start by wresting some of the control from the yeshiva arm of the institution and not encouraging students to swap a year of on-campus study of academic religious topics for study abroad programs in Israel, some of which exhibit antiacademic positions.

Many yeshiva alumni have an encyclopedic knowledge of rabbinic approaches to the content of the sacred books they have studied and have absorbed dozens of medieval commentaries responding to those texts, but they lack understanding of the larger context surrounding those works. For example, yeshiva curricula rarely address the historical settings that surrounded the various rabbinic figures whose words they commit to memory; it would, no doubt, come as a surprise to many yeshiva students to learn that when the Talmud choreographs a debate between Rabbi Aleph and Rabbi Bet, or explores what seems like a conversation between two rabbis, the two did not necessarily live in the same region, let alone the same century.

The conversations are essentially manufactured, almost like the Socratic dialogues in Plato's works. This is not to say that the Talmud is misrepresenting itself; rather, the way it is presented as an ahistorical and flat text no doubt misleads many students. And with all of the Rabbi Joshuas, Eliezers, Gamliels, Jochanans, Samuels, and others, it can be particularly tough to keep track of which one is which when the curriculum does not place any emphasis on who lived where and when, and how a rabbi's cultural and family upbringing, national identity, and sociopolitical milieu may have helped shape his theological positions.

There also tends to be a lack of attention to the historicity of the sacred texts themselves. Confronted with handsomely bound modern editions of biblical and rabbinic texts, yeshiva students are rarely, if ever, encouraged to consider how those texts were passed down for generations and how they arrived in their current form in students' hands.

For example, 2 Kings 22:8 recounts how Hilkiah, the high priest, discovered a copy of the Torah—which had apparently been lost for some time—and passed it along to the scribe Shaphan, who in turn shared the manuscript with King Josiah. The notion that every copy of the Jewish scriptures was lost for a period of time, of course, is "a pivotal source for the history of biblical composition," as Eve Krakowski notes. She adds,

> The biblical account does not directly describe the scroll's contents. Classical rabbinic treatments of the story assume that Hilkiah discovered a copy of the Pentateuch itself and suggest that the entire pentateuchal text was at that time unknown, having been lost or forgotten during the dark days of the Judean monarchy. Rabbinic discussion of this story is sparse and neutral, reflecting an outlook comfortable with, but largely uninterested in, the theme of loss and recovery of scripture.[2]

Particularly given the emphasis in some Orthodox institutions on an argument of "reliable tradition"—echoing the view of the twelfth-century philosopher Rabbi Yehuda Halevi in his book *Kuzari* that Jewish traditions were passed down from generation to generation from Sinai until today in an unbroken chain that ought to be treated like the testimony of reliable witnesses—the Hilkiah and Josiah narrative presents a bit of a biblical monkey wrench.

As Rabbi Ken Spiro writes on the website of Aish Hatorah, an Orthodox outreach organization, "Jews say that we have kept the Torah for thousands of years, not because of miracles or any other supernatural phenomena of Jewish history, but because we *all* stood at Mount Sinai and heard God speak and for generation after generation that very fact was passed down."[3] That the loss of all copies of the Torah during a certain time

2. See Krakowski, "Many Days," 122.

3. See Spiro, "History Crash Course," para. 8.

period raises questions about that supposedly continuous chain ought to be at least worth examining in the yeshiva curriculum. Of course, arriving at the position that there was a possibility of someone manufacturing and inventing scriptures in Josiah's time and passing off the fake text as canonical and divinely inspired would be anathema for Orthodox Jews—as, indeed, it would be for many faith groups—but raising a discussion in the classroom is not akin to embracing that position.

This is just one example of many that could be cited to point to the failure of many yeshivas to approach their own sacred texts with the humility, skepticism, and critical eye[4] that those texts are subjected to in secular institutions, and that yeshivas even unleash on the elements of the secular canon that they engage in the classroom. If yeshivas want to operate as distinctive institutions that function in a radically different fashion from Jewish studies departments at secular universities, that is their prerogative, of course. But if they make that choice, as many of them have, they ought to have transparent and clear signage in their marketing materials and their mission statements to that effect.

Controversial Study Abroad in Israel

One of the most telling signs of Yeshiva University's questionable decisions when it comes to misrepresenting its academic rigor is its S. Daniel Abraham Israel Program (SDAIP), which, it proudly states on its website, brings most undergraduate students at the university to Israel for a gap year of study—essentially a freshman year abroad at one of more than forty-five yeshivas (for men) and seminaries (for women).

"For the more than 600 young men and women each year who choose to begin their Yeshiva University education with a year of Torah study in Israel, the program provides structure, support, guidance and programming

---

4. See Renz, "Teaching Biblical Criticism," para. 8, who notes, "At Yeshiva University, I can learn about musical composers, painters of the Renaissance, and African-American authors of the twentieth century, and about all these things, I am entrusted to study them with an open yet critical mind, and to come to my own thoughtful conclusions. Yet when it comes to Bible, an area in which I am certainly offered a variety of courses with some truly fantastic professors, there is suddenly no room for my opinion on Biblical Criticism. All of a sudden, the most powerful theory towards Bible in the last four hundred years is apparently too risqué and heretical for reasonably knowledgeable and thoughtful students."

during their first year as members of the YU family,"[5] states the Yeshiva website, which adds:

> Most Yeshiva University undergraduates find a year of study in Israel to be an invaluable and enriching experience, academically and spiritually. By incorporating study at Israeli yeshivot [plural of yeshiva], seminaries or universities that are formal partners with SDAIP into their overall college experience, students dramatically enhance their future academic experience. Learning with Israel's leading educators, students engage in intense study of Jewish subjects including Talmud, Bible, Jewish law, Jewish thought, philosophy, Zionism and Jewish history. The Israel experience increases proficiency in oral and written Hebrew and enables students to learn firsthand about Israel's land, people, history and culture.

But it has been a matter of controversy in the Orthodox Jewish community that many universities do not give credit for studies at the yeshivas in the YU Israel program—which is seen as a rite of passage for Orthodox high school graduates.[6] And at least one Orthodox high school advises students accepted to universities other than YU to consider attending an Israeli yeshiva through Yeshiva University's program, and then transferring those YU credits to the other university.[7]

On a webpage devoted to frequently asked questions, Columbia University's Middle Eastern, South Asian, and African Studies Program notes that the university does not allow students to transfer credit from Israeli yeshivas or *michlalot* (seminaries for women), "because these programs are not recognized as college-level schools by the Israeli Council on Higher Education."[8] Not only are the programs not recognized as college level by Israel's education department, but in 2005, Israel's Ministry of Education announced that it would not recognize degrees from U.S. universities that gave credit for the gap year of yeshiva study in Israel.[9]

5. See Yeshiva University, "S. Daniel Abraham," paras. 1, 3.

6. For a great resource, see Berger, "Year of Study," although Berger focuses on the degree to which Israel programs produced alumni whose religious observance increased, rather than examining the academic merits of the programs. He does note that "many yeshiva high schools now feature Israel guidance departments that rival their college guidance departments in stature, assisting seniors in choosing among available programs, in the application process, in arranging for financial assistance and in working out transfer of credit to American universities" (ibid., 3).

7. See Yeshiva of Flatbush, "Making Israel Happen," para. 4.

8. See Columbia University, "Frequently Asked Questions," para. 16.

9. See Berman, "U.S. Degrees," para. 3, who quotes Yeshiva University's president

The University of Pennsylvania likewise notes on the website of its Jewish Studies Program that it will not recognize transfer credit from Israeli yeshivas:

> All students matriculating in or after September 2008 should be aware that yeshiva study will not be considered for credit within the interdisciplinary major or minor in Jewish Studies. This policy extends to all other non-accredited study programs. Only courses taken at accredited colleges and universities may be considered for credit.
>
> All courses submitted for credit approval will be evaluated on an individual basis and will be judged on the basis of number of course hours, reading assignments, exams, written work, and other criteria. Students should apply for credit to the appropriate department . . . rather than to the Jewish Studies Program.[10]

Given that the overwhelming majority of yeshivas in Israel do not have tests or written assignments, and only issue grades of pass or fail, the University of Pennsylvania's standards are particularly telling in their call for more educational oversight and better standards.

The University of Maryland, which has a large number of Jewish students, also rejects transfer credit from Israeli yeshivas, albeit more delicately and with a heavier dose of deliberately massaged PR-speak (which is worth quoting at length):

> The University of Maryland greatly values its diverse student body and encourages students and prospective students to take advantage of opportunities to work, live, and study abroad. These opportunities can be invaluable for individual students and help us to build a multi-lingual and multi-talented student community on campus.
>
> Many students choose to spend a year or semester in Israel either before entering the University or during their junior year. Currently students accepted to the University of Maryland are studying at over twenty different Israeli institutions. These

---

Richard Joel: "Never, ever has an accrediting body or a graduate school ever had the slightest question about the stature of a Yeshiva University degree. . . . Harvard University gladly accepts our undergraduates to their law schools and medical schools. The notion that the Ministry of Education questions the integrity of Yeshiva University degrees boggles the mind."

10. See http://ccat.sas.upenn.edu/jwst/undergraduate/jewish-studies-transfer-credit-credit-away-and-ap-policies/.

students will bring a great deal of knowledge and experience back with them to College Park.

While we encourage students to take advantage of the broad array of Israel programs, not all of them are appropriate for the transfer of credit towards graduation. The University of Maryland can only accept credits from accredited, baccalaureate-granting institutions of higher learning.

Credits received from the Hebrew University of Jerusalem, Tel Aviv University, Ben Gurion University of the Negev, Haifa University, and the regular Bar Ilan University courses, whether offered in Hebrew or English, will be evaluated on a course-by-course basis. . . . Courses taken in yeshiva programs, irrespective of denomination and including the Institute for Advanced Torah Studies, Midrasha for Women and Kollel for Men at Bar Ilan University, are not eligible for transfer credit. We take seriously the rigorous and high-level study in such programs *but recognize that both the method of instruction and goals of these programs differ markedly from those in standard academic institutions* [emphasis mine].[11]

If an institution such as the University of Maryland recognizes that studies at Israeli yeshivas tend to "differ markedly from those in standard academic institutions," one wonders why many of the schools admit Yeshiva University alumni as graduate students without questioning the academic merit of their freshman year studies, as the Israeli educational ministry did.

Critics of the programs also cite a variety of cultural aspects. Noting that over the past twenty-five years more and more young Orthodox students have spent a year or two studying in Israel, Naomi Schaeffer Riley records a conversation with a Yeshiva University student and then-editor of the student newspaper, who tells her that many of the schools in Israel "'do try to de-emphasize the value of the secular education because they feel that religious education is really their primary goal.' Beyond that, though,

11. See University of Maryland, "Transfer," paras. 2, 3, 4, 6. See also University of Maryland, "Prospective & New Students," para. 6, which adds this caveat: "Administrators at many programs will sometimes tell parents 'Maryland gives college credit for our programs.' This is not always the case, and you must not assume it unless the Admissions office or Jewish Studies has evaluated a specific course, and even that evaluation is revisited periodically. In fact, there are some programs where credit is given for some courses but not for others. Students would be wise to check with the undergraduate advisor before taking a specific course elsewhere."

many of them also instill a sort of disgust with modern American culture in their students."[12]

A series of webpages on the Yeshiva University website devoted to the Israeli programs underscores the irony of any college actually accepting these credits by featuring, in its descriptions of the various yeshivas, a tab for their "Attitude towards University Studies." At Kerem B'Yavneh, an Israeli yeshiva known for catering to the most serious and religious high school graduates and whose website connects its history to the ancient yeshiva that Rabbi Jochanan ben Zakkai established in Jabneh,[13] the yeshiva's attitude toward university studies is tolerant.

> Almost all of KBY's overseas alumni attend college afterwards. While the Yeshiva views Torah as the supreme learning ideal for those capable of it, it recognizes the practical value of a college education and degree in order to succeed in the world, and values the application of Torah in all professions and worldly endeavors as Am Yisrael's [the nation of Israel] unique role. The natural course of most American talmidim [students] is to attend YU, with a small percentage going to other combined programs such as Lander's [*sic*] College, HTC [Hebrew Theological College], Ner Yisrael [a rabbinical college in Baltimore], etc.[14]

Another school, Ateret Yerushalayim, answers the *hashkafa* (religious philosophy) question about university study thus: "For those students qualified and interested in continuing their secular education we do recommend YU. After completing our program boys continue in YU, Touro, other colleges or Yeshiva Gedola."[15] And another school, HaKotel, claims to offer, at the end of the school year, "special shiurim [classes] to help prepare our students for secular college and the challenges it presents to the Torah observant Jew."[16] Not the challenges that secular college *may* present to Torah observant Jews; the school formulates the challenges as fundamental and inherent, rather than potential hazards.

Another school, Ohr David, is more blunt. "Students who feel they want to pursue full-time Torah study are encouraged to do so even if that

---

12. See Riley, *God on the Quad*, 105. For more on the culture at yeshivas in Israel, see Chabin, "Fast Times."

13. See Yeshivat Kerem B'Yavneh, "KBY History," para. 1.

14. See Yeshiva University, "Guide to Israel Schools: Kerem," para. 4.

15. Yeshiva University, "Guide to Israel Schools: Ateret," para. 4.

16. Yeshiva University, "Guide to Israel Schools: HaKotel," para 4.

means they will attend a night college. Students not interested in full-time Torah study are encouraged to attend Yeshiva University and not to attend secular colleges," it states.[17]

It is clear that there is a problem when an institution such as Yeshiva University encourages students to spend a gap year—and even proudly shares statistics about student participation in studies at those Israeli institutions—when the best that one of the preferred schools can say about the value of a college education is that it recognizes that there can be practical and professional value in undergraduate study. And given some of what other schools in the program have to say about college in general, it seems akin to PETA recommending internships at butcheries.

On the opposite side, some schools, including Yeshiva University, are happy to transfer credits from Israeli yeshivas, whose transcripts, they claim, are parallel to the offered courses at the university. Hebrew Theological College in Illinois,[18] also known as the Skokie Yeshiva, states that the study abroad program "enables a student to spend a year of intensive study in an Israeli yeshiva or seminary while earning college credit" and that most students find that gap year "a challenging and enriching experience that serves as a guide in developing a lifestyle consonant with Torah values."[19] Skokie Yeshiva staff, the site continues, can "help students ensure that they receive maximum benefit in Torah achievement as well as attain additional educational goals both in Israel and upon their return."

Lander College for Men, a division of Touro College,[20] encourages students to study at one of the more than thirty postsecondary schools in the Touro College Israel Option,[21] whose objectives, it states, are to

- enable young men and women to explore their tradition without distraction, exposing them intensively to the concentrated study of Torah Texts: Talmud and Tanach [Old Testament] with their respective commentaries, Jewish Law, History, and Philosophy;

- increase the students' knowledge and fluency in the oral and written expression of Hebrew;

17. Yeshiva University, "Guide to Israel Schools: Ohr," para 4.

18. The school is accredited by the North Central Association of Colleges and Schools. See Higher Learning Commission, "Hebrew."

19. See Hebrew Theological College, "Israel Experience Program," para. 1.

20. For more on Touro and criticism of its Israel program, see Zeveloff, "Touro Under Scrutiny."

21. See Lander College for Men, "Israel Option," para. 1.

- provide students with a rare opportunity to immerse themselves in the culture, history and land of Israel;

- enhance students' collegiate experience by enabling them to incorporate accredited study at Israeli institutions into their academic career;

- provide students with necessary structure, support and assistance to gain the most from their Israel experience.

For that experience, Lander College offers students up to thirty-six credits—or, it seems, an additional sixteen credits for a second year in Israel, for a maximum of forty-eight credits—which appear on official Touro transcripts.

This acceptance of Israel credits seems to be in line with the school's religious identity, characterized in a message from Moshe Sokol, the dean. "The bulk of the day and evening is spent in the study of gemarah [Talmud], but college classes are offered Monday through Thursday, from mid-afternoon to evening," the dean writes. "This makes it possible to continue intensive gemarah study, while receiving the kind of superb education requisite for success."[22]

Brooklyn College, which is part of the City University of New York (CUNY), also welcomes credits from Israeli yeshivas, but that policy is buried on its website and it requires prospective students to be creative excavators to locate it. Like many other schools, Brooklyn College offers study abroad options at accredited Israeli universities—particularly Bar Ilan University,[23] Ben Gurion University of the Negev, Haifa University, Hebrew University, and Tel Aviv University—through its CUNY Study in Israel program.[24] But the college's Department of Judaic studies, on its homepage, praises one of its faculty members, Professor Jonathan Helfand (the longest-serving professor in the department's history, who retired in 2013), for supervising "the program that grants students up to 30 transfer credits for intensive study in yeshivas and seminaries in Israel, as well as in the United States."[25]

It takes digging through the college's Faculty Handbook to find more information: "Yeshiva credit. A maximum of 32 equivalency credits may be

---

22. See Lander College for Men, "Message," para. 2.

23. At Bar Ilan, however, there have been other issues. See Maltz, "Director."

24. See Brooklyn College, "CUNY Program Study in Israel," para. 2.

25. Ibid., "Mission Statement," para. 13.

granted for postsecondary studies at a yeshiva. Cases are decided individually. Details are available in the Office of Transfer Evaluations."[26]

Given the controversy surrounding these Israeli yeshiva credits—and the ways that some institutions seem to conceal the fact that they transfer those credits—Yeshiva University sends a message to its undergraduates and sets a larger tone for the institution and its academic priorities by hawking its Israeli gap year program. It is not that surprising that an institution would defund a student publication that publishes an article about premarital sex or would denounce a panel addressing homosexuality and Orthodox Judaism, after all, if the academic standards that that institution embraces do not differentiate, in many contexts, between religious apologetics and religious studies.

It is important to be clear, though, that Yeshiva University's departments of Bible, (biblical) Hebrew, Jewish History, and Jewish Philosophy and Thought are very serious programs, and the faculty associated with those departments is stellar and teaches from an academic perspective. Some of the Bible courses taught within the university arm of YU do address biblical criticism and other scholarly perspectives that are not necessarily compatible with an Orthodox Jewish perspective and set of values.

But that very sort of open-minded inquiry is anathema in much of the yeshiva arm of the institution, and certain Bible professors are known to have a reputation for being "unkosher"; some rabbis even tell their students not to study in certain Judaic studies courses at the university, for fear of being exposed to *kfirah* (heresy). That is precisely why it is so problematic that a year of coursework within such a rigorous framework is deemed equivalent to a year of Jewish apologetics at an Israeli institution, without any tests or written assignments and a teaching method that focuses on what is often religious propaganda rather than religious studies.[27]

One of the most fundamental solutions to the academic freedom challenges at Yeshiva University might begin with reviewing its academic mission and priorities and ensuring that those priorities place it firmly within the academic community that it hopes to inhabit. Alternatively, Yeshiva

26. Brooklyn College, "Faculty Handbook," 97.

27. One might recognize a tremendous embrace of academic freedom in Yeshiva University's propensity to encourage students to study at institutions that, in a sense, do not recognize the university's right to exist, but if one does entertain such a line of argument, one would hope that Yeshiva University would then recommend a subsequent gap year at an institution that would balance out that perspective from the opposite side of the academic spectrum.

could tweak its mission statement and come clean about what it prioritizes as an institution. If it wants to be the sort of university that represents a safe place for students to be Orthodox Jews and to take some college courses on the side—as many of the members of its community describe it—the university would do well to be upfront about that orientation in its mission statement and marketing materials.

A Greater Assortment of Institutions

In the course of my interviews, I have been asked frequently why I was devoting so much ink and attention to Yeshiva University, rather than other institutions such as Touro, the Skokie Yeshiva, and Yeshivat Chovevei Torah Rabbinical School in Manhattan. The truth is that I have dwelled on Yeshiva University for several reasons. First, I studied for three years on campus at YU (with a freshman year of study in Israel), and I have kept a fairly close eye on the institution since graduating about eight years ago. Yeshiva not only self-identifies as the flagship institution of Modern Orthodox Judaism, but it also tells *U.S. News & World Report*—and its millions of readers—that it is not a religious institution, which makes it a particularly intriguing test case for academic freedom issues in religious higher education. Also, I am using YU as a case study that can be extended, albeit with various limitations, to other institutions.

I also recognize that Jewish Theological Seminary (Conservative) and Hebrew Union College (Reform) are sure to have their own academic freedom challenges, and that such challenges are in no way endemic and restricted to Orthodox academies. If a professor does not feel comfortable sharing a creationist position in the classroom at a more liberal institution, or if someone is denied tenure because she or he is perceived as being too religious for the institution—that poses the same challenge to the integrity and efficacy of the academy as censorship by conservatives of more liberal viewpoints.

It has been frequently noted that Yeshiva University is facing competition on the left from Chovevei and on the right from Lander College. Chovevei is a rabbinical school that believes that "the future of Orthodoxy depends on our becoming a movement that expands outward non-dogmatically and cooperatively to encompass the needs of the larger Jewish community and the world," according to its website.[28] "For this vision

---

28. See Yeshivat Chovevei Torah, "About Us," para. 1.

to succeed, we require a new breed of leaders—rabbis who are open, non-judgmental, knowledgeable, empathetic, and eager to transform Orthodoxy into a movement that meaningfully and respectfully interacts with all Jews, regardless of affiliation, commitment, or background."

Since ordaining its first class of rabbis in 2004, Chovevei—which elsewhere on its website identifies itself as "modern and open Orthodox"[29]—has carved out an interesting niche for itself. It has failed to gain widespread acceptance within the Orthodox Jewish world, although its new president, Rabbi Asher Lopatin, seems to be set on improving the rabbinical academy's reputation within the Orthodox community.[30] Rabbi Avi Weiss, the founding president of Chovevei, whom Lopatin replaced, is notorious in Orthodox circles for ordaining a "rabba," a quasi-rabbinical role for women.[31] Only time will tell if Weiss's openness to Orthodox feminism will spread and if Chovevei, under its new leadership, will really compete with Yeshiva University for pulpit placements.[32]

However well the competition fares, it is probably safe to assume that a more crowded rabbinical college space will force the players—particularly the more established ones like Yeshiva University—to improve their academic freedom track record and to examine their policies and practices.

The Hope for a More Tolerant Academic Neighborhood

Academic standards that are not up to snuff at rabbinical schools and Orthodox Jewish universities are not necessarily the fault or responsibility of secular colleges and universities, but as long as Orthodox students and parents cite dormitory environments[33] that are incompatible with a religious lifestyle, yeshivas—with all of their academic warts—may be the only viable option.

Brokering any sort of understanding between Orthodox Jewish students hoping to study at secular institutions without sampling much of the

29. See Yeshivat Chovevei Torah, "Mission," para. 1.

30. See Heilman, "Asher Lopatin."

31. For more on Weiss, see Hoffman, "New 'Morethodox' Rabbi," and Ungar-Sargon, "Orthodox Yeshiva Set to Ordain Three Women."

32. See Cattan, "Upstart Rabbinical School."

33. A recent article in the *New York Times*, for example, argues that collegiate women are increasingly comfortable with casual sex rather than seeking dating or marital partners. See Taylor, "Sex on Campus."

culture at those universities and the schools themselves, who are no doubt proud of their campus life and lifestyle, can be a difficult task without offending either party or both parties. But particularly in the higher education space, the social media era seems to be amplifying certain customer service issues that had previously been easier to ignore than to address.[34]

Perhaps in the coming years secular institutions will find it expedient and wise to recognize that certain segments of their student populations have religious needs that are worth accommodating when it comes to everything from single-sex or Shabbat-friendly dorms to religious food requirements. Some schools are very accommodating of these sorts of needs—and indeed there has been much progress since the so-called Yale Five[35]—but it might take a more widespread change in this regard to convince Orthodox students that they do not need to select Yeshiva University for their studies or compromise on their religious lifestyle.

At New York University, for example, the vice president of student affairs recently announced that students could no longer request roommates based on a shared faith—a move that, he said, would increase "global and inclusive campus community." As the *New York Jewish Week* reported, "Some students 'may face conflict' [according to the vice president] but that 'could ultimately be conducive to personal growth.'"[36] Rabbi Yehuda Sarna, the director of the Bronfman Center for Jewish Student Life at New York University, is advising Orthodox students who want to room together to select a particular dorm at NYU, which has the worst reputation, because they are likelier to get assigned to one another there, but that is more like putting a Band-Aid on the problem than performing reconstructive surgery.

If there were more viable academic options for Orthodox students at a wider range of colleges and universities, Yeshiva University might have to consider making certain changes to its academic offerings rather than relying on its monopoly on kosher lifestyle.

---

34. For a partial discussion of this topic, see Wecker, "Colleges Get Mixed Reviews."

35. See Associated Press, "Orthodox Jews Protest."

36. See Mark, "NYU Dorm Changes," para. 3, who quotes an incoming freshman, currently studying in Israel on a gap year, who wrote NYU: "Walking into a room on the Sabbath where there is music playing from a computer, poses a threat and challenge to my religion. I had hoped that in my room, there would be an aura of religiosity but in the halls, classes, and socially, there, I would have a diverse circle of friends."

Student and Alumni Pressure

When I first started working on this book, I envisioned the community surrounding the *Beacon* as a sort of Occupy Yeshiva movement, in large part because of the massive national and international dialogue it inspired, but also for the many conversations it sparked among Yeshiva University alumni. In my conversation with former *Beacon* coeditor Simi Lampert, I was told that it was flattering, yet overstating the case, to refer to Occupy Yeshiva. But one can be optimistic that in the social media era, perhaps student and young alumni voices—even if they do not donate in the amounts of older and more traditional alumni—might make a difference.

Yeshiva is currently at a crossroads of sorts, and it is struggling with a series of exposés about its cover-up of rabbinic involvement in sexual abuse.[37] No doubt, Yeshiva has its work cut out to ensure that its students, rather than its rabbinic offenders, are protected moving forward, but while the institution is in a period of self-evaluation and growing pains, it has the opportunity to rethink some other aspects of its culture—including those that may have elevated certain rabbis to positions in which they were beyond reproach.

If Yeshiva University looks to students, alumni, and faculty during this period of introspection and renovation, rather than falling back on the *Daat Torah* and conferral of demigod status to certain members of its rabbinic faculty, as I described in chapter 4, the institution could greatly improve not only its administrative operations but also its academic offerings.

And there are takeaways for students at other schools as well. With so many resources available online that can offset official, slanted university websites—from social media comments to blogs to news articles—there is really no excuse for parents and prospective students not to do their research and find out how the schools they are considering operate. If they want an environment that prioritizes religious study—in Yeshiva University's case, Torah studies—above all else, then so be it, but if they are hoping for an academic atmosphere in which liberal arts are taken seriously, or even a full secular education, they should make sure that they have chosen an appropriate institution.

That doesn't mean, however, that administrators at YU—or any other religious school—are not shirking their responsibility and acting immorally

37. See Paul Berger's excellent coverage for the *Jewish Daily Forward*, including Berger, "Third Alleged Yeshiva U. Abuser," "Yeshiva Rocked," and "Former Y.U. High School Students." See also Nathan-Kazis, "Norman Lamm Leaves."

by obscuring their academic and religious values. With a somewhat confusing mission of being both modern and orthodox, Yeshiva University can often seem to speak in riddles, but an institution either is or is not religious. Clearly, a university can report whatever it wants to *U.S. News & World Report*, but if it censors student publications on religious grounds, accepts credits from certain Israeli institutions that barely tolerate the institution of the academy, and otherwise exhibits behavior that would solidify its standing as a religious institution, it ought to own up to that religious identity. Of course, institutions often evolve and grow over time, so dusting off the old mission statement and making sure that it still reflects the reality on the campus ground is something that could benefit every college and university.

Conclusion

Menachem Wecker

Thou shalt not" is famously "writ over the door" of the chapel—whose gates, tellingly, are bolted—in the 1794 poem "The Garden of Love" by William Blake, the enigmatic poet, illustrator, and painter. Blake, who appeared to exhibit an aversion to organized religions but had a penchant, according to some scholars, to invent his own,[1] knew more about a life of faith from his own studies and experience than just the proclivity to prohibit anything and everything. But he chose to adorn the signage above the entrance to the chapel with the cautionary language that introduces 70 percent of the Decalogue; and the Garden of Love, which ought to be overgrown with "sweet flowers," instead is a church graveyard where priests clad in black robes bind the narrator's joys and desires with thorns.

The religious academy, like the church, is by no means the exclusive domain of tombstones and thickets where all joys, desires, and fun go to die, although by secular standards, some of those are curtailed somewhat in the hallowed halls of theological seminaries and religious chapels of all sorts. The important component of Blake's chapel for our purposes is which aspect of the institutional identity the church leads with in its signage. The eighteenth century's sign over the door is today a Facebook page, a LinkedIn group, a Twitter handle, an official website, or a Tumblr, but the principle remains the same—it's a mechanism that is understood to be self-promotional rather than objective journalism, but it is supposed to actually reflect the values and the operative mechanisms of the establishment.

As the previous chapters in this book have underscored time and again, it can be difficult enough to unpack how secular colleges and universities

---

1. For a partial discussion of how Blake's grasp of Jewish mysticism is often inflated, see Wecker, "William Blake."

ideally and realistically ought to operate. When the school in question has a dual identity—a religious mandate as well as a secular, academic one—composing and staying true to a hyphenated identity can be exponentially more complicated, just as living a traditional, religious life in a fast-evolving modern world poses many difficulties.

If the bulk of this book has shone a light on what the casualties often are—for students, faculty, and all of those who value academic scholarship—when the "Thou shalt not" charge is overzealously and unilaterally applied as a bully pulpit (literally) to censor others, it is not because we believe that the religious academy is necessarily problematic and destructive. One can point to countless examples of religious students and faculty thriving in the domain of the theological seminary that is governed by "Thou canst," "Thou is free to," and "Thou shalt." Many would also cite aspects of campus life in the secular academy that could afford to be curtailed a bit, although others might question whether prohibition is really the most effective way to influence behavior. The Talmud in *b. San.* 107b recommends that the left hand ought to be used when it is necessary to discipline, while the more powerful right hand[2] is always to be used for reconciliation, and that is the spirit of this manuscript, which recognizes that some of the greatest scholarship throughout the ages, and indeed today, was the brainchild of researchers funded by Christian, Islamic, and Jewish academies, as well as institutions that operated in Eastern and other faith traditions. As Brandon notes in chapter 3, the history of the Western academy is, in fact, utterly inseparable from Christianity, and I would add that this important history is not necessarily something that many of the critics of the conservative bent of many religious schools are aware of, let alone acknowledge.

In my experience, both working in higher education communications and subsequently in reporting on higher education, where I was on the receiving rather than composing and distributing end of press releases, it can be very easy for those within the academy to fall prey to a limited worldview that allows the bubble of their own campus to overshadow the larger landscape outside of their own ivory tower. Many higher educational institutions, like many news publications, have swapped transparent and effective communication for hackneyed and atmospheric language, which aims for the holy grail of search engine optimization. Even as much of the

2. Online: http://www.come-and-hear.com/sanhedrin/sanhedrin_107.html#PARTb. In the Bible the right hand is held to be more powerful. See Judges 3:15, which refers to Ehud the son of Gera as being "left handed" in the King James Version, but the original Hebrew more appropriately means "with weakened/restricted right hand."

news industry and private enterprise has been embracing the absurd "expertise" of certain so-called digital strategists and swapping creative and witty language on their websites with terms designed to "trick" search engines into sending unsuspecting visitors to their sites, higher educational institutions, where senior staff are often academics themselves, tend to cling to vocabularies accentuated by scholarly hobbyhorses that are surely well known within their halls and faculty offices, but quite opaque to laypeople.

At religious schools, the addition of religious terminology and concepts—such as God communing directly with senior staff, whether fortuitously when those staff happen to be under some sort investigation or more broadly when the institution needs to make a major decision—may further solidify an us-versus-them mentality, or a clear demarcation of the boundary between the safety of the institution and the challenges posed by the outside world. But it's not only a linguistic challenge, confined to marketing brochures that applaud the schools (affectionately known in graduate legal programs as "law school porn"); it's also a radical difference between the ways that faculty and staff, who are at least semi-permanent denizens of the academy, sometimes view the continuity of the institution and the manner in which students, who might be said to be "just visiting" rather than in Monopoly jail, envision the institution.

Many alumni of undergraduate programs will not seek graduate education, and the completion of their four years on campus will mark the culmination of their association with formal education. For religious students, that means that their college experience will be an opportunity to question, interrogate, better understand, and solidify their religious identities in a controlled environment; the religious toolkit they cultivate in college, the hope would be, will serve them as alumni when they try to make their way in a comparatively less hospitable world. To be sure, many university and college administrations could not care less about undergraduates, and only pay attention to them when there is a prospect of litigation or a PR crisis; and higher education staff can comfortably count on waiting out any student complaints, since the student body's collective memory is as fickle and short-term as the constant revolving door of graduates and new incoming students.

In addition to taking action to ensure the continuity of the school's mission and its upholding of narrow missions that can be packed with inside-baseball references, there is a need for schools to approach faculty and students who have difficult questions and perspectives that aren't mainstream with more Christian and Jewish charity. It ought to be as essential to a religious school's mission to allow for the development and growth of its students and to provide a safe place for its faculty to create its best research as it is to circle the wagons and protect its religious mandate. Of course, there will be absolute heresies that the institution will decide it cannot suffer in silence, but the degree to which it can be as tolerant as possible ought to be viewed as a badge of courage, rather than cause for threats that donors will yank funding.

In chapter 7, Brandon did some deep wading into the case law surrounding academic freedom both at religious and secular institutions, and it seems pretty clear that it might be high time for some significant reexamination of those laws. It will remain true, however, that private religious institutions will not be bound by the same restrictions as public colleges and universities, and that will give them a good deal of power.

Some of the most poignant messages of the Bible—both the Old and New Testaments—that even nonreligious readers can take away involve boldly speaking truth to power. Whether it is Jesus overturning corporate tables on sacred ground and standing up to the Pharisees or Moses and Aaron confronting Pharaoh and his legions of guards, magicians, and advisers, and indeed the entire bureaucracy of the ancient Egyptian state, the protection of the ethically minded underdog is championed early and often in scripture.

Moving forward, as digital communication makes it easier and easier for students and professors to publicize controversial positions and for administrations to monitor and document those views, it will be interesting to watch which institutions offset the power they wield with a sense of responsibility. It also will be fascinating to see which religious academies continue to conceive of their central administrations as the sole voices of the institution and which act like communities, where even wayward children get a voice in defining the school. The schools that are bold enough to allow that might just find more Prodigal Sons in their alumni ranks.

Bibliography

Abelard, Peter. *Letters of Peter Abelard: Beyond the Personal.* Translated by Jan M. Ziolkowski. Washington, DC: Catholic University Press of America, 2008.

Aberbach, Moses. "Shem: In the *Aggadah.*" In *Encyclopaedia Judaica,* edited by Michael Berenbaum and Fred Skolnik, 18:453. 2nd. ed. Detroit: Macmillan Reference, 2007.

Abramowitz, Benjamin. "Rabbi Yona Reiss Unveils Plan for Internet Censorship: Dormitory Pornography to Be Blocked." *Yeshiva University Commentator,* December 9, 2011, http://www.yucommentator.org/2011/12/rabbi-yona-reiss-unveils-plan-for-internet-censorship-dormitory-pornography-to-be-blocked/.

Aleman, Ana M. Martinez, and Kristen A. Renn. "Southern Baptist Colleges." In *Women in Higher Education: An Encyclopedia,* edited by Ana M. Martínez Alemán and Kristen A. Renn, 52–57. Santa Barbara: ABC-CLIO, 2002.

Alliance of Confessing Evangelicals. "An Appeal to Fellow Evangelicals: The Alliance of Evangelicals Reply to 'The Gift of Salvation.'" *Modern Reformation* 7 (1998) 29–32.

———. "Cambridge Declaration." In *Here We Stand: A Call from Confessing Evangelicals,* edited by James M. Boice and Benjamin E. Sasse, 14–20. Grand Rapids: Baker, 1996.

American Association of University Professors (AAUP). "1915 Declaration of Principles on Academic Freedom and Academic Tenure." http://www.aaup.org/AAUP/pubsres/policydocs/contents/1915.htm.

———. "1940 Statement of Principles on Academic Freedom and Tenure." http://www.aaup.org/report/1940-statement-principles-academic-freedom-and-tenure.

———. "Academic Freedom and Tenure: Cedarville University (Ohio)." January-February 2009. http://www.aaup.org/report/academic-freedom-and-tenure-cedarville-university.

———. "Academic Freedom and Tenure: Olivet Nazarene University (Illinois)." January-February 2009. http://www.aaup.org/sites/default/files/Academic-Freedom-and-Tenure-Olivet.pdf.

———. "Joint Statement on Rights and Freedoms of Students." http://www.aaup.org/AAUP/pubsres/policydocs/contents/stud-rights.htm.

———. "Letter to President Donald Dowless of Shorter University." December 12, 2011, http://www.insidehighered.com/sites/default/server_files/files/Shorter%20University%20-%20December%2012,%202011(1).pdf.

———. "Protecting an Independent Faculty Voice: Academic Freedom after *Garcetti v. Ceballos.*" http://www.aaup.org/file/Protecting-Independent-Voice.pdf.

———. "Supreme Court Issues New Rulings." June 25, 2013, http://www.aaup.org/news/supreme-court-issues-new-rulings.

Anderson, Gary A. "The Status of the Torah before Sinai: The Retelling of the Bible in the Damascus Covenant." *Dead Sea Discoveries* 1 (1994) 1–29.

Bibliography

Anonymous. "How Do I Even Begin to Explain This." *The Beacon*, December 5, 2011, http://thebeaconmag.com/2011/12/the__written_word/how-do-i-even-begin-to-explain-this/.

Anonymous. "Transcript of the Report on the March 26, 2008 Westminster Theological Seminary Special Board Meeting 10:30 A.M., April 1, 2008, Van Til Auditorium, Westminster Theological Seminary, Philadelphia, PA." Author copy.

Arenson, Karen W. "Yeshiva Students Say the University Is Behind Removal of Campus Paper." *New York Times*, December 15, 1999, B15, http://www.nytimes.com/1999/12/15/nyregion/yeshiva-students-say-the-university-is-behind-removal-of-campus-paper.html.

Armstrong, John H. *Your Church Is Too Small: Why Unity in Christ's Mission Is Vital to the Future of the Church.* Grand Rapids: Zondervan, 2010.

Associated Press. "Orthodox Jews Protest Yale's Required Coed Dormitories." *Los Angeles Times*, October 4, 1997, http://articles.latimes.com/1997/oct/04/local/me-39253.

———. "Professor: Seminary Ousted Her over Gender: Baptist School Cited Biblical Ban against Women Teaching Men, She Says." *NBCNews.com*, January 26, 2007, http://www.nbcnews.com/id/16828466/ns/us_news-education/t/professor-seminary-ousted-her-over-gender.

Baptist Press. "Cedarville Calls SWBTS' White as President." June 5, 2013, http://www.bpnews.net/bpnews.asp?id=40455.

Barrick, Audrey. "Judge Dismisses Gender Discrimination Suit against Baptist Seminary." *Christian Post*, March 21, 2008, http://www.christianpost.com/news/judge-dismisses-gender-discrimination-suit-against-baptist-seminary-31607.

Bartlett, Thomas. "Cedarville U. Board Says Officials Followed Procedure in Professor's Dismissal." *The Chronicle of Higher Education*, April 4, 2008, http://chronicle.com/article/Cedarville-U-Board-Says/40752/.

Basu, Kaustuv. "Tenure at Risk at Seminaries." *Inside Higher Ed*, July 20, 2012, http://www.insidehighered.com/news/2012/07/30/kentucky-court%E2%80%99s-decision-questions-tenure-seminaries.

Bebbington, David. "Christian Higher Education in Europe: A Historical Analysis." *Christian Higher Education* 10 (2011) 10–24.

Benedict. *Saint Benedict's Rule.* Translated by Patrick Barry. 2nd ed. Mahwah, NJ: HiddenSpring, 2004.

Berger, Paul. "Former Y.U. High School Students File $380M Suit Claiming Sex Abuse Cover-Up." *Jewish Daily Forward*, July 8, 2013, http://forward.com/articles/180007/former-yu-high-school-students-file-m-suit-cla/.

———. "Third Alleged Yeshiva U. Abuser Accused of Preying on Boys in Dorms and Apartment." *Jewish Daily Forward*, July 12, 2013, http://forward.com/articles/180331/third-alleged-yeshiva-u-abuser-accused-of-preying/.

———. "Yeshiva Rabbi Hershel Schachter Stirs Hornet's Nest with Remarks—Again." *Jewish Daily Forward*, March 21, 2013, http://forward.com/articles/173452/yeshiva-rabbi-hershel-schachter-stirs-hornets-nest/.

———. "Yeshiva Rocked as 6 More People Accuse School of Sex Abuse Cover-Up." *Jewish Daily Forward*, July 11, 2013, http://forward.com/articles/180235/yeshiva-rocked-as--more-people-accuse-school-of-s/.

Berger, Shalom. "A Year of Study in an Israeli Yeshiva Program: Before and After." PhD diss., Azrieli Graduate School of Jewish Education and Administration, Yeshiva University, January 1997, http://lookstein.org/articles/sberger_dissertation.pdf.

Berman, Daphna, "U.S. Degrees Based on Yeshiva Credits Not Valid, Says Ministry." *Ha'aretz*, January 21, 2005, http://www.haaretz.com/u-s-degrees-based-on-yeshiva-credits-not-valid-says-ministry-1.147917.

Berrett, Dan. "Fired Professor Says Seminary Forcibly Raised Students' Grades." *The Chronicle of Higher Education*, August 7, 2012, http://chronicle.com/article/Fired-Professor-Says-Seminary/133437/.

Billing, Michael. *The Hidden Roots of Critical Psychology*. Thousand Oaks, CA: Sage, 2008.

Bland, Kalman P. *The Artless Jew: Medieval and Modern Affirmation and Denials of the Visual*. Princeton: Princeton University Press, 2001.

Borst, Arno. *Medieval Worlds: Barbarians, Heretics and Artists in the Middle Ages*. Chicago: University of Chicago Press, 1991.

Bortniker, Elijah. "In the Middle Ages: Northern France and Germany." In *Encyclopaedia Judaica*, edited by Michael Berenbaum and Fred Skolnik, 18:162–214. 2nd. ed. Detroit: Macmillan Reference, 2007.

Botticini, Maristella, and Zvi Eckstein. "Jewish Occupational Selection: Education, Restrictions, or Minorities?" *The Journal of Economic History* 65 (2005) 922–48.

Bowden, John, and Hugh Bowden. "University." In *Encyclopedia of Christianity*, edited by John Bowden, 1218. New York: Oxford University Press, 2005.

Brickman, William W. "Universities: In the Middle Ages." In *Encyclopaedia Judaica*, edited by Michael Berenbaum and Fred Skolnik, 18:407. 2nd. ed. Detroit: Macmillan Reference, 2007.

Brooklyn College. "CUNY Program Study in Israel." http://www.brooklyn.cuny.edu/web/academics/international/cunypsi.php.

———. "Faculty Handbook." http://www.brooklyn.cuny.edu/web/aca_faculty/090901_FacultyHandbook.pdf.

———. "Mission Statement." http://depthome.brooklyn.cuny.edu/judaic/.

Calvin College. "FAQ about Recent Scholarship by Professors Harlow and Schneider." http://www.calvin.edu/admin/provost/origins-discussion.

——— and John Schneider. "Joint Statement." http://media.mlive.com/grpress/news_impact/other/Calvin%20statement.pdf.

Calvin College Biology Department. "Perspectives on Evolution." http://www.calvin.edu/academic/biology/why/evolution-statement10May2010.pdf.

Cargill, Robert. "Call for Letters in Support of Christopher Rollston." *Excavator*, November 8, 2012, http://robertcargill.com/2012/11/08/call-for-letters-in-support-of-christopher-rollston/#list.

———. "Winners and Losers in the Emmanuel Christian Seminary Scandal." *Excavator*, December 31, 2012, http://robertcargill.com/2012/12/31/winners-and-losers-in-the-emmanuel-christian-seminary-scandal.

Carhart, Michael C. *The Science of Culture in Enlightenment Germany*. Cambridge: Harvard University Press, 2007.

Carpenter, Joel A. *Revive Us Again: The Reawakening of American Fundamentalism*. New York: Oxford University Press, 1997.

Cattan, Nacha. "Upstart Rabbinical School Set to Fight for Pulpit Jobs." *Jewish Daily Forward*, June 13, 2003, http://forward.com/articles/7445/upstart-rabbinical-school-set-to-fight-for-pulpit/.

Cedarville University. "Academic Freedom." http://www.cedarville.edu/Job-Openings/Academic-Freedom.aspx.

———. "Accreditation: Self-Study Report." Spring 2007. https://www.cedarville .edu/accreditation/selfstudy/document/CedarvilleUniversitySelfStudyReport.pdf.

———. "Cedarville University Board of Trustees Resolution: Truth and Certainty August 21, 2006." http://web.archive.org/web/20070423090143/http://www.cedarville.edu/ cf/truthandcertainty/showpdf.cfm.

———. "Doctrinal Statement." http://www.cedarville.edu/About/Doctrinal-Statement .aspx.

———. "FAQ: Recent Personnel Actions." http://web.archive.org/web/20070711165101/ http://www.cedarville.edu/academics/avp/truth/personnelfaq.cfm.

Chabad. "Bereishit—Genesis—Chapter 25." http://www.chabad.org/library/bible_cdo/ aid/8220/showrashi/true20#showrashi=true.

———. "Devarim—Deuteronomy—Chapter 17." http://www.chabad.org/library/bible_ cdo/aid/9981#showrashi=true.

———. "Melachim II—II Kings—Chapter 22." http://www.chabad.org/library/bible_ cdo/aid/15928#showrashi=true.

Chabin, Michele. "Fast Times at 'Gap Year' High." *New York Jewish Week*, January 10, 2010, http://web.archive.org/web/20100218130055/http://www.thejewishweek.com/ viewArticle/c40_a17661/News/Israel.html.

Chernikoff, Helen. "Pressure on YU as Budget, Enrollment Woes Persist: Less Expensive Colleges to the Left, New Yeshivas on the Right: Yeshiva University Seeks a Perch for Itself as Joel Nears 10th Year." *New York Jewish Week*, March 27, 2012, http://www .thejewishweek.com/news/new_york/stuck_middle_yu_special_report.

Cobban, Alan. *English University Life in the Middle Ages*. London: University College London, 1999.

Colish, Marcia L. *Medieval Foundations of the Western Intellectual Tradition, 400–1400*. Yale Intellectual History of the West. New Haven: Yale University Press, 1998.

Colling, Richard G. *Random Designer: Created from Chaos to Connect with the Creator*. Bourbonnais, IL: Browning, 2004.

Colson, Charles, and Richard John Neuhaus. *Evangelicals and Catholics Together: Toward a Common Mission*. Dallas: Word, 1995.

Columbia University. "Frequently Asked Questions." http://www.columbia.edu/cu/mesaas/ languages/hebrew/faqs.html.

Contreni, John J. "The Carolingian Renaissance." In *Renaissances Before the Renaissance: Cultural Revivals of Late Antiquity and the Middle Ages*, edited by Warren Treadgold, 59–74. Stanford: Stanford University Press, 1984.

———. "The Carolingian Renaissance: Education and Literacy Culture." In *The New Cambridge Medieval History II, c.700–c.900*, edited by Rosamond McKitterick, 709–57. New York: Cambridge University Press, 1995.

Cornman, Thomas. "Trustees, White Papers, and Christ-Centered Education." *Fiat Lux*, August, 31, 2012, http://fiatlux125.wordpress.com/old-ltbl/articlesetc/trustees-white-papers-and-christ-centered-higher-education/.

De Dreuille, Mayeul. *The Rule of St. Benedict: A Commentary in Light of World Ascetic Traditions*. Manwah, NJ: Newman, 2000.

De Ridder-Symoens, Hilde. "The Intellectual Heritage of Ancient Universities in Europe." In *The Heritage of European Universities*, edited by Nuria Sanz and Sjur Bergan, 79–90. 2nd ed. Council of Europe Higher Education Series 7. Strasbourg: Council of Europe Publishing, 2006.

———. "Management and Resources." In *Universities in Early Modern Europe, 1500–1800*, edited by Hilde de Ridder-Symoens, 155–209. History of the University in Europe 2. Cambridge: Cambridge University Press, 1996.

Delbanco, Andrew. *College: What It Was, Is, and Should Be.* Princeton: Princeton University Press, 2012.

DelFattore, Joan. "Defending Academic Freedom in the Age of *Garcetti*." *Academe*, January-February 2011, http://www.aaup.org/article/defending-academic-freedom-age-garcetti.

———. "To Protect Academic Freedom, Look Beyond the First Amendment." *The Chronicle of Higher Education*, October 21, 2010, http://chronicle.com/article/To-Protect-Academic-Freedom/125178.

Del Verme, Marcello. *Didache and Judaism: Jewish Roots of an Ancient Christian-Jewish Work.* New York: T. & T. Clark, 2004.

Deutsch, Nathaniel. "The Forbidden Fork, the Cell Phone Holocaust, and Other Haredi Encounters with Technology." *Contemporary Jewry* 29 (2009) 3–19, http://www.nabilechchaibi.com/resources/Deutsch.pdf.

Dunn, Sydni. "As Part-Time Faculty Wait for Payday, Peers Help Out with a Food Drive." *The Chronicle of Higher Education*, January 17, 2013, http://chronicle.com/article/As-Part-Time-Faculty-Wait-for/136723.

Enns, Peter. "The Authority of Scripture Is a Function of Its Divine Origin, Not Its Cultural Expression, Although the Bible That the Spirit Has Given the Church Is a Thoroughly Encultured Product." http://peterennsonline.com/ii/authority-of-scripture.

———. "Bible in Context: The Continuing Vitality of Reformed Biblical Scholarship." *Westminster Theological Journal* 68 (2006) 203–18, http://peterennsonline.com/wordpress/wp-content/uploads/2007/11/Enns_inaugural_address_dr_6_23_06.pdf.

———. *The Evolution of Adam: What the Bible Does and Doesn't Say about Human Origins.* Grand Rapids: Brazos, 2012.

———. *Inspiration and Incarnation: Evangelicals and the Problem of the Old Testament.* Grand Rapids: Baker Academic, 2005.

Estes, Adam Clark. "Yeshiva University Is in an Uproar Over a Not-Very-Saucy Sex Column." *The Atlantic*, December 9, 2011, http://www.theatlanticwire.com/national/2011/12/yeshiva-university-uproar-over-not-very-saucy-sex-column/45994/.

Evangelicals and Catholics Together. "The Gift of Salvation." *Christianity Today*, December 8, 1997, http://www.christianitytoday.com/ct/1997/december8/7te034.html.

Evans, Gillian Rosemary. *John Wyclif: Myth and Reality.* Downers Grove, IL: InterVarsity, 2005.

Fernández-Enguita, Mariano. "Ethnic Groups, Class, and Gender in Education." In *Transnational Perspectives on Culture, Policy, and Education: Redirecting Cultural Studies in Neoliberal Times*, edited by Cameron McCarthy and Cathryn Teasley, 257–76. New York: Peter Lang, 2008.

Fine, Steven. *Sacred Realm: The Emergence of the Synagogue in the Ancient World.* New York: Oxford University Press, 1996.

Fish, Stanley. *Save the World on Your Own Time.* New York: Oxford University Press, 2008.

Frohlich, Yaelle. "President Richard Joel and Menahel Rabbi Yona Reiss Issue Statement Addressing Religious Proscription of Homosexual Activity." *Yeshiva University Observer*, December 21, 2009, http://www.yuobserver.com/news/president-richard-joel-and-menahel-rabbi-yona-reiss-issue-statement-addressing-religious-proscription-of-homosexual-activity-1.2470600#.Ubqb89y1GSq.

Gerber, Larry. "Professionalization as the Basis for Academic Freedom and Faculty Governance." *Journal of Academic Freedom* 1 (2010) 1–26.

Gieysztor, Aleksander. "Management and Resources." In *Universities in the Middle Ages*, edited by Hilde de Ridder-Symeons, 108–43. History of the University in Europe 1. New York: Cambridge University Press, 1992.

Ginther, James R. *The Westminster Handbook to Medieval Theology*. Louisville: Westminster John Knox, 2009.

Glick, Thomas, Steven J. Livesey, and Faith Wallis, eds. "Cathedral Schools." In *Medieval Science, Technology, and Medicine: An Encylopedia*, 121–22. New York: Routledge, 2005.

Golden, Daniel. "A Test of Faith: A Professor's Firing after His Conversion Highlights a New Orthodoxy at Religious Colleges." *Wall Street Journal*, January 7, 2006, http://online.wsj.com/article/SB113659805227040466.html.

Goldfish, Ezzie. "YoU Are Sub-Par II . . ." *SerandEz*, April 15, 2008, http://serandez.blogspot.com/2008/04/you-are-sub-par-ii.html.

Grafton, Anthony, and Megan Williams. *Origen, Eusebius, and the Library of Caesarea*. Cambridge: Harvard University Press, 2006.

Grant, Iain Hamilton. "Postmodernism and Science and Technology." In *The Routledge Companion to Postmodernism*, edited by Stuart Sim, 94–107. 3rd ed. New York: Routledge, 2011.

Graves, Shawn, and David Mills. "Why I Am Not Voting for Romney." *Cedars*, October 13, 2012, http://cedars.cedarville.edu/article/481/Why-I-am-Not-Voting-for-Romney.

Gray, Madeleine. *The Protestant Reformation: Belief, Practice, and Tradition*. Portland, OR: Sussex Academic, 2003.

Greer, Rowan A. "Introduction." In *Origen: An Exhortation to Martyrdom, Prayer, First Principles*, translated by Rowan A. Greer. New York: Paulist, 1979.

Gregory the Great. *Dialogues*. Translated by Odo John Zimmerman. Washington, DC: Catholic University of America Press, 1959.

Grendler, Paul F. *Renaissance Education: Between Religion and Politics*. Burlington, VT: Ashgate, 2006.

Gross, Netty C. "Bittersweet Harvest." *The Jerusalem Post*, October 29, 1993, 6.

Grovois, John. "University Timed Firing of 2 Professors to Avoid Affecting Accreditation, Recording Suggests." *The Chronicle of Higher Education*, March 13, 2008, http://chronicle.com/article/University-Timed-Firing-of-2/591.

Gutmann, Joseph. "The Illustrated Jewish Manuscript in Antiquity: The Present State of the Question." *Gesta* 5 (1966) 39–44.

———. "The Jewish Origin of the Ashburnham Pentateuch Miniatures." *The Jewish Quarterly Review*, New Series, 44 (1953) 55–72.

Harlow, Daniel C. "After Adam: Reading Genesis in an Age of Evolutionary Science." *Perspectives on Science and Christian Faith* 62 (2010) 179–95, http://www.asa3.org/ASA/PSCF/2010/PSCF9-10Harlow.pdf.

Harris, Harriet A. *Fundamentalism and Evangelicals*. Pbk. ed. Oxford: Oxford University Press, 2008.

Haskins, Charles Homer. *The Rise of the Universities*. Edited by Lionel S. Lewis. Piscataway, NJ: Transaction, 2004.

Hauerwas, Stanley. *The State of the University: Academic Knowledges and the Knowledge of God*. Malden, MA: Blackwell, 2007.

Heaney, Thomas. "Democracy, Shared Governance, and the University." *New Directions for Adult and Continuing Education* 128 (2010) 69–79.

Hebrew Theological College. "Israel Experience Program (IEP)." http://www.htc.edu/divisions-and-programs/programs/iep-israel-experience-program.html.

Heckel, Jodi. "E-mail that Prompted Complaint over UI Religion Class Instructor." *The News-Gazette*, July 9, 2010, http://www.news-gazette.com/news/local/2010-07-09/e-mail-prompted-complaint-over-ui-religion-class-instructor.html.

Heilman, Uriel. "Can Asher Lopatin Secure Yeshivat Chovevei Torah's Place in the Orthodox World?" *Jewish Telegraphic Agency*, September 7, 2012, http://www.jta.org/2012/09/07/life-religion/can-asher-lopatin-secure-yeshivat-chovevei-torahs-place-in-the-orthodox-world.

Heller, Jan, et al., eds. "The Old Testament as Inspiration in Culture: International Academic Symposium—Prague, September 1995." Třebenice: Mlýn, 2001. http://www.etf.cuni.cz/~prudky/OTculture/9-Illustrations.pdf.

Higher Learning Commission. "Hebrew Theological College." http://www.ncahlc.org/component/com_directory/Action,ShowBasic/Itemid,/instid,2054/.

Hill, Charles E. "Polycarp *Contra* Marcion—Irenaeus' Presbyterial Source in *AH* 4.27–32." *Studia Patristica* 40 (2006) 399–412.

Hill, Jonathan. *The History of Christian Thought*. Oxford: Lion, 2003.

Hoffman, Allison. "The New 'Morethodox' Rabbi." *Tablet*, April 29, 2013, http://www.tabletmag.com/jewish-life-and-religion/130760/the-new-morethodox-rabbi.

Hyman, Nathan. "Internet Filtration at YU." *Yeshiva University Commentator*, December 26, 2011, http://www.yucommentator.org/2011/12/internet-filtration-at-yu/.

Ingersoll, Julie. *Evangelical Christian Women: War Stories in the Gender Battles*. New York: New York University Press, 2003.

International Council on Biblical Inerrancy. "The Chicago Statement on Biblical Inerrancy." 1978. library.dts.edu/Pages/TL/Special/ICBI_1.pdf.

Jaeger, C. Stephen. *The Envy of Angels: Cathedral Schools and Social Ideals in Medieval Europe, 950–1200*. Philadelphia: University of Pennsylvania Press, 1994.

Jaschik, Scott. "Academic Freedom and Evolution." *Inside Higher Ed*, December 10, 2007, http://www.insidehighered.com/news/2007/12/10/evolution.

———. "Battle of Wills and Faith." *Inside Higher Ed*, March 1, 2010, http://www.insidehighered.com/news/2010/03/01/erskine.

———. "Conceding Defeat at Shorter." *Inside Higher Ed*, July 11, 2005, http://www.insidehighered.com/news/2005/07/11/shorter.

———. "A Dissenter Is Fired." *Inside Higher Ed*, September 8, 2011, http://www.insidehighered.com/news/2011/09/08/english_professor_at_erskine_known_for_defending_science_is_fired.

———. "Faith, Science and Academic Freedom." *Inside Higher Ed*, January 15, 2009, http://www.insidehighered.com/news/2009/01/15/aaup.

———. "Fall from Grace." *Inside Higher Ed*, August 15, 2011, http://www.insidehighered.com/news/2011/08/15/a_professor_s_departure_raises_questions_about_freedom_of_scholarship_at_calvin_college.

———. "A Separation and a Return." *Inside Higher Ed*, July 30, 2010, http://www.insidehighered.com/news/2010/07/30/illinois.

Bibliography

———. "Skepticism about Tenure, MOOCs and the Presidency: A Survey of Provosts." *Inside Higher Ed*, January 23, 2013, http://www.insidehighered.com/news/survey/skepticism-about-tenure-moocs-and-presidency-survey-provosts.

———. "Tests of Faith." *Inside Higher Ed*, January 12, 2006, http://www.insidehighered.com/news/2006/01/12/faith.

Jeauneau, Édouard. *Rethinking the School of Chartres*. Translated by Claude Paul Desmarais. Toronto: University of Toronto, 2009.

Jeynes, Wiliam H. *American Educational History: School, Society, and the Common Good*. Thousand Oaks, CA: Sage, 2007.

June, Audrey Williams. "Jobs for Historians Rose Last Year, but Competition Remains Tough." *The Chronicle of Higher Education*, January 2, 2013, http://chronicle.com/article/Jobs-for-Historians-Rose-Last/136403.

Kaplan, Lawrence. "Rabbi Isaac Hutner's 'Daat Torah Perspective on the Holocaust': A Critical Analysis." *Tradition* 18 (1980) 235–48.

Kaplin, William A., and Barbara A. Lee. *The Law of Higher Education: A Comprehensive Guide to Legal Implications of Administrative Decision Making*. 4th ed. San Francisco: Jossey-Bass, 2006.

Katz, Jacob. "Da'at Torah—The Unqualified Authority Claimed for Halakhists." *Jewish History* 11 (1997) 41–50.

Kelley, Mary. *Learning to Stand and Speak: Women, Education, and Public Life in America's Republic*. Chapel Hill: University of North Carolina Press, 2006.

Keohane, Nannerl O. "The American Campus: From Colonial Seminary to Global Multiversity." In *The Idea of a University*, edited by David Smith and Anne Karin Langslow, 48–67. Philadelphia: Jessica Kingsley, 1999.

Kleinman, Rachel. "Joel: Gay Panel 'Could Send the Wrong Message.'" *The Cardozo Jurist*, March 3, 2010, http://www.cardozojurist.com/2010/03/joel-gay-panel-%E2%80%98could-send-the-wrong-message%E2%80%99/.

Koerner, Joseph Leo. *The Reformation of the Image*. London: Reaktion, 2004.

Krakowski, Eve. "'Many Days without the God of Truth': Loss and Recovery of Religious Knowledge in Early Karaite Thought." In *Pesher Nahum: Texts and Studies in Jewish History and Literature from Antiquity through the Middle Ages Presented to Norman (Nahum) Golb*, edited by Joel L. Kraemer, Norman Golb, and Michael G Wechsler, 121–40. Chicago: Oriental Institute of the University of Chicago, 2012.

Lahey, Stephen E. *John Wyclif*. New York: Oxford University Press, 2009.

Lambert, Malcolm. *Medieval Heresy: Popular Movements from the Gregorian Reform to the Reformation*. New York: Barnes and Noble, 1998.

Lampe, Peter. *Christians at Rome in the First Two Centuries: From Paul to Valentinus*. London: Continuum, 2003.

———. *Die stadtrömischen Christen in den ersten beiden Jahrhunderten: Untersuchungen zur Sozialgeschichte*. Wissenschaftliche Untersuchungen zum Neuen Testament 18. Series 2. Tübingen: Mohr, 1989.

Lander College for Men. "Israel Option." http://lcw.touro.edu/prospective-students/israel-option/.

———. "Message from the Dean." https://web.archive.org/web/20130730042934/http://lcm.touro.edu/about/message-from-the-dean/.

Langer, Ruth. "Response to William Bellinger: Exploring Covenant in a World of Faiths." Delivered at Houston Clergy Institute, March 6, 2007, 1–3, http://napoleon.bc.edu/ojs/index.php/scjr/article/download/1440/1449.

Larsen, Andrew E. *The School of Heretics: Academic Condemnation at the University of Oxford, 1277–1409*. Leiden: Brill, 2011.

Lederhendler, Eli. *Who Owns Judaism? Public Religion and Private Faith in America and Israel*. New York : Oxford University Press. 2001.

Levi, Arieh. "New Internet Filters Block Pornographic Content in Dorms." *Yeshiva University Commentator*, September 11, 2012, http://www.yucommentator .org/2012/09/new-internet-filters-block-pornographic-content-in-dorms/.

Lewis, Jack P. "What Do We Mean by Jabneh?" *Journal of Bible and Religion* 32 (1964) 125–32.

Lipman, Steve. "Gay YU Panel Broadens Discussion, Debate." *New York Jewish Week*, December 30, 2009, http://www.thejewishweek.com/news/new_york/gay_yu_panel_ broadens_discussion_debate.

Liss, Sara. "Censorship Committee Stirs Up Debate at Yeshiva University." *The Cardozo Jurist*, February 1, 2011, http://www.cardozojurist.com/2011/02/censor ship-committee-stirs-up-debate-at-yeshiva-university/.

Long, Nancy A. "July 2012 AAUP Summer Institute: Legal Round-Up: What's New and Noteworthy for Higher Education!" http://www.aaup.org/sites/default/files/files/ SummerInstitute2012LegalRoundUpFINAL72512.pdf.

Lundin, Roger. *Emily Dickinson and the Art of Belief*. Grand Rapids: Eerdmans, 2004.

Maltz, Judy. "Director of Orthodox Gap-Year Program at Bar-Ilan Fired for Installing Cameras in Girls' Dorms." *Haaretz*, May 2, 2013, http://www.haaretz.com/jewish-world/director-of-orthodox-gap-year-program-at-bar-ilan-fired-for-installing-cameras-in-girls-dorms-1.518916.

Marenbon, John. *The Philosophy of Peter Abelard*. New York: Cambridge University Press, 1997.

Mark, Jonathan. "NYU Dorm Changes Worry Observant Jews." *New York Jewish Week*, April 15, 2013, http://www.thejewishweek.com/news/breaking-news/nyu-dorm-changes-worry-observant-jews.

Marsden, George M. *The Soul of the American University: From Protestant Establishment to Established Nonbelief*. New York: Oxford University Press, 1994.

Mastricht, Peter van. *Treatise on Regeneration*. Edited by Brandon G. Withrow. Translated by Anonymous. Morgan, PA: Soli Deo Gloria, 2002.

Matheson, Stephen. "Silence Camouflages Suspicious Procedures." *Chimes*, October 22, 2010, http://clubs.calvin.edu/chimes/article.php?id=7034.

McClellan, James E., and Harold Dorn. *Science and Technology in World History: An Introduction*. 2nd ed. Baltimore: Johns Hopkins University Press, 2006.

McGrath, James F. "In Support of Christopher Rollston." *Exploring Our Matrix*, October 9, 2012, http://www.patheos.com/blogs/exploringourmatrix/2012/10/in-support-of-christopher-rollston.html.

McMurthrie, Beth. "Do Professors Lose Academic Freedom by Signing Statements of Faith?" *The Chronicle of Higher Education*, May 24, 2002, http://metis.findlay .edu:3990/article/Do-Professors-Lose-Academic/3577.

Merrim, Stephanie. *Early Modern Women's Writing and Sor Juana Inés de la Cruz*. Nashville: Vanderbilt University Press, 1999.

Metzger, Walter P. "Profession and Constitution: Two Definitions of Academic Freedom in America." *Texas Law Review* 66 (1988) 1265–1322.

Milavec, Aaron. *The Didache: Text, Translation, Analysis, and Commentary*. Collegeville, MN: Liturgical, 2003.

Moll, Rob. "Mark Noll Leaving Wheaton for Notre Dame." *Christianity Today*, February 9, 2006, http://www.christianitytoday.com/ct/2006/februaryweb-only/106-43.0.html.

———. "Two Degrees of Separation: GARBC Distances Itself from College after Southern Baptist Endorsement." *Christianity Today*, September 2006, http://www.christianitytoday.com/ct/2006/september/16.24.html.

Moore, Melissa Partain. "Continuing Our Series of 'Things That Don't Add Up' ..." *Under the Sun*, May 22, 2008, http://windofhebel.blogspot.com/2008/05/continuing-our-series-of-things-that.html.

Murdoch, Murray. "Cedarville University." In *Cradles of Conscience: Ohio's Independent Colleges and Universities*, edited by John William Oliver Jr., James A. Hodges, and James H. O'Donnell, 109–19. Kent, OH: Kent State University Press, 2003.

N., Yitzchak. "Yeshiva University Rabbis, Students Decry Gay Forum Calling It a Chillul Hashem." *Vos Iz Neias?*, December 30, 2009, http://www.vosizneias.com/45816/2009/12/30/new-york-city-yeshiva-university-rabbis-students-decry-gay-fourm-calling-it-a-chillul-hashem/.

Naden, Corinne J., and Rose Blue. *Cornel West*. Chicago: Raintree, 2006.

Nadler, Steven M. *Spinoza's Heresy: Immortality and the Jewish Mind*. New York: Oxford University Press, 2004.

Nathan-Kazis, Josh. "Norman Lamm Leaves Outsized Legacy in Modern Orthodoxy—And a Cloud." *Jewish Daily Forward*, July 3, 2013, http://forward.com/articles/179745/norman-lamm-leaves-outsized-legacy-in-modern-ortho/.

Nazworth, Napp. "Calvin College Professor Claims Administration Not Truthful over Colleague's Resignation." *Christian Post*, August 17, 2011, http://www.christianpost.com/news/calvin-college-professor-claims-administration-not-truthful-over-colleagues-resignation-54046.

Nedava, J. "Who Were the 'Biryoni.'" *The Jewish Quarterly Review*, New Series 63 (1973) 317–22.

Nelson, Cary. "Defining Academic Freedom." *Inside Higher Ed*, December 21, 2010, http://www.insidehighered.com/views/2010/12/21/nelson_on_academic_freedom.

———. *No University Is an Island: Saving Academic Freedom*. New York: New York University Press, 2010.

Nelson, Libbey A. "Banned." *Inside Higher Ed*, December 1, 2011, http://www.insidehighered.com/news/2011/12/01/controversy-shorter-over-faith-statements.

———. "A Campus in Turmoil." *Inside Higher Ed*, January 22, 2013, http://www.insidehighered.com/news/2013/01/22/several-controversies-converge-ohio-baptist-college.

———. "Refusing to Sign." *Inside Higher Ed*, May 14, 2012, http://www.insidehighered.com/news/2012/05/14/shorter-university-faculty-leaving-over-new-lifestyle-statements.

———. "Shorter's Exodus, a Year Later." *Insider Higher Ed*, November 14, 2012, http://www.insidehighered.com/news/2012/11/14/cultural-change-tears-georgia-baptist-college-apart.

———. "Tenure vs. Donors." *Inside Higher Ed*, October 15, 2012, http://www.insidehighered.com/news/2012/10/15/seminary-threatens-discipline-professor-offending-prospective-students-donors.

Neuhofer, M. Dorothy. *In The Benedictine Tradition: The Origins and Early Development of Two College Libraries*. Lanham, MD: University Press of America, 1999.

New York Times. "U.N. Plea Halts Firing." November 1, 1965, http://select.nytimes.com/gst/abstract.html?res=F60916F73454177A93C3A9178AD95F418685F9.

Newman, M. G. *The Boundaries of Charity: Cistercian Culture and Ecclesiastical Reform, 1098–1180.* Stanford: Stanford University Press, 1996.

Nielsen, Lauge O. "Peter Abelard and Gilbert of Poitiers." In *The Medieval Theologians,* edited by G. R. Evans, 102–28. Malden, MA: Blackwell, 2001.

Noll, K. L. "The Ethics of Being a Theologian." *The Chronicle of Higher Education,* July 27, 2009, http://chronicle.com/article/The-Ethics-of-Being-a/47442.

Oppenheimer, Mark. "An Ohio Christian College Struggles to Further Define Itself." *New York Times,* February 15, 2013, http://www.nytimes.com/2013/02/16/us/a-christian-college-struggles-to-define-itself.html.

Orthodox Union. "Great Leaders of Our People." http://www.ou.org/about/judaism/rabbis/feinstein.htm.

Otterman, Sharon. "Orthodox Jewish Student's Tale of Premarital Sex, Real or Not, Roils Campus." *New York Times,* December 10, 2011, A23, http://www.nytimes.com/2011/12/10/nyregion/yeshiva-university-stunned-by-tale-of-a-tryst.html.

Pahl, Michael. *The Beginning and the End: Rereading Genesis's Stories and Revelation's Visions.* Eugene, OR: Cascade, 2011.

———. "It's True." *Rustlings in the Grass,* October 29, 2012, http://rustlingsinthegrass.blogspot.com/2012/10/its-true.html.

Pearson, Birger A. "Egypt." In *The Cambridge History of Christianity: Origins to Constantine,* edited by Margaret M. Mitchell and Frances M. Young, 331–50. Cambridge: Cambridge University Press, 2006.

Penn, Ascher. "Advanced Talmudic Academies." In *Jewish Education in the United States: A Documentary History,* edited by Lloyd P. Gartner, 212–13. New York: Teacher's College, 1969.

Pirkle, Richard. "Richard Pirkle—Letter of Resignation." *Save Our Shorter,* May 22, 2012, http://saveourshorter.com/personal-narratives/letters/richard-pirkle/.

Poskanzer, Steven G. *Higher Education Law: The Faculty.* Baltimore: Johns Hopkins University Press, 2002.

Pulliam, Sarah. "Cedarville's Tenure Tremor: The Baptist University Is Embroiled in a Long-Running Dispute over the Firing of Two Professors." *Christianity Today,* April 3, 2008, http://www.christianitytoday.com/ct/2008/aprilweb-only/114-43.0.html.

Renz, Rachel. "Teaching Biblical Criticism: A Proposal to Yeshiva University." *The Beacon,* December 2011, http://thebeaconmag.com/2011/12/uncategorized/teaching-biblical-criticism-a-proposal-to-yeshiva-university-administration-and-faculty/.

Riley, Naomi Schaeffer. *God on the Quad: How Religious Colleges and the Missionary Generation Are Changing America.* Chicago: Dee, 2005.

Roach, David. "GARBC Severs Ties with Cedarville Because of SBC Ties." *Baptist Press,* September 25, 2006, http://www.bpnews.net/BPnews.asp?ID=24043.

Rollston, Christopher. "The Marginalization of Women: A Biblical Value We Don't Like to Talk About." *The Huffington Post,* August 31, 2012, http://www.huffingtonpost.com/christopher-rollston/the-marginalization-of-women-biblical-value-we-dont-like-to-talk-about_b_1833648.html.

Rosenberg, Shmarya. "Exclusive! YU Sanitizes Website—New York Times Falls for YU Deception." *Failed Messiah,* December 12, 2008, http://failedmessiah.typepad.com/failed_messiahcom/2008/12/exclusive-yu-sa.html.

Bibliography

Rosenblatt, Gary. "Rabbinically Incorrect." *New York Jewish Week*, July 30, 2004, http://www.thejewishweek.com/news/new_york/rabbinically_incorrect.

———. "Where Will Joel Take Yeshiva U?" *New York Jewish Week*, August 22, 2003, http://www.thejewishweek.com/news/new_york/where_will_joel_take_yeshiva_u.

———. "YU's Schachter Accused of Obsolete Views on Church." *New York Jewish Week*, August 28, 2012, http://www.thejewishweek.com/news/new-york-news/yus-schachter-accused-obsolete-views-church.

Roth, Cecil. "Jewish Intellectual Life in Medieval Sicily." *The Jewish Quarterly Review*, New Series, 47 (1957) 317–35.

Rubin, Nissan, and Admiel Kosman. "The Clothing of the Primordial Adam as a Symbol of Apocalyptic Time in the Midrashic Sources." *Harvard Theological Review* 90 (1997) 155–74.

Rüegg, Walter. "The Europe of Universities: Their Tradition, Function of Bridging across Europe, Liberal Modernisation." In *The Heritage of European Universities*, edited by Nuria Sanz and Sjur Bergan, 39–48. 2nd ed. Council of Europe Higher Education Series 7. Strasbourg: Council of Europe Publishing, 2006.

———. "Themes." In *Universities in the Middle Ages*, edited by Hilde de Ridder-Symoens, 3–34. History of the University in Europe 1. New York: Cambridge University Press, 1992.

SCOTUSblog. "Vance vs. Ball State University." http://www.scotusblog.com/case-files/cases/vance-v-ball-state-university/.

Schmidt, Peter. "Court Dismisses Wrongful-Termination Claim against Cedarville U. as a Religious Matter." *The Chronicle of Higher Education*, September 24, 2009, http://chronicle.com/article/Court-Dismisses/48610/.

Schneider, John. "Recent Genetic Science and Christian Theology on Human Origins: An 'Aesthetic Supralapsarianism.'" *Perspectives on Science and Christian Faith* 62 (2010) 196–212, http://www.asa3.org/ASA/PSCF/2010/PSCF9-10Schneider.pdf.

Schneider, Zach, and Josh Steele. "On the Firing of Dr. Pahl." *The Ventriloquist*, October 2012, http://theventriloquist.us/article/on_the_firing_of_dr_pahl.

Shipper, William. "Benedict of Nursia." In *The Rise of the Medieval World, 500–1300: A Biographical Dictionary*, edited by Jana K. Schulman. Westport, CT: Greenwood, 2002.

Schwartz, Howard. "Narrative and Imagination: The Role of Texts and Storytelling in Nurturing Spirituality in Judaism." In *Nurturing Child and Adolescent Spirituality: Perspectives from the World's Religious Traditions*, edited by Karen Marie Yust et al., 61–63. Lanham, MD: Rowman & Littlefield: 2006.

———. *Tree of Souls: The Mythology of Judaism*. New York: Oxford University Press, 2004.

Shabazz, Amilcar. *Advancing Democracy: African Americans and the Struggle for Access and Equity in Higher Education in Texas*. Chapel Hill: University of North Carolina Press, 2004.

Shogimen, Takashi. "Academic Controversies." In *The Medieval Theologians: An Introduction to Theology in the Medieval Period*, edited by G. R. Evans, 233–49. Oxford: Blackwell, 2001.

Shorter University. "Faculty Handbook, 2012–2013." August 2012. http://www.shorter.edu/academics/provost/faculty_handbook_2012_13.pdf.

———. "Shorter University Trustees Adopt New Logo and Faith Statements for The University." *Shorter News*, October 25, 2011, http://www.shorter.edu/about/news/2011/10_25_11_logo_statements.htm.

Sloan, Kim. "Shorter Librarian Prepares to Leave, Would Love to Stay." *Rome News-Tribune*, May 2012, http://saveourshorter.com/2012/05/08/shorter-librarian-prepares-to-leave-would-love-to-stay/.

Society of Professional Journalists. "Resources for Students." http://www.spj.org/students.asp.

Solomont, E. B. "YU Holds Discussion on Homosexuality." *The Jerusalem Post*, December 24, 2009, http://www.jpost.com/Jewish-World/YU-holds-discussion-on-homosexuality.

Soloveitchik, Joseph B. *The Lonely Man of Faith*. New York: Doubleday, 1965.

Spiro, Ken. "History Crash Course #11: Mount Sinai." *Aish HaTorah*, http://www.aish.com/jl/h/cc/48932202.html.

Steffan, Melissa. "After Turbulent Year, Cedarville University Selects Theologian as New President." *Christianity Today*, June 5, 2013, http://www.christianitytoday.com/gleanings/2013/june/after-turbulent-year-cedarville-university-selects.html.

———. "Crisis of Faith Statements: Does It Matter 'Why' Christian Professors Agree with Their Colleges' Doctrine?" *Christianity Today*, October 29, 2012, http://www.christianitytoday.com/ct/2012/november/crisis-of-faith-statements.html.

Story, Ronald, ed. *Five Colleges: Five Histories*. Amherst: University of Massachusetts Press, 1992.

Swan, Laura. *Spirituality in History: The Benedictine Tradition*. Edited by Phyllis Zagano. Collegeville, MN: Liturgical, 2007.

Sweeney, Douglas A. *The American Evangelical Story: A History of the Movement*. Grand Rapids: Baker, 2005.

Taylor, Kate. "Sex on Campus: She Can Play That Game, Too." *New York Times*, July 12, 2013, http://www.nytimes.com/2013/07/14/fashion/sex-on-campus-she-can-play-that-game-too.html.

Thijssen, J. M. M. H. *Censure and Heresy at the University of Paris*. Philadelphia: University of Pennsylvania Press, 1998.

Tolley, Kim. "Mapping the Landscape of Higher Schooling, 1727–1850." In *Chartered Schools: Two Hundred Years of Independent Academies in the United States, 1727–1925*, edited by Nancy Beadie and Kim Tolley, 19–43. New York: RoutledgeFalmer, 2002.

Trueman, Carl R. "Being Presbyterian in the Church of Scotland." *Heidelblog*, May 2009, http://heidelblog.net/2009/05/trueman-being-presbyterian-in-the-church-of-scotland/.

Ungar-Sargon, Batya. "Orthodox Yeshiva Set to Ordain Three Women: Just Don't Call Them 'Rabbi.'" *Tablet*, June 10, 2013, http://www.tabletmag.com/jewish-life-and-religion/134369/orthodox-women-ordained.

United Nations. "The Universal Declaration of Human Rights." 1948. http://www.un.org/en/documents/udhr/index.shtml.

University of Maryland. "Prospective & New Students." http://jewishstudies.umd.edu/undergraduate/prospective-new-students.

———. "The Transfer Credit Section." http://www.tce.umd.edu/StAbIsrael.htm/.

U.S. Civil Rights Act of 1964 (Sec. 702, 703.3.e). http://www.ourdocuments.gov/doc.php?flash=true&doc=97&page=transcript.

U.S. Equal Employment Opportunity Commission. "Questions and Answers: Religious Discrimination in the Workplace." http://www.eeoc.gov/policy/docs/qanda_religion.html.

Bibliography

U.S. News & World Report. "Yeshiva University." http://colleges.usnews.rankings andreviews.com/best-colleges/yeshiva-university-2903.

U.S. Supreme Court. *Garcetti et al. v. Ceballos,* 547 U.S. 410 (2006). http://www .supremecourt.gov/opinions/05pdf/04-473.pdf.

———. *Sweezy v. New Hampshire* 354, U.S. 234 (1957). *Findlaw,* http://laws.findlaw.com/ us/354/234.html.

———. *Vance v. Ball State University et al.* (No. 11–556, 2013 BL 167357, 118 FEP Cases 1481). June 24, 2013. http://www.supremecourt.gov/opinions/12pdf/11-556_1102. pdf.

Van de Sandt, Huub, and David Flusser. *The Didache: Its Jewish Sources and Its Place in Early Judaism and Christianity.* Assen, Netherlands: Royal Van Gorcum and Fortress, 2002.

Van den Hoek, Annewies. "The 'Catechetical' School of Early Christian Alexandria and Its Philonic Heritage." *Harvard Theological Review* 90 (1997) 59–87.

Van Farowe, Roxanne. "Calvin Profs Say Evolution Evidence." *The Banner,* January 22, 2011, http://www.thebanner.org/news/2011/01/calvin-profs-say-evolution-evidence.

Vrettos, Theodore. *Alexandria: City of the Western Mind.* New York: Free Press, 2001.

Weber, Jeremy. "Bruce Waltke Headed to Knox Theological Seminary?" *Christianity Today,* April 12, 2010, http://www.christianitytoday.com/gleanings/2010/april/ bruce-waltke-headed-to-knox-theological-seminary-updated.html.

Wecker, Menachem. "Colleges Get Mixed Reviews When Using Twitter for Customer Service." *U.S. News & World Report,* October 17, 2011, http://www.usnews.com/ education/best-colleges/articles/2011/10/17/colleges-get-mixed-reviews-when-using-twitter-for-customer-service.

———. "Did William Blake Know Hebrew?" *Jewish Daily Forward,* December 11, 2009, http://forward.com/articles/120109/did-william-blake-know-hebrew/.

Weeda, Claire. "Ethnic Stereotyping in Twelfth-Century Paris." In *Difference and Identity in Francia and Medieval France,* edited by Meredith Cohen and Justine Firnhaber-Bake, 115–36. Burlington, VT: Ashgate, 2010.

Weiner, Marcella Bakur, and Blema Feinstein. *A Woman's Voice: Bibical Women: Divine Wisdom Transformed into Action for Today's Woman.* Northvale, NJ: J. Aronson, 2001.

Weinreb, Tzvi Hersh. "Preserving Our Mesorah in Changing Times: Tzvi Hersh Weinreb." *Jewish Action,* Winter 2010, http://www.ou.org/jewish_action/10/2010/preserving_ our_mesorah_a_symposium3/.

Westminster Theological Seminary. "Faculty Pledge." http://www.wts.edu/about/beliefs/ statements/facultypledge.html.

———. "Official Documents Collected by Westminster Theological Seminary, Philadelphia, PA, 2008." http://files.wts.edu/uploads/images/files/Official Theological Documents for Web.pdf.

———. "Précis to the Board on Theological Tensions on the Faculty." http://files.wts.edu/ uploads/images/files/Hermeneutics FC-Prcis-Dec06.pdf.

White, Carolinne. "Introduction." In *The Rule of St. Benedict,* translated by Carolinne White. New York: Penguin, 2008.

Wilson, Charles W. "A Vision for Erskine as Articulated by the Erskine Facebook Participants." *ARP Talk,* July 28, 2011, http://www.arptalk.org/2011/07/28/a-vision-for-erskine-as-articulated-by-the-erskine-facebook-participants.

Wilson, Ellen Judy. "Universities." In *Encyclopedia of the Enlightenment*, edited by Peter Hanns Reill, 606–7. Rev. ed. New York: Facts on File, 2004.

Wilson, John K. "Interview with Bill Crenshaw." *College Freedom*, October 14, 2011, http://collegefreedom.blogspot.com/2011/10/interview-with-bill-crenshaw.html.

Wineman, Aryeh. "A Hasidic View of Dreams, Torah-Text, and the Language of Allusion." *Hebrew Studies* 52 (2011) 353–62.

Wissema, J. G. *Towards the Third Generation University: Managing the University in Transition*. Northampton: Edward Elgar, 2009.

Withrow, Brandon. *Becoming Divine: Jonathan Edwards's Incarnational Spirituality within the Christian Tradition*. Eugene, OR: Cascade, 2011.

———. "Finding Empathy in Religious Studies." *The Chronicle of Higher Education*, November 17, 2011, http://chronicle.com/article/Finding-Empathy-in-Religious/129779.

———. "Jonathan Edwards as a Resource for Current Evangelical Discussion over the Language of Justification." MA thesis, Trinity Evangelical Divinity School, 1999.

———. *Katherine Parr: The Life and Thought of a Reformation Queen*. Philipsburg, NJ: P&R, 2009.

———. "Mary Astell's Unlikely Feminist Revolution: Lessons on the Role of Religion in Fighting for Gender Rights in Eighteenth-Century England." *Journal of Inter-Religious Studies* 8 (2012) 9–16.

———. "Not Your Father's Ph.D." *The Chronicle of Higher Education*, April 15, 2008, http://chronicle.com/article/Not-Your-Father-s-PhD/45752.

Yeshiva of Flatbush. "Making Israel Happen . . ." http://www.flatbush.org/content.aspx?rec_id=100099.

Yeshiva Ohr Yerushalayim. "Faculty." http://yoy.org.il/faculty/?id=61.

Yeshiva University. "About YU." http://yu.edu/about/.

———. "Guide to Israel Schools: Ateret Yerushalayim." http://yu.edu/israel-program/men-schools/ateret-yerushalayim/.

———. "Guide to Israel Schools: HaKotel." http://yu.edu/israel-program/men-schools/hakotel/.

———. "Guide to Israel Schools: Kerem B'Yavneh." http://yu.edu/israel-program/men-schools/kerem-byavneh/.

———. "Guide to Israel Schools: Ohr David." http://yu.edu/israel-program/men-schools/ohr-david/.

———. "Mission Statement." http://yu.edu/about/mission.

———. "President Carter at Cardoza." http://blogs.yu.edu/news/2013/04/08/president-carter-at-cardozo/.

———. "Rabbi Hershel Schachter." http://www.yutorah.org/Rabbi_Hershel_Schachter.

———. "S. Daniel Abraham Israel Program." http://www.yu.edu/Israel-Program/.

———. "Shabbat Programming." http://yu.edu/student-life/living-at-YU/shabbat-programming/beren/.

———. "Where Will Joel Take Yeshiva U? In His First Interview as President, Richard Joel Speaks of Moving Forward, but Cautiously." http://blogs.yu.edu/news/2003/08/02/where-will-joel-take-yeshiva-u-in-his-first-interview-as-president-richard-joel-speaks-of-moving-forward-but-cautiously/.

Yeshivat Chovevei Torah. "About Us." http://www.yctorah.org/content/blogcategory/13/49/.

Bibliography

————. "Mission and Values." http://www.yctorah.org/content/view/1/49/.

Yeshivat Kerem B'Yavneh. "KBY History." http://www.kby.org/english/history/?id=1.

Yeshivat Sha'alvim. "Overview and History." http://www.shaalvim.org/yeshiva/about/.

Yuter, Josh. "The Unmaking of a Gadol." *YUTOPIA*, March 12, 2008, http://www.joshyuter.com/2008/03/12/judaism/jewish-culture/the-unmaking-of-a-gadol/.

Zanger, Walter. "Jewish Worship, Pagan Symbols: Zodiac Mosaics in Ancient Synagogues." *Bible History Daily*, August 24, 2013, http://www.biblicalarchaeology.org/daily/ancient-cultures/ancient-israel/jewish-worship-pagan-symbols/.

Zeveloff, Naomi. "Touro Under Scrutiny over Israel Class: College Faces Questions about Credits for Advocacy Session." *Jewish Daily Forward*, November 25, 2011, http://forward.com/articles/146221/touro-under-scrutiny-over-israel-class/.

Scripture Index

Name and Subject Index

Carolingian Empire, 45–46
cathedral schools, 44, 46–49
catechetical schools, 42–44, 45
Ceballos, Richard, 138–39
Charlemagne, 46
"Chicago Statement on Biblical Inerrancy," 90
Cobban, Alan, 51
Code of Hammurabi, 17
Colleges,
    Calvin, 141–42, 147
    Erskine, 133–43
    Kalamazoo Valley Community, xiv
    Milligan, 143
    Mount Holyoke (see also seminaries, Mount Holyoke Female), 60–61, 61n68
    Oberlin, 58
    Wheaton, 13, 140–41
    Yale (early), 59 (see also University, Yale)
collegia, 50
Colling, Richard G., 147–48, 150
Colson, Charles 13, 17
communitas, 144, 150
controversy, nature of, 10, 12–13, 15, 21–23, 86–87, 152
Cornman, Thomas, 100, 102
Councils,
    Council of Toledo (527), 46
    Second Council of Constantinople (553), 44
    Council of Sens (1140), 48
    Council of Soissons (1121), 48
    Third Lateran Council (1179), 46
    Fourth Lateran Council (1215), 47
    Council of Trent (1545–63), 55
craft guilds, medieval, 50
Crenshaw, 133–34
Cutler, Timothy, 59

DelFattore, Joan, 139–40
dispensationalism, 6, 10–11, 21
Dixon, A. C., 16
D'Ailly, Pierre, 52
Dickinson, Emily, 61
Didache, 41–42, 45
Dowless, Donald, 88, 88n5

Dulles, Avery, 13
Dryer, Emma, 61

Edgar, William, 93
education,
    New Learning, 55
    triviium, 47
    of women, 54, 57–59
    quadrivium, 47
    postmodernism, 56n52, 91n12, 96
Edward of Woodstock, 51
Eliezer (Talmud), 28–29, 71–76, 155
English Civil War, 90n10, 148
Enlightenment (movement), 55–59
    Epistemology and, 56
    postmodernism and, 56n53
    Enns, Peter (see also, Westminster Theological Seminary); 17–19, 22, 90–94, 96, 103, 141n26, 148
Epistle to Diognetus, 152
Erasmus of Rotterdam, 53
Establishment Clause, xv
Ethics of the Fathers, 65, 78
Evangelicals and Catholics Together, 12–15, 16, 17, 21–22
    "An Appeal to Fellow Evangelicals," 14, 22
    Alliance of Confessing Evangelicals, 13–14
    "The Cambridge Declaration," 14
    "Evangelicals and Catholics Together: The Christian Mission in the Third Millennium," 13
    "The Gift of Salvation," 14
    "Resolutions for Roman Catholics and Evangelical Dialogue," 14
evolution, 6, 16, 56, 62, 86, 88, 89, 91, 140–41, 147, 151, 152, 154
    Adam (Genesis), 47, 98–99, 141–142, 147, 151, 152
excommunication (Talmudic), 72, 72n37

faculty search process, xii–xiv
Feinstein, Rabbi Moshe, 29–30
Fish, Stanley, 145–46, 151
Fiske, Fidelia, 61
Fosdick, Harry Emerson, 17

Name and Subject Index